SOCIAL CHANGE AND ECONOMIC LIFE INITIATIVE

Series Editor: Duncan Gallie

TRADE UNIONISM IN RECESSION

THE SOCIAL CHANGE AND ECONOMIC LIFE INITIATIVE

———

This volume is part of a series arising from the Social Change and Economic Life Initiative—a major interdisciplinary programme of research funded by the Economic and Social Research Council. The programme focused on the impact of the dramatic economic restructuring of the 1980s on employers' labour force strategies, workers' experiences of employment and unemployment, and the changing dynamics of household relations.

ALSO PUBLISHED IN THIS SERIES

Social Change and the Experience of Unemployment
Edited by Duncan Gallie, Catherine Marsh, and Carolyn Vogler

Skill and Occupational Change
Edited by Roger Penn, Michael Rose, and Jill Rubery

Employer Strategy and the Labour Market
Edited by Jill Rubery and Frank Wilkinson

Gender Segregation and Social Change:
Men and Women in Changing Labour Markets
Edited by Alison MacEwen Scott

The Social and Political Economy of the Household
Edited by Michael Anderson, Frank Bechhofer, and
Jonathan Gershuny

TRADE UNIONISM IN RECESSION

Edited by

DUNCAN GALLIE, ROGER PENN,

and

MICHAEL ROSE

OXFORD UNIVERSITY PRESS
1996

Oxford University Press, Walton Street, Oxford OX2 6DP

Oxford New York
Athens Auckland Bangkok Bombay
Calcutta Cape Town Dar es Salaam Delhi
Florence Hong Kong Istanbul Karachi
Kuala Lumpur Madras Madrid Melbourne
Mexico City Nairobi Paris Singapore
Taipei Tokyo Toronto
and associated companies in
Berlin Ibadan

Oxford is a trade mark of Oxford University Press

Published in the United States
by Oxford University Press Inc., New York

British Library Cataloguing in Publication Data
Data available

Library of Congress Cataloging in Publication Data
Trade unionism in recession / edited by Duncan Gallie, Roger Penn, and
Michael Rose
—(Social change and economic life initiative)
Includes bibliographical references and index.
1. Trade-unions—Great Britain. I. Gallie, Duncan. II. Penn,
Roger, 1949– . III. Rose, Michael, 1937– . IV. Series.
HD6664.T7214 1995 331.88'0941—dc20 95–16229
ISBN 0–19–827920–5. ISBN 0–19–827977–9 (Pbk.)

1 3 5 7 9 10 8 6 4 2

Set by Hope Services (Abingdon) Ltd.
Printed in Great Britain
on acid-free paper by
Biddles Ltd., Guildford and King's Lynn

FOREWORD

This volume forms part of a series of publications arising from the Social Change and Economic Life Initiative—a programme of research initiated and supported by the Economic and Social Research Council. Fieldwork for the Work Histories/Attitudes survey, and the Household and Community survey, was undertaken by Public Attitude Surveys (High Wycombe) Ltd. The authors and editors wish to thank the many colleagues and others who commented on earlier drafts or versions of the chapters, several of which appeared in the SCELI Working Papers series.

DUNCAN GALLIE
National Co-ordinator and Series Editor

CONTENTS

Contents

LIST OF FIGURES

LIST OF TABLES

ABBREVIATIONS

ACAS	Advisory and Conciliation Service
ACTSS	Association of Clerical, Technical and Supervisory Staffs
AEU	Amalgamated Engineering Union
APEX	Association of Professional and Executive Staff
ASE	Amalgamated Society of Engineers
ASLEF	Association of Locomotive Engineers and Firemen
ASTMS	Association of Scientific, Technical and Managerial Staffs
ATWU	Associated Textile Workers Union
AUEW	Amalgamated Union of Engineering and Electrical Workers
BALPA	British Airline Pilots Association
BIFU	Banking, Insurance and Finance Union
BREL	British Rail Engineering Limited
BTD	Beamers, Twisters, and Drawers Union
BTEA	British Textiles Employers' Association
COHSE	Confederation of Health Service Employees
CPSA	Civil and Public Services Association
CSEU	Confederation of Shipbuilding and Engineering Unions
CSO	Central Statistical Office
DoE	Department of Employment
EEF	Engineering Employers Federation
EETPU	Electrical, Electronic Technicians and Plumbing Union
EPEA	Electrical Power Engineers Association
ESRC	Economic and Social Research Council
FUMPO	Federated Union of Managerial, Administrative and Professional Officers
G&M	See 'GMWU' and 'GMBU'
GCHQ	Government Communications Headquarters (Cheltenham)
GMBU	General, Municipal and Boilermakers Workers Union

GMWU	General and Municipal Workers Union
HRM	Human Resources Management
IER	Institute of Employment Research
ISTC	Iron and Steel Trades Confederation
MATSA	Managerial, Administrative, Technical and Supervisors Association
MSC	Manpower Services Commission
MSF	Management, Science and Finance Union
NAHT	National Association of Head Teachers
NAIRU	Non-Accelerating Inflation Rate of Unemployment
NALGO	National Association of Local Government Officers
NASUWT	National Association of Schoolmasters Union of Women Teachers
NATFHE	National Association of Teachers in Further and Higher Education
NESDA	North East of Scotland Development Agency
NGA	National Graphical Association
NSOAC	North Sea Oil Action Committee
NUM	National Union of Mineworkers
NUPE	National Union of Public Employees
NUR	National Union of Railwaymen
NUS	National Union of Seamen
OILC	Oil Industry Liaison Committee
PSI	Policy Studies Institute
SAUS	School of Advanced Urban Studies
SCELI	Social Change and Economic Life Initiative
SCS	Society of Civil Servants
SOGAT	Society of Graphic and Allied Trades
TASS	Technical and Supervisory Staff (division of AUEW)
TEC	Training and Education Council
TGWU	Transport and General Workers Union
TSSA	Transport Salaried Staffs Association
TUC	Trades Union Congress
UCATT	Union of Construction Allied Trades and Technicians
UDM	Union of Democratic Miners
UKOOA	United Kingdom Offshore Operators Association
WIRS	Workplace Industrial Relations Surveys

NOTES ON THE CONTRIBUTORS

PETER ELIAS is a Professorial Fellow at the Institute for Employment Research, University of Warwick.

DUNCAN GALLIE is an Official Fellow at Nuffield College, Oxford.

BRIAN G. M. MAIN is Professor of Economics at The University, Edinburgh.

ROGER PENN is a Reader in Economic Sociology, at the University of Lancaster.

MICHAEL ROSE is a Visiting Fellow in Economic Sociology at the University of Bath.

HILDA SCATTERGOOD is at the University of Lancaster.

JOHN SEWEL is Professor of Sociology at the University of Aberdeen.

1

The British Debate on Trade Unionism: Crisis and Continuity

DUNCAN GALLIE, MICHAEL ROSE, AND ROGER PENN

1. INTRODUCTION

Most studies of British industrial relations and trade unionism over the last decade have been characterized by the twin themes of crisis and discontinuity. During the 1980s, British trade unionism confronted its greatest challenge, and suffered its greatest reverses, since the inter-war period. After a decade of rapid growth, for much of which trade unions exercised significant influence in the corridors of power, they experienced a steep decline in their membership, a marked erosion of their ability to mobilize a depleted following, and, in national political affairs—even in the affairs of the Labour Party itself at times—virtual marginalization. Once self-assured actors on the national scene, no less than in the industrial arena, trade unions seemed to have lost confidence in playing any role; indeed they appeared at times to have become increasingly confused over what their role *could* be, and *should* be, as the century drew to a close.

Trade union membership reached its peak in 1979, when it stood at 13,289,000. By 1990 it had fallen by over 3 million to 9.9 million, the lowest membership figure since 1961. At the same time trade union density fell from over half of the workforce in 1979 to 32 per cent in 1990 (Department of Employment, May 1993: 189). Loss of membership was paralleled by a well-publicized decline of industrial militancy as indicated by the frequency and duration of strikes. In the 1970s, in only one year did the number of working days lost fall under 6 million, whereas this was the case in 6 out of 9 years between 1980 and 1988 (Department of Employment, 1989: 350). This difficulty in mobilizing their membership raises the possibility that there was a major loss in workplace support over this period. Finally, from active partnership in national tripartite institutions, the trade union leadership found itself ignored by government, while a series of major legislative acts were passed to curb strikes and to make recruitment more difficult. By 1990, what had been, in the eyes of many outsiders and members ten years earlier, a united, self-confident social movement as well as a powerful industrial bargainer, often seemed more closely akin to a demoralized collection of special interest groupings.

The record of these years raises a number of fundamental questions. Did membership loss imply a change in the relationship between employers and trade unions and a significant weakening of traditional union influence in the workplace? What factors lay behind the loss of trade union membership? Were they attributable to a difficult period of transition, or did they reflect longer-term attitudinal and structural changes that implied that the unions had entered a phase of irreversible decline? Finally, what steps had the unions taken to react to their falling membership, what were the main difficulties they confronted in doing so, and was there evidence that under certain conditions they could successfully revive their former support?

Such questions themselves point to a more general issue still. Is it appropriate to regard the 1980s as marking a fundamental break with the past? Should we interpret this period as one of cumulative displacement resulting in an irretrievable loss by British trade unionism of its former important position in British society and the British workplace? Alternatively, has any such break been overstated, to the extent that trade unions might regain a substantial measure of their former influence at some later date, provided economic, social, and political conditions once again turned favourable to them?

Improbable as such an eventuality now (1994) might seem, it should be remembered that many unknowns must be discounted in *any* forecast intended to hold good for the longer term. At the very least, the historical record on union influence in Britain suggests that any such prediction should be carefully qualified. The experience of the inter-war years should not be overlooked. Although the decline of British trade unionism in the 1920s and 1930s was massive and long-lasting, and the cause of demoralization in many parts of the labour movement, it had later to be viewed in significant part as cyclical and contingent, above all as an outcome of the structural change and recurrent economic recession of the inter-war years. However it is nowadays interpreted, it cannot be read as a permanent retreat. In the context of such a comparison, the unions' losses in the 1980s might appear to have been remarkably well-contained. Union density fell by nearly a third in the early 1920s, compared with less than a fifth between 1979 and 1984 (Batstone, 1988). In sum, a degree of caution—more caution certainly than is apparent in much of everyday political and economic analysis—should be exercised before concluding that trade union influence has receded once and for all, and is not merely undergoing another protracted recession from which it may recover.

The title of this book marks the caution with which the editors believe such questions should continue to be approached by social scientists. Despite the record of the 1980s, with the sharp falls of membership and the contraction of the sphere of trade union influence, it may still be premature to conclude that the decline of British trade unionism is irreversible.

2. THE END OF VOLUNTARISM?

Until the 1980s, the distinctive tradition of the British industrial relations system had been that of voluntarism. It was a tradition, supported by both employers and trade unions, which relegated legal intervention to a relatively minor role in industrial relations in favour of the regulation of the employment relationship through voluntary collective bargaining (Fox, 1985).

There is general agreement that the most notable feature of the period since 1979 is the challenge that was made to several of the key structural supports of voluntarism. The five changes that are most frequently cited as undermining voluntarism can be summarized as the *exclusion* of the trade unions from the policy process; the *pacification* of industrial conflict; the *contraction* of union membership and political influence; the *juridification* of industrial relations procedures and union organization; and the *demoralization* of trade unionism as a social movement (Rose, 1993). But despite this common picture of the broad processes of change, the scale of each type of change, its permanence, and its implications for the future, may be subject to considerable debate.

The central lever of change in most accounts is the legislative programme introduced by the successive Conservative governments. It is commonly concluded that the Thatcher governments were successful in achieving their main policy aims for 'taming' British trade unionism. This view has been advanced not only by writers supporting or sympathizing with Thatcherism (Kavanagh, 1987; Kavanagh and Seldon, 1988; Minford, 1988), or by prominent former members of those administrations (Tebbit, 1989; Lawson, 1992); it is accepted, albeit with sometimes important reservations, by many others less sympathetic to Thatcherite policies, or openly critical of them (Crouch, 1986; Gamble, 1988; Roberts, 1988). Nevertheless, it remains open to social observers concerned with the effect of more fundamental structural factors to question the exact nature, and the degree, of the discontinuity with the traditional pattern of industrial relations that occurred.

The clearest case by far can be made for discontinuity in the position of trade unionism at the national level. The themes stressed in many appraisals are the completeness of exclusion, and the extent and success of juridification. Union leaders were rapidly deprived of their *de facto* national influence in the early 1980s and their resulting inability to rally their membership to resist the legislative programme further undermined their power and authority. The declared aims of policy were the imposition of 'orderliness' in the internal affairs of unions and in industrial relations processes and procedures. However, it can be argued that juridification also had an accumulating normative and ideological impact far beyond this, diluting, or even dissolving, the previously strong tradition of voluntarism in British industrial relations. Dating back to mid-Victorian times, the voluntarist system, and its attendant sets of beliefs and values, had grown out of the readiness of governments and employers to accede to the wish of the trade unions to avoid close legal regulation of employment and workplace relations, in return for the acquiescence of trade unions in the continuation of capitalism and their scrupulous respect for the rule of law outside the workplace itself. Appearing in 1985, Alan Fox's *History and Heritage*, the most systematic, and sympathetic, treatment of the voluntarist tradition, itself already noted many advance signs in the first years of Thatcherism pointing towards the steady withdrawal of support for voluntarism within government circles, and a consequent erosion of the values that sustained it in industry. Above all, the growing legislative programme expressed the right of the State to regulate not only the relations of employers and trade unions in the workplace, but also to intervene in union governance itself. The whole spirit of the new legislative apparatus, and much of its letter, abandoned the voluntarist tradition and its ideology. For their part, many government spokesmen and ministers openly disparaged voluntarist practice and its accompanying moral code, as part of the accommodative ('wet') consensus politics they blamed for Britain's economic decline.

At the national level, then, the voluntarist tradition may well have been displaced in a relatively enduring way. In this sense, the case for a radical and enduring break with the past during the 1980s seems a powerful one indeed. However, a decisive break with the voluntarist tradition would involve rather more than this. It would imply that voluntarist norms and practices at workplace level have been abandoned, and the replacement of the system of representation they allowed by some new one. Yet, this is an area that has received rather less attention from commentators. In practice, the importance attached to the new political agenda led to a tendency for studies of British trade unionism over the last ten or so years to focus heavily on what was in reality only one aspect of the position of the trade unions in British society. Until recently, the broader debate over the position of trade unions and the nature of industrial relations in Britain has been weighted towards discussion of the loss of trade union influence at the national level, and has been too little grounded in well-researched information about changes within workplaces.

Moreover, care must be taken as to what would constitute adequate evidence of general and permanent discontinuity at workplace level; it cannot be assumed to have occurred simply because change at national level was intended by its authors to produce it. There has been a growing awareness among industrial relations researchers that such a break in the voluntarist system at a workplace level, and its extent, must be *shown* rather than merely assumed, as a 'necessary' result of the retreat at national level (MacInnes, 1987; McCarthy, 1992).

The new employment laws undoubtedly gave employers the means to repudiate voluntarism, if they so wished, and it may seem logical that they would try to make full use of them for this

purpose. Such rationality was evidently assumed by the legis-
lators. Whether employers did so, successfully replacing voluntarism with new institutions and belief-systems, required
empirical confirmation. Early in the Thatcher period it was
widely—and not unreasonably—expected that British employers
would move rapidly against trade unions in the workplace, taking every advantage of a friendly government, the growing body
of employment legislation, and public opinion hostile to unionism, to mount a determined 'Employers' Offensive' (Hyman and
Elger, 1982). After marginalizing shop-floor representatives and
bypassing existing workplace institutions, it was suggested, many
employers would move on towards constructing non-union methods of consultation and negotiation, and finally withdraw recognition from, or simply expel from the workplace, those unions
that had not already withered.

This was by no means an implausible scenario, given the
record of tough bosses in some still nationalized firms, nor in
view of the success of just such an employers' offensive in
American industry over the previous decade. The bellicose industrial relations rhetoric of the Prime Minister and such
Employment Secretaries as Norman (now Lord) Tebbit gave it
further credibility. But if the prediction of an early and widespread employers' offensive was not an unreasonable one, given
the climate of the times and the legacy of resentment within
British management of the spread of the power of shop-floor
leaders during the previous decade, the reality of change may
well have been less dramatic.

As survey and case-study evidence of workplace industrial relations slowly accumulated (Batstone, 1984; Cressey, Eldridge, and
MacInnes, 1985; Rose and Jones, 1985; Millward and Stevens,
1986), surprisingly few signs were found of employers moving in
such a direction, even in unionized private firms. Indeed, what
struck some observers was the extent to which existing institutions and arrangements, though often weakened, remained in
place, despite the sudden opportunity to abolish them with relative impunity (Kelly, 1987; McInnes, 1987; McIlroy, 1988). To be
sure, the claim continued to be made (McKay, 1986) that 'muscular' or 'macho' managers were replacing those with a more
constitutionalist or voluntarist-minded approach, and trampling
over the traditional forms of bargaining, consultation, and nego-

tiation. Yet fewer living specimens of the breed than might have been expected were produced for inspection, and it was always difficult to separate the element of *ad hoc* opportunism from strategic choice in the behaviour of these comparatively rare cases.

3. BEYOND A THATCHER EFFECT

The relative neglect of developments at workplace level was accompanied by a tendency to place primary emphasis on government policy as the main source of change. This was perhaps understandable given the dramatic changes in policy and the effort taken to give them visibility. As has been seen, the years preceding the research were marked by a sharp reversal of many previous policies affecting the economy by a government intent on engineering a switch from a 'culture of dependency' to an 'enterprise culture' through its social and economic reforms. The name of the Prime Minister leading this political programme to transform British economic life had become linked directly with both the policies and with most of their immediately obvious social and economic outcomes.

The research programme of the Social Change and Economic Life Initiative (of which this volume constitutes one component) was concerned to research the nature of underlying social change rather than to focus upon policies *per se*. There were grounds for thinking that deep changes were under way in British society—for example, in family structure, in attitudes and values, or in gender roles—that had major implications for economic life, quite apart from the more visible political events and policy changes.

True enough, any such concern with 'fundamental change', rather than with the implications of particular government policies, may seem more valid in some domains than in others. For example, if we consider the household, there appears to be no a priori reason for believing that a profound effect on the domestic division of labour may have been produced directly by Thatcherism. (The analysis of this domain is reported in Anderson *et al.*, 1994.) Yet on the other hand, industrial relations and trade unions had been specifically targeted by Conservative strategists for remodelling through policy changes long before Margaret Thatcher came to power. The Thatcher governments were to carry out the greater part of their initial programme of industrial relations reform before the end of the decade: indeed, it was to become an even more ambitious programme than that originally envisaged. Given the radicalness of this programme and the public controversies it aroused, the temptation to focus primarily on policy effects is clearly substantial.

However, even with respect to trade unionism, such an approach may well be profoundly misleading. Social change, at least over the short to medium term, may be produced less by policies than by the social and economic fundamentals of structural and technological change in industry, with their knock-on effects on the distribution of skills or the composition of occupations. Government policy, to be sure, may amplify some of these trends and check others, even in the short term; in the longer term it may indeed override or reverse some of them; but the underlying trends exist independently of the policies, and their possible significance should not be overlooked. Indeed, it may be that the political and legal aspects of change in the situation of trade unions have been overstated, at the expense of others that are less evident or dramatic, in many reviews of the 1980s.

While the political context must be a central component of any social analysis of employment and the labour market, a focus on government aims, policies, and style of leadership, distracts attention from less dramatic underlying factors having little to do with government policy. Unless such factors—the degree of opposition, acceptance, or indifference of employers towards unions for example, or the subjective meaning of trade unionism to employees—are examined systematically any effect they *did* have is likely to be overlooked, or ignored. The evidence on such matters for the 1980s, it should be noted, is remarkably sparse compared to the massive documentation on changes in government policies and on the changing *political* position of trade unions. It is the nature and effects of such underlying social changes that constitute the principal concern of the research reported in this volume.

4. THE SCOPE OF THE DATA

The findings of the research programme, and their relationship to other work in the field, have to be seen in the light of the types of data that the Social Change and Economic Life Initiative collected. The overall programme of research, and the core surveys in particular, are described in the Methodological Appendix at the end of this volume. The concern here is to give some idea of the distinctive characteristics of the data for the study of trade unionism. To begin with, the research programme was based on a research design involving a very detailed analysis of different aspects of economic life in six localities—Aberdeen, Coventry, Kirkcaldy, Northampton, Swindon, and Rochdale. A locality design was chosen with the aim of studying both employers and the labour force within a common setting. At the same time, it made it possible to assess arguments about the implications of different local labour market contexts for employment experience. The localities selected differed both in terms of their experiences of unemployment and of their history of industrial development. Both factors could have had important implications for the organizational strength of trade unions with the onset of severe recession in the 1980s.

In each locality, there were several phases of data collection. The first and essential feature of the resulting data-sets, relatively uncommon in British social research, is their complementarity. The Work Histories/Attitudes survey provided information on the involvement in and attitudes towards trade unionism of over 6,000 individuals; while the Employers Baseline survey (involving over 1,300 workplaces), supplemented by an intensive follow-up survey of 191 workplaces, documented the policies and attitudes of employers. The complementarity of data (and perspectives) that results is increased by the quite different *methods* of data collection used in the smaller-scale Related Studies, designed to gain a more qualitative understanding of the dynamics of industrial relations and of the experiences and attitudes of managers, union officials, and employees, in situations chosen for their theoretical importance. As will be seen from Chapters 3, 7, and 8, these studies relied upon intensive case-study work, open-ended interviewing, observation, and historical documentation. This provided a rare chance to examine the consistency of findings—which proved to be of a high order—produced by contrasting methods of enquiry and analysis.

A second feature of the data is its comprehensiveness. The survey enquiries were not restricted to employees who were currently union members; they were also concerned with the attitudes to trade unionism of the non-unionized. As well as providing information on 4,000 employees, the full sample of the Work Histories/Attitudes survey included almost 2,000 people who were either self-employed, currently unemployed, in full-time training or education, or currently non-active. The surveys collected information not only about people's current relationship to trade unions, but also about their experience of trade union membership in the course of their earlier work histories. Similarly, the research on employers was concerned not only with workplaces where trade unions were present, but also with those where trade unions were not recognized. Unlike the other major source of data on workplace relations (the Workplace Industrial Relations Survey) it includes small establishments (with 25 employees or fewer) as well as larger. This is important in that there are good reasons for thinking that both the nature of employee contracts and the pattern of employment relations is quite distinctive in small establishments. It is in this sector for instance that a large proportion of part-time work is concentrated.

It will be seen also from the chapters that authors have made use of varied, but complementary techniques of analysis. Statistically based treatments—themselves adopting very varied techniques—are employed in Main's chapter on the union wage mark-up, Elias's longitudinal handling of the work histories to explore long-run trends in membership, Gallie's exploration of the issue of union allegiance and decline between the localities, and Gallie and Rose's chapter on employer policies to unionism. Largely qualitative approaches (though they too make use of 'hard' data where appropriate) are adopted in Rose's examination of union survival in Swindon, Penn and Scattergood's exploration of the challenges to unionism in Rochdale which recurred throughout the 1980s, and Sewel and Penn's extended case-history of attempts to unionize the North Sea oil industry up to 1990. As will be argued shortly, these different techniques of analysis produced results which together build an integrated picture of trade unionism in the six localities in the later 1980s.

The type of data collected by the Social Change and Economic Life Initiative differed in some important ways from that of other studies concerned with the development of trade unionism. As was emphasized earlier, the overall programme was intended to throw light on the longer-run, underlying social changes affecting economic life. In this sense, it can be regarded as an effort to understand, and to document, continuing processes in contemporary social and economic history, as these were experienced by—and in turn affected by—*the actors themselves*. It is concerned above all with drawing a representative picture of what was happening at local level in the different labour markets. This contrasts sharply with most studies of British trade unionism over this period, which have focused either on developments at national level or on case studies of industrial relations, selected because they involved particularly dramatic (but not necessarily representative) examples of change.

The aims of this study can most closely be compared with those of the three Workplace Industrial Relations surveys (WIRS) (Millward *et al.*, 1992; Millward and Stevens, 1986; Daniel and Millward, 1983). The well-recognized strengths of the WIRS studies (see Rose, 1993) are their provision of nationally representative data on workplace relations, as these are reported by management and employee representatives. It will be noted that many of the basic findings from employers in this study correspond with the results from the WIRS reports for the period in question.

However, the data used in the present study have a rather different emphasis. The WIRS surveys—rooted primarily in the research tradition of industrial relations—focus primarily on the institutions of representation and bargaining. The Social Change and Economic Life Initiative—influenced primarily by work in Economic Sociology and Labour Economics—was concerned with trade unionism as one aspect of a much broader set of issues relating to the experience of employment. Thus the enquiries on trade unionism were set in the context of others dealing, in some detail, with pay, technical change, work organization, trends in skills development, and employment policies with regard to women, part-time workers, and other peripheral employees. The findings on trade unionism *per se* can thus be set in a broader context than they can be with the WIRS material—although they lack an equivalent national representativeness.

Second, the present study was concerned not only with the description of institutional change, but with the motivation of the actors involved. An important way in which the Initiative data complements that of WIRS lies in the more extensive evidence it can provide on the attitudes and intentions of individual and collective actors. Moreover, whereas WIRS had primarily examined the perception of change by employers and trade unionists, the Initiative was just as centrally concerned with the experiences of ordinary employees and particularly with the factors that underlay their decisions about whether or not to be members of trade unions.

5. OVERVIEW OF THE RESEARCH

5.1. Employer Policies and Trade Unionism

As was noted earlier, the principal objective of the research programme was to chart changes in the position and strength of trade unions at local level. Our first concern was with whether or not there had been major changes in employer attitudes to the unions. The conventional wisdom of the 1960s and 1970s was that British employers had come, over the decades, largely to accept the ethos of collective bargaining. They were prime models of what has been termed the 'constitutional' approach to management (Harbison and Myers, 1959; Kerr *et al.*, 1973). Collective bargaining was recognized as the most effective way of winning consent and co-operation to workplace rules; institutionalized relationships with the unions prevented the irruption of unpredictable wildcat strikes that had devastating effects for production; and, in any event, negotiation was a realistic response to employers' awareness of the coercive power of a strong trade union movement (Batstone, 1988).

For many commentators, the 1980s was a decade characterized by a sharp break with the dominant trend in employer attitudes to the unions. Employers, it was argued, began to move away from a policy of building collaborative relationships with the unions to a policy of bypassing them in favour of direct links between management and employees. A particularly clear statement of this view was advanced by Beaumont in 1987 in a book significantly titled *The Decline of Trade Union Organisation.* For Beaumont, a major change in management attitudes to the unions 'could be held to constitute the major threat to union density in the UK, given that existing recognition arrangements are generally viewed to be largely the result of management (and government) policies and practices' (p. 15). The major incentive for employers to seek to reduce union influence, he argued, was the sharp increase in the union mark-up on pay, although it had been facilitated by the move away from centralized bargaining arrangements, the growth of a 'secondary' workforce of workers on fixed-term contracts or working for sub-contractors, and industrial relations legislation designed to weaken the unions (ibid. 15 ff.).

Another factor that has been viewed as altering employer attitudes to trade unions was the rapidly changing technical and product market environment of the 1980s. Employers had been faced by a sharp increase in competition in the product market and one of their principal responses to this was to accelerate the introduction of new technology. A characteristic of automation is that it frequently cuts across conventional skill demarcations in the workforce and encourages employers to seek greater flexibility in the use of labour. More generally, employers have been seen as becoming increasingly preoccupied with increasing flexibility in the use of labour (Atkinson, 1985; Atkinson and Meager, 1986), although the extent of such a development has been a matter of considerable debate (Pollert, 1991). Arguably, confronted by a trade union movement still profoundly influenced by historic craft traditions, the achievement of such flexibility requires a marked reduction in union influence.

Finally, the 1980s saw the advocacy of a new philosophy of employee relations—human resource management (for overviews see Storey, 1989; Sisson, 1989). This conflicted in many ways with the assumptions of the traditional industrial relations model. In the latter, employee commitment was to be secured through the process of *collective* bargaining. Participation in the formulation of the rules that governed work life was regarded as the key to consent. Human resource management, on the other hand, advocated a sharply individualistic approach to the relationship between employer and employee. Employee motivation was seen as depending upon the development of better direct communications with individual employees, the closer monitoring and evaluation of performance, the development of rewards that recognized individual effort and performance, and the construction of opportunities for personal development and for advancement within the organization. With their emphasis on equality of treatment between employees, the trade unions could well be seen as a major constraint on the possibilities of implementing the new principles of effective management.

The evidence adduced for such a profound change in employer strategies is often little more than anecdotal. The data in the present study has made it possible to examine the issue in a far more systematic way.

It was evident from the main survey of establishments that the picture of a marked change in employer attitudes to unions has little empirical basis. To begin with, as Chapter 2 shows, strong anti-union feeling was very rare. Only 5 per cent of managers claimed that their establishments discouraged union membership, a far smaller proportion than that of establishments that actively encouraged membership (28 per cent). Further, the great majority (77 per cent) of managers in establishments with unions, when asked whether there had been any change in their policies over the previous five years, claimed that there had been no change. Nor was there any sign that they wanted to change the existing level of union influence in the foreseeable future. The reasons that were given for the preference of maintaining the *status quo* were remarkably evocative of the factors that had emerged as important in the 1960s (McCarthy, 1966). The unions were seen as helping to ensure effective communications in the workplace, as making it possible to build up higher levels of trust, and as permitting more rational forms of negotiation. In short, there was no evidence of widespread anti-unionism among employers and those employers that had unions present emphasized the continuity rather than change in their policies.

What had happened to union influence within the workplace? The evidence confirmed that there were substantial variations by industry. For instance, in engineering, there was a clear tendency for the unions' influence over both pay and work organization to decline, whereas it had increased sharply in financial services. Taking the overall pattern, however, there was no evidence of a general tendency for union power to be undermined. The most frequent pattern with respect to both pay and work organization was one of stability. It was clear that union power at workplace level proved much more resilient than would be anticipated from loss of union power at the national level. The explanations that managers gave of this again suggested the strong continuity with earlier decades. Union influence has been maintained in part because managers found unions useful and in part because they recognized that the cost in conflict of trying to undermine them would be too great.

A closer examination shows that the principal reasons that have been advanced for a shift in managerial attitudes are unconvincing. There was no sign, for instance, that organizations that had been in the forefront of introducing new technology were particularly unfavourable to trade union membership or had seen a decline in union influence. In part, this reflects the fact that the picture often held of union resistance to technical change is heavily exaggerated. Research on the introduction of new technology has shown that in reality shop stewards have tended to co-operate with the introduction of new technology and new working practices and have focused their efforts primarily on receiving a share of the financial gains of technical progress (Flanders, 1964; Gallie, 1978). For the 1980s the Workplace Industrial Relations surveys indicated that there was very little bargaining, as distinct from consultation about technical change, and that strong resistance was only encountered in 2 per cent of cases affecting manual employees (Daniel, 1987: 130, 185). This general co-operativeness of employees and their representatives in the introduction of technical change should be seen in the context of our evidence that technical change clearly leads to an enrichment of the skill levels of employees at almost all levels of the workforce (see Penn, Rose, and Rubery, 1994). Finally, doubts about the view that the unions were a significant obstacle to technical change can only be reinforced by the finding that workplaces which recognized manual trade unions were consistently more likely to introduce change affecting manual workers than establishments which did not (Daniel, 1987: 22). Overall, there seems little support for the notion that technological change has had major impact on industrial relations. The character and strength of British trade unionism has been little affected by the new technology 'revolution'.

The evidence also casts considerable doubt on the argument

that employers are changing their attitudes to the unions and to collective bargaining as a result of their conversion to new philosophies of employee relations emphasizing direct contact between the managerial hierarchy and the workforce. Our survey data certainly indicate that 37 per cent, a significant minority, of employers had been introducing alternative forms of involvement for employees. But there is no evidence that these were designed to undercut union influence. Indeed, organizations that had introduced employee involvement schemes were more likely than other establishments to actively encourage union membership and, most crucially, union influence over work organization was more likely to have increased than where such schemes had not been introduced. The data suggest that employee involvement schemes were closely linked to management's perceptions of the motivational needs generated by technical change and to the adoption of more strategic types of overall workforce policy (involving for instance personal development through training and promotion). There was no evidence that they reflected anti-unionism or had the effect of weakening the unions.

The implications of the spread of new employee relations policies are explored in greater depth by Michael Rose in Chapter 3. He draws on four case studies, carried out in Swindon, that represent the types of establishments where such developments should have been particularly evident, if they were occurring. They included the subsidiary of an American-owned multinational, the parent company of which advocated a strong employee communications policy; a non-union firm in the electronics sector, with an explicit attachment to a team-work conception of the employment relationship; the administrative headquarters of a larger British-owned multinational, which was experiencing the extensive introduction of information technology; and a public sector research establishment, which had been exposed to new government pressures to introduce market criteria.

Two points emerged particularly strongly from this research. First, employer policies in general consisted of relatively fragmented and *ad hoc* introductions of particular elements of the new employee philosophy, rather than forming a systematic and well-thought-out strategy. There was evidence of a change in the direction of greater informality, the reduction of formal status differences, increased discretion for employees in their jobs, and a reduction in the autocratic control of supervisors. But beyond this, policies varied substantially and focused in a very piecemeal way on particular experiments in work organization. The rather partial nature of this 'new employee philosophy' in firms that were apparently ideal candidates for developing it could be attributed to diverse factors: the cultural difficulty of transferring American communication styles to a British workplace, the difficulties of maintaining any type of coherent personnel policy in a rapidly changing organizational environment, the lack of expertise of managers in how to run such systems and in many cases their scepticism about their effectiveness, or in the case of the public sector, about the principles underlying them.

Second, it was clear that such partial new employer strategies had relatively little success in transforming the employment relationship or in generating very different employee attitudes to trade unions. Employees in two of the companies failed to perceive the closer relations and the new atmosphere of trust that management was trying to introduce. In general, the increased pressure of work was as noted as the growth of job discretion. There was little sign in any of the establishments of strong anti-union feeling, and in the public sector research organization, support for the unions and the willingness to take industrial action had grown stronger. Certainly, the non-union electronics company which had the most developed of the new employee relations policies had been successful in keeping away the growth of demands for union representation. But it was clear that non-unionism among employees remained conditional upon the company maintaining its current concern for employees and its advantageous employment conditions. As the company expanded, the conditions for achieving this were becoming steadily more problematic. Perhaps the final irony was that the company with the highest level of employee commitment was not one that had sought to limit the role or even the presence of the unions, but rather one that had maintained traditional bargaining arrangements.

Overall, these intensive case studies strongly confirm the evidence of the survey data. Even in conditions that were in principle highly favourable to a major restructuring of the employment relationship, new employer policies have been introduced in a very partial and often half-hearted way and have had very little impact on the underlying attitudes of employees to either management or the unions.

Finally, it has been noted that one of the major arguments for why employers in the 1980s should have become more aggressive towards unions was the supposed increase in the trade union mark-up. In Chapter 6, Brian Main uses the survey data on employees to subject this to empirical scrutiny. In the past, there have been very varying estimates of the extent of the union mark-up; but as Main points out, the critical factor in ensuring an adequate analysis is the ability to control for as wide a range as possible of other characteristics that could influence pay levels. Here the data provided by the Initiative is of unusual richness. It contains not only indicators of the conventional human capital variables, but a very considerable amount of detail on the demands and characteristics of people's current job, their family union backgrounds, their political allegiances, and their household characteristics. Further, as Main argues, when estimating the mark-up, care has to be taken to allow for the possible selectivity bias created by workers with high productivity characteristics choosing to move into better-paid unionized jobs.

The substantive conclusions that emerge from Main's analysis show that the level of trade union mark-up varies substantially depending on the particular type of worker. Allowing for selectivity bias, it was 6.2 per cent for manual males and 8.1 per cent for non-manual males. However, a notable finding was that it tended to be considerably higher for women—18.7 per cent for full-timers and 13.5 per cent for part-timers. Is there any evidence of the sharp increase in the pay differential created by trade union membership that underlies arguments such as Beaumont's? Earlier studies have focused on manual workers and this group must therefore be the point of reference for change. Stewart (1983), using data from 1975, found a wage gap of 7.7 per cent for the average manual male trade union member, a figure which is very close to that revealed by Main's analysis for 1986. The evidence, then, points to a substantial continuity, rather than major change, in the trade union mark-up. The financial motive that is supposed to lie at the heart of any new employer offensive—namely, a sharp rise in the mark-up—would appear to have little empirical basis and is unlikely to have been a significant factor influencing employer policy.

Overall, then, the evidence suggests that commentators who have pointed to a widespread change in employer attitudes to the unions have been misled by a reliance on selective and largely atypical evidence. The general pattern has been one of very considerable continuity. Employers have maintained their relationships with trade unions within the workplace rather than trying to undermine them. The explanation for this is primarily that they consider unions to play a valuable role in mediating their relations with the workforce. At the same time, the constraints that unions in practice impose on management's ability to introduce technical change, to initiate new employee relations policies, and to pay competitively, appear to have been heavily exaggerated.

5.2. Structural Change and Trade Union Membership

A second factor that could be seen as greatly weakening the traditional system of industrial relations is the decline in trade union membership. This is sometimes depicted as a necessary and remorseless outcome of long-term structural and cultural changes in British society. Such accounts have emphasized, in particular, changes in the class structure, the sectoral shift away from manufacturing and towards service sector employment, the growing feminization of the workforce, and broad cultural changes emphasizing individualist rather than collectivist values.

Historically the heartland of the trade union movement has been the manual working class. Its strength could be seen as deriving from a number of distinctive conditions of traditional working class life: the organization of work in large factory settings; the sharp status divide between manual and non-manual work; the vulnerability of jobs in periods of economic downturn; and the strength of community sociability outside work. All these factors were likely to generate a sense of collective identity and an awareness that improvement was more likely to come about through collective action than through individual effort.

However, the central feature of the changing occupational structure is the relative decline of manual work and the expansion of non-manual occupations. In the period immediately prior to the First World War, some 80 per cent of the workforce were manual workers. By 1987, the proportion had fallen to 52 per cent (Routh, 1987: 28, 38). Indeed, non-manual workers now represent a majority of those currently in employment. The growth of non-manual work was partly linked to the sectoral shift from a manufacturing to a service-based economy. For authors such as Daniel Bell (1974) this implied a fundamental change in the organization of work of a type which was likely to undermine the traditional strength of trade unionism. The typical work units of the expanding non-manual strata are smaller in size and have greater autonomy. Hierarchical forms of management are superseded by more egalitarian forms of professional control. The dehumanization of work dominated by the rhythms of the machine disappears with the emergence of a form of work that is centred on interactions with people (ibid. 40–2, 162–3). Thus, it is argued, the major sources of resentment that gave rise to the collective organization of labour are steadily undermined, while rising levels of skill and education encourage meritocratic principles and cultural individualism.

The move to a society dominated by the service sector was also accompanied by a marked increase in the labour market participation of women and this, too, has been seen as aggravating the difficulties of trade union organization. In 1954 women constituted 29.8 per cent of all employees; by the end of the 1980s this had risen to 43.8 per cent (IER, 1987: 98; CSO, 1991: 72). Indeed, between 1971 and 1989, some 90 per cent of the increase of the labour force by 3.1 million can be accounted for by the increase in the number of women (CSO, 1991: 67). A number of studies have suggested that women are less likely to join trade unions. Some (for instance, Bell, 1974: 146) argue that this is due to a lower commitment of women to continuing participation in the labour market and hence to a lower incentive to join unions. Others have pointed to the influence of the typical work situation of women—in particular, the prevalence of part-time work—and to work cultures that emphasize the subordinate status of women, in heightening the obstacles for unionization.

These different structural changes, it has been argued, have contributed to a long-term shift in social values, a shift away from the traditional collectivist values that have underpinned trade unionism and towards values that emphasize individual choice and achievement. Some evidence supporting such a trend could be found in the results of surveys' questions into public

attitudes to trade union power (Nielson, 1985: 15). Trade unionism, it was implied, survived largely through its ability to coerce
employees into membership through institutional arrangements
such as the closed shop. In this context, the membership crisis of
the 1980s could be viewed as a natural result of the sharp decline
in commitment to trade unionism, at a time when the coercive
powers of the unions had been fundamentally weakened.

In this volume, the data from the Initiative is used to assess
these explanations of trade union decline. Chapter 4 focuses on
the argument that membership can be explained in terms of a
declining commitment to collectivism among trade union members. Using a variety of different types of evidence, it concludes
that such a view is highly implausible. To begin with there is very
little evidence of widespread alienation from the unions among
trade union members. While it is correct that a significant minority (41 per cent) had initially become members out of some element of constraint—whether because it was a condition of the
job or because they had experienced strong informal pressures to
join from their work colleagues—their experience of membership
had led them to develop a much more positive type of commitment to membership over time. It is notable too that few trade
union members (15 per cent) had come to feel that membership
had become less important to them over the previous five years.
In contrast, 39 per cent felt that it had become more important.
Turning to those that had left union membership, the striking
fact is that the explanations that they gave overwhelmingly
reflected structural constraints rather than any disagreement in
principle with trade unionism. A large proportion had left
because they had become unemployed or non-active. Of those
that had stayed in employment, the major reason for having
ceased to be a member was that there was no union present in
the establishment that they had joined. In short, the evidence
from current members and from ex-members points in a very
similar direction. The current members showed no signs of
declining commitment to the unions (if anything it was the
reverse), while the former members had given up their membership for reasons that were largely outside their control and that
had nothing to do with anti-union feeling.

Is there any evidence that changes in the class structure are
fundamentally undercutting union support? The research results

reported by Gallie in Chapter 4 cast considerable doubt on the view that trade union decline is an inevitable feature of the growth of non-manual occupations. It should be noted that the differential commonly cited between manual and non-manual membership rates depends on the use of a particular (and rather crude) classification scheme for distinguishing manual and non-manual occupations. It disappears once a more rigorous scheme of class classification is adopted. Certainly, it is misleading to think of non-manual employees, in general, as less committed to trade unionism than manual workers. The level of membership in the rapidly expanding service class, which brings together professionals, administrators, and managers, is fully comparable with that among the declining class of non-skilled manual workers. Moreover, in terms of the extent to which the decision to join and to stay a member was voluntary, in terms of frequency of attendance at trade union meetings, and in terms of the extent to which the importance of membership was felt to have increased over time, trade unionism in the expanding service class is, if anything, more robust than in the manual working classes. Overall, there is little convincing evidence that the growth of non-manual occupations has any necessary effect in weakening trade unionism.

Was sectoral change of greater importance? Our evidence also conflicts with the view that the shift to a 'service-based' economy inherently undercuts trade unionism. The overall levels of membership in the manufacturing and service sectors were very much the same. Far more important than the growth of the service sector *per se* was the nature of ownership. Levels of unionization were very much higher in the public sector (69 per cent) than in the private (31 per cent). This could not be explained away in terms of the size of establishments in the two sectors. Rather more significant was the more widespread favourability to union membership among managers in the public sector, perhaps reflecting the fact that, historically, government action has played a significant role in encouraging the institutionalization of industrial relations in this sector. The growth of public services has proved favourable to the unions, the growth of private services has weakened them.

While our evidence undermines the importance frequently placed on class changes in the structure and on broad sectoral changes, it does confirm that there is a substantial difference in the membership levels of men and women. However, a close examination suggests that this is not specifically to do with gender differences in the value attached to collectivism. Where women were employed in full-time jobs, their membership levels were very similar to those of men. The major difference is not between men and women, but between full-timers (whether male or female) and women part-timers. Further, our data show that it is not possible to account for the lower unionization of part-time female employees in terms of lower commitment to employment. It seems probable that it reflects the structural conditions in which part-timers work and the nature of trade union recruitment efforts, rather than anything distinctive about women's attitudes.

As well as such longer-term structural arguments concerning changes in trade union membership, other arguments have been advanced which emphasize shorter-term cyclical factors. In particular, it has been suggested that trade union membership is heavily affected by changes in the rate of inflation and by changes in the rate of unemployment. Inflation, it is suggested, tends to lead to an increase in membership. Workers perceive a threat to their standard of living and join unions to counter it. At the same time employees will be more willing to make concessions that reinforce the union's reputation for efficacy, since higher costs can be passed on to customers. Unemployment, on the other hand, depresses union membership levels, because employers feel in a stronger position to oppose unionism and to withstand strikes.

In Chapter 5 Peter Elias extends the analysis to examine business-cycle theories of union membership changes. He draws on the detailed work histories that were collected from the 6,000 respondents. These provide information on all the jobs that the people had held since they left school (together with details about periods of unemployment and non-employment). As part of the information about the characteristics of each job, the people were asked whether or not they were trade union members. This provided an exceptionally rich set of data about the histories of trade union membership over time and their relationship to patterns of labour market change. Using the full set of 17,000 employment years, Elias develops a series of statistical models to examine the influence of business-cycle factors, individual characteristics, and job characteristics on the probabilities of being a trade union member. He finally estimates a 'fixed-effects' model of the factors that influence the propensity to join or to leave a union.

His analysis shows that there is in fact no significant relationship between changes in the national rate of inflation and trade union membership. There is somewhat more evidence in favour of an effect of the national unemployment rate, but the effect is rather weak. In general, he concludes that business-cycle theories have little explanatory power and that the more important influences on membership lie in individual labour market experiences and in the characteristics of the employment situation. Much more important than the national unemployment rate was people's personal experience of unemployment. The strongest influences of all were the characteristics of the jobs people held. Those who were employed in the public sector, in larger-sized establishments, in manufacturing, or in transport and communications were notably more likely to be union members. Although using the data in a rather different way, his analysis confirms many of the cross-sectional conclusions about the determinants of trade union membership.

The data presented cast considerable doubt on deterministic scenarios of trade union decline. The major shift in the occupational structure with the relative expansion of non-manual work has been exaggerated as a factor undermining union strength. The trade unions have been able to successfully expand their membership among non-manual employees and our evidence suggests that in terms of active commitment the rapidly expanding 'service' class may be one of the strongest bastions of union influence. Integrally related to this, it is clear that the growth of a service-based economy does not in itself undercut trade unionism. Rather what is crucial is the influence of the public sector on service provision. That is ultimately a matter of political decision and, as such, is a contingent rather than deterministic aspect of social structural development. Finally, despite the persisting evidence of a difference in levels of trade unionism between men and women, it is clear from our evidence that this is in no sense a necessary outcome of differences in gender values. Women working full-time are very similar in membership levels to men.

The shortfall in the unionization of women is related to the recruitment difficulties in part-time work, the extent of which is a very distinctive, and again contingent, aspect of the British pattern of employment.

Instead our evidence points to the continuing effects of a period of unusually rapid transition and restructuring. A great deal of the membership loss suffered by the unions can be accounted for in terms of the collapse of traditional industrial sectors in the 1980s. The rapid change in economic structure confronted the unions with greatly increased organizational difficulties relating to the expansion of new industrial sectors and smaller-sized establishments. A trade union movement which had come to experience relatively easy membership growth in the 1970s as a result of government protection was clearly faced by a major challenge of organizational renewal in order to be able to recruit effectively in new areas. However, there is little evidence of any extensive or increasing disenchantment with trade unionism in the workforce and, as we shall see in the final section, the logic of the employment relationship is likely to provide fertile terrain for recruitment in hitherto unionized sectors.

5.3. The Trade Union Response: Constraints and Opportunities

If there are few grounds for adhering to a deterministic view of the evolution of trade union membership and influence, it becomes essential to consider the nature of the organizational problems that the unions have had to confront and the policies they have adopted in trying to overcome them. The latter part of the volume provides case study evidence relating to two of the localities that were at different ends of the spectrum in terms of the recent experience of economic growth—Rochdale and Aberdeen.

In Chapter 7, Roger Penn and Hilda Scattergood focus on the implications of the recession in the 1980s for the organizational structure of trade unionism in Rochdale and on the nature of the unions' response to membership loss. Their interviews with local employers and trade unionists confirmed the conclusions of the first part of this volume that the unions were not significantly threatened by a change in employers' attitudes. It was the dramatic collapse of large sectors of traditional manufacturing industry in the locality that posed the major threat to union strength. These changes confronted the unions with a major new challenge, which, in many cases, they were slow to meet. What were the major reasons for this?

The authors examine a number of possible constraints on local union effectiveness. One factor that may have undermined union organization at local level was the structural change in union organization occurring at national level. Faced with falling membership and revenues, there was a sharp increase in the pressure for an amalgamation of unions and a simplification of union structure. Increasingly, smaller occupation- or industry-based unions were being assimilated within the giant union conglomerates. What was the implication of this for the effectiveness of the unions at local level and for the services they were able to provide their members?

Penn and Scattergood show that such rationalization did not inevitably weaken local union organization. Depending on the nature of the union and its locational decision, the process in some cases weakened and in some cases strengthened local unionism. Amalgamation could lead to the weakening of local unionism when it implied an increased distancing of union officers from their membership. Such distancing could also occur within unions that had maintained their identities. The AEU, for instance, dissolved its Rochdale district in the mid-1980s, amalgamated it with that of Oldham, and placed the administrative centre in Oldham. In such cases, the increased geographical distance between officials and membership made it more difficult for overstretched union officials to keep closely attuned to developments in the locality.

However, there were also cases where amalgamation strengthened local union organization. A clear example was the case of the textile workers. In 1986, the ATWU was amalgamated with the GMB and this led to a radical transformation of union structure for members in the industry, involving the development of an extensive shop steward system in the textile mills. The outcome of changes in union structure in textiles was, then, a strengthening of grass-roots organization and the adoption of a pattern of unionism much closer to that prevalent in the engineering industry.

Another factor that might have seriously weakened the unions' local effectiveness was a growth in union division. Apart from the amalgamation movement, perhaps the most visible change in union relations was the increased sharpness of inter-union conflict. Union solidarity appeared more threatened than at any time since the Second World War. In particular, the EETPU and the AUEW found themselves locked in a series of disputes with the other unions over respect of the Bridlington principles at the Isle of Grain, over the acceptance of government financial assistance for postal ballots, and over the principle of single union deals with employers. The exclusion of the EETPU from the TUC in 1988 raised the spectre of a major split in British trade unionism, that might have produced a divided and conflictual unionism of the type that has characterized post-war France. However, Penn and Scattergood show that, despite the media publicity they attracted, these inter-union disputes had little impact on the everyday relations between unions at local level. Relations between unions in Rochdale remained generally good. Although the expulsion of the EETPU from the TUC might have led to a fierce membership war, as other unions took advantage of its loss of protection under the Bridlington rules, in practice there were no significant attempts to capture the EETPU membership. An awareness of the mutual risk and of the organizational resources that would be required for a membership war led to a preference to maintain the traditional pattern of inter-union relations at local level.

The central source of weakness of the local unions was not then a growth of inter-union division, it was rather the acute understaffing of the unions at local level and the deeply entrenched traditionalism of views about recruitment. The local union offices were hopelessly under-resourced. Officials in three of the major unions were unable even to provide estimates of the number of members that they had in Rochdale. In some cases, union officials were unaware that they had members in certain establishments. The picture that emerges is of local officials, sometimes at a distance from the locality, working exceptionally long hours, lacking relevant information and overloaded by the demands upon them. This helps, in part, to account for the fact that local union organizations showed relatively little initiative in trying to widen their recruitment bases. Despite calls from the national union organizations to launch major campaigns to extend recruitment among women and to find ways of incorporating peripheral workers into union structures, there was little evidence of any substantial drive at local level to open up major new areas of membership. The traditionalism of the unions was reflected in their structure, with women and Asians still heavily under-represented within the unions' own local leadership. Their internal structure made them poorly equipped to formulate the types of demands that would extend their membership.

Trade union organization in Rochdale, then, was clearly on the defensive, but there was nothing deterministic about the strategic passivity that prevailed. On Penn and Scattergood's analysis, the key source of union weakness lay in the inadequate resourcing of local officials and in the failure to develop programmes that responded better to the needs of categories of employee that had not been part of the traditional membership.

While the structural problems that trade unions have faced in devising an adequate response to the large-scale shifts in the economy in recent decades are clearly very substantial, there have none the less been cases where the trade unions have developed their organizational strength even under exceptionally difficult conditions. An interesting example of the ability of British trade unionism to respond to adverse structural change is the recent history of industrial relations in the North Sea off-shore oil industry. This represents in many ways an extreme case of the rapid growth of a new industry, which provided very unfavourable terrain for the extension of union influence. The employers were strongly opposed to union representation. The American-owned companies in the industry had brought with them a more sharply crystallized non-union philosophy than was prevalent in British non-union firms in general. At the same time, given the profits generated by the industry, employers were able to provide pay levels that were likely to weaken the sense that unions were necessary. Finally, the conditions of work in the industry had created a workforce that was particularly difficult to organize. It was physically cut off from easy access by union officials. It was highly dispersed, both in terms of the work setting and of the residential areas from which employees were drawn. Also it was sharply divided between a set of core employees who were employed directly and on a permanent basis by the oil companies, and an extensive periphery of employees working for sub-contractors on short-term contracts.

Yet, as John Sewel and Roger Penn show in Chapter 8, despite this wide variety of factors that might be expected to lead to stable non-unionism, the oil industry employers have been unsuccessful in maintaining the legitimacy of a non-unionized employment relationship. They have had to concede trade union recognition and negotiating rights to certain sectors of the workforce, they have increasingly granted an important informal role to the unions in resolving disputes, and they have been confronted by steadily more effective types of collective action.

How was this possible? To begin with, Sewel's account points to a number of ways in which the employers' non-union policies had effects which de-stabilized the employment relationship and thereby provided opportunities for union mobilization. The unrestricted nature of managerial power in the oil industry made it relatively easy to intensify work practices, a process that was particularly marked in the period of restructuring and cost reduction in the 1980s. However, such intensification can easily occur at the expense of safety standards. The growing worry about this culminated in the tragedy at the Piper Alpha oil rig in 1988, when 167 employees lost their lives. It seems likely that the disaster heightened the awareness of the need for a greater degree of employee control and gave a major stimulus to the militancy of the close of the decade.

The 'dualistic' system—with its sharp distinction between the terms of employment of the core and the peripheral workers—was also a major potential source of resentment. It has been suggested that this type of employment system offers employers significant advantages in terms of flexibility and is likely to become increasingly prevalent. However, such an employment system has its costs. While the insecurity of contract work had been concealed during the long period of growth, it was made apparent with a vengeance when oil prices collapsed in the mid-1980s. The contract workers bore the brunt of staff reductions and their pay levels were slashed. The action of the employers could but generate a much keener awareness of the logic of the dualist system and highlight the disadvantages to employees of the lack of union organization and collective agreements.

In short, the very effectiveness of the new employment system in making it easier for employers to intensify work, to cut pay, and to reduce the workforce provided the conditions for a

greater awareness on the part of employees of the need for collective organization. By refusing to accept mechanisms of
employee representation and control, the oil employers were able
to suppress the expression of dissatisfaction and grievance in the
short term. In the longer term, however, this led to an accumulation of tensions and finally to the eruption of particularly sharp
forms of unofficial industrial action.

Moreover, over time, the unions themselves became more
effective at developing appropriate organizational forms and finding power resources that could be used to put pressure on the
employers. Chapter 8 highlights the internal difficulties the
unions had to resolve in devising an effective strategy to recruit
and to gain bargaining rights in a new industrial sector. They
were very slow to understand the strategic importance of the new
industry, and inter-union rivalry about who should represent the
oil workers hampered effective action. Yet, despite these difficulties, there appeared to be a learning experience over time,
marked by increased co-operation between different unions and
between union officials and grass-roots activists. Further, the
unions discovered that there were ways in which they could bring
pressure to bear on employers, even in a context as unfavourable
as that of the oil industry.

Finally, it is clear that the ability of the unions to extend their
influence was as much dependent on the support that they could
count on from government as on the purely industrial power
resources that they could muster. The advances that the unions
made in the 1970s in extending collective bargaining rights to certain categories of workers and in securing union officials' rights
of access to workers, took place in a context of active government support. By the 1980s, however, the political climate had
been transformed and the unions' attempts to extend their influence were seriously hampered by the Conservative Government's
removal of the unions' right to obtain recognition ballots in the
face of employer opposition.

Overall, then, the case of the off-shore oil industry reinforces
the view that there is no deterministic process by which structural
changes lead to the marginalization of union influence. This was
an industry where the barriers to unionization were particularly
great. Yet despite this, once the unions had taken the task of
organization seriously, they showed that they could make signifi-

cant progress in extending their influence and in developing collective action. This was partly because a non-union employment
situation generated sources of strain that provided opportunities
for mobilization and partly because of the growing skill of the
unions in using their local power resources. However, it is also
clear that a major factor affecting the unions' capacity to organize is the support available from government in setting the general climate of industrial relations, in intervening directly with
employers, and in providing a legislative framework that facili-
tates union recognition.

6. THE INEVITABILITY OF TRADE UNION DECLINE?

It is clear that the British trade union movement was severely
weakened in the 1980s, both in terms of its membership and its
national power. But our results suggest that at local level its
influence held up much better and, indeed, that the underlying
support for the traditional voluntaristic structures of collective
bargaining remained much more resilient than is commonly
believed.

While some employers clearly took advantage of the economic
and political climate of the 1980s to reduce union influence, there
was no evidence of a growth of widespread employer hostility to
trade unions. Indeed, where trade unions were present employers
generally saw them as exercising a useful function in facilitating
communications with the workforce and in providing a more
orderly system of industrial relations. The introduction of new
managerial policies with a stronger emphasis on direct communications with employees was seen as complementary to, rather
than in contradiction to, the desirability of maintaining more traditional forms of collective bargaining. While employer culture
may change in the future, it seems improbable that it was a
major factor contributing to the decline of union strength over
this period.

It is also clear that there was no major decline in employee
commitment to trade unions. The great majority of trade union
members felt that their membership was voluntary and they were
more likely to feel that the importance of membership to them

had increased over the previous five years than that it had decreased. There was no evidence that the long-term shift towards higher-skilled occupations was undercutting commitment to the unions. Those who had left trade unions consisted of two major groups. The first were people who were no longer in jobs either because they had become unemployed or because they had left the labour market altogether. The second were people who had moved to new jobs where there were no unions present. Hostility to the principles of trade unionism appears to have been of negligible importance in accounting for membership loss.

The major structural factors undercutting the unions were the sharp rise in unemployment and changes in the pattern of employment. The 1980s saw a collapse of employment in the manufacturing industries, a marked decline in public sector employment, a shift towards smaller workplaces, and a growth of part-time work. These changes involved a serious erosion of the types of employment setting from which the trade unions had traditionally drawn their strength. The unions were confronted by the need to adapt their policies and organization to recruit from new sectors of the workforce. At the same time new recruitment was made more difficult by high unemployment and the withdrawal of any effective government support for the extension of collective bargaining.

While the economic changes of the 1980s greatly increased the difficulties that the unions faced in maintaining their membership, they do not imply a deterministic scenario of union decline. As we have shown, the re-orientation of union policies and the organizational changes needed to recruit new types of employee entail a long and very difficult process of adjustment, but there is no reason in principle why they should not occur. Indeed, the experience of the 1980s has clearly led to a considerable rethinking of union structures, with a shift towards a smaller number of unions with broader coverage. But, equally important, the future of the unions is likely to depend upon the policies of government with respect to unemployment, the public sector, and the encouragement of collective bargaining. It is a future, then, in which political and organizational factors will play the decisive role.

2

Employer Policies and Trade Union Influence

DUNCAN GALLIE AND MICHAEL ROSE

There are a number of grounds for thinking that employer attitudes to the trade unions might have hardened in the 1980s. First, there was a shift in the size distribution of establishments. It is generally thought that employers are more favourable to the unions in larger establishments, where there is a greater need to ensure formal communications with the workforce and to negotiate agreements about employment conditions. However, the direction of change in the 1980s had been for the growth of smaller, and the relative decline of larger, establishments. Second, it was a period of rapid technological change. Arguably employers were encouraged to reduce union influence by a desire to implement change more rapidly, without being constrained by detailed negotiations over pay and work organization. Third, changes in the labour market, particularly the high level of unemployment in some local labour markets, might have given employers a sense that cheap labour would be available if trade union influence could be reduced while giving them an increased confidence in their power to curb the unions in a context of employee insecurity. Fourth, sharpening national and international product market competition might have led to much greater emphasis being placed on the efficiency of working practices and the reduction of costs, thereby increasing anti-union feeling among the employers most affected. Finally, the 1980s saw an ambitious legislative programme designed to weaken trade union power and this may have both encouraged employers, and given them the means, to roll back union controls in the workplace.

But how much did employer policies change in practice over this period? This chapter is concerned with examining the nature

of managerial attitudes to union organization in the mid-1980s
and with assessing the extent to which effective union influence
had changed within the workplace. It provides the essential context both for the analysis of employees' involvement in unionism
(Chapter 4) and for the intensive case studies of management–
union relations (in Chapters 3, 7, and 8). The chapter will
explore the major contextual influences on managerial policies
and union influence and will consider whether or not the spread
of new types of managerial policy for communication with the
workforce posed a fundamental threat to the traditional influence
of the unions. It draws on two sources of data: the employers'
baseline survey (involving 1,311 establishments) and the in-depth
follow-up interviews in 191 establishments (see Methodological
Appendix).

1. MANAGERIAL POLICIES TOWARDS UNION ORGANIZATION

The first question to be addressed must be how far employers in
these localities were disposed to continue supporting existing
trade union representation and involvement, rather than merely
tolerating it or actually reducing it, at a time when government
policy and prevailing political rhetoric were unfavourable to the
unions. Is there any evidence that hostility to the unions had
become widespread among employers? The managers of the organizations in our sample were asked whether, as employers, they
encouraged trade union membership, accepted it, or disapproved
of it. The striking feature of Table 2.1 is just how rare anti-union

TABLE 2.1. *Policy towards trade union membership*

	All	Private sector	Public sector
Encourages	28	12	47
Accepts	44	39	49
Disapproves	5	8	1
No policy	23	40	2
Other	1	1	1
N	935	660	275

Source: Baseline Employers Survey.

feeling was among employers. Overall only 5 per cent of organizations disapproved of trade union membership. A far higher proportion (28 per cent) were to be found actively encouraging it, while 44 per cent accepted it without strongly positive or negative feelings. A substantial proportion of employers (23 per cent) appeared not to have formulated a policy in the absence of any attempt by employees to organize.

There is no evidence that those who had experience of trade union organization in the workplace were thereby made more hostile to the unions. On the contrary, a mere 2 per cent of managers in organizations where the unions had a presence disapproved of them. The general impression that managers in unionized plants were generally sympathetic, rather than hostile, to the unions is reinforced by the data collected in the intensive follow-up interviews. For instance, when asked how management found its contacts with shop stewards, the great majority (64 per cent) thought they were helpful and a mere 5 per cent described them as conflictual. Some 20 per cent said that relations varied between stewards and 7 per cent that they were neutral—neither particularly harmonious nor conflictual. A similar pattern emerges with respect to relations with local union officials, with 57 per cent considering these helpful, 2 per cent conflictual, and 34 per cent with no strong view either way. In our intensive studies, we were also concerned to explore further whether or not policies had changed over time. To begin with, management was asked whether it had changed its policy towards the unions in any significant way in the previous five years. Overall, 77 per cent of establishments claimed that there had been no change in policy. Although the proportion that had changed tended to be higher in establishments that were more favourable to trade unions, it is still the case that 70 per cent of those encouraging membership and 73 per cent of those accepting it reported that policy had remained the same. Further, among those that had changed policy, it is notable that only a third said that management had become tougher.

If preferences for the future are considered, a very similar picture emerges. When asked whether or not they would like a change in the level of union influence, over 80 per cent of managers were happy with the existing state of affairs. In the small proportion of establishments that favoured a change, however, it was certainly the case that the preference was for a reduction (16 per cent), rather than for an increase (2 per cent), in union influence. The more general pattern of satisfaction with the *status quo* was evident whatever the current policies of the organization. It also held true for both the public and the private sectors, although satisfaction was particularly widespread in the private sector. Whereas, in the public sector, 61 per cent of those that encouraged union membership and 75 per cent of those that accepted it, would wish to see no change in the current situation, the proportions in the private sector rose to 82 per cent and 83 per cent respectively.

Why was it that the great majority of managers in organizations that either encouraged or accepted trade unionism were favourable to preserving existing union influence? The most common reason given (32 per cent) was that the unions helped to ensure effective communications with the workforce (Table 2.2).

TABLE 2.2. *Reasons trade union influence should be maintained*

	Count (no.)	Proportion (%)
Social explanation		
Effective comms. allow this	39	32
Wish to build trust	16	12
Subtotal social		44
Technical explanation		
Simplifies negotiation	16	12
Eases change	7	5
Subtotal technical		17
Non-technical explanation		
Can't give coherent reason	14	10
Union good policeman	13	9
Contains militants	2	2
Unions lack real influence	7	5
Other	7	5
Subtotal non-technical		39
TOTAL	121	100

Note: Number of employers giving reason for saying 'happy with present influence' = 97.

Source: 30 Establishment Survey of Employers.

A number of other factors mentioned also reflected the view that the unions were an important source of social integration. For instance, 12 per cent said that the presence of unions helped to build up trust in the organization, 12 per cent mentioned that it led to more rational forms of negotiation, and a further 5 per cent that it eased social change. The borderline between these types of responses and the perception of the unions as a source of social control is clearly a thin one. Some 10 per cent of managers gave reasons that suggested that they saw the unions as useful in containing militants and in helping to keep order on the shop floor. The principal difference between those who actively encouraged membership and those who just accepted unions was that the former were more likely to give explanations in terms of building up trust and easing social change, while the latter placed more emphasis on the rationalization of negotiations and the usefulness of the unions in controlling the workforce.

The minority of managers who wished to reduce union influence were also asked what differences a reduction of union influence would make to the way they organized the workforce. The factor most frequently mentioned was that it would make it possible to increase flexibility in work and to reduce the numbers employed. A small proportion mentioned the advantages it would bring for the control of work performance.

Overall, then, the picture provided by our data is a clear one. Even in the mid-1980s, there was evidence of strong anti-union feeling among only a very small minority of employers. A far higher proportion actively encouraged union membership and, in a majority of the establishments, managers at least accepted a union presence. The explanations given for this indicate that the unions were seen as having a positive function in contributing to social integration in the establishment and, in some cases, towards improved social control over the workforce. Managerial policies towards the unions appeared to have changed little over the preceding five years and there was little sign that managers wanted them to change in the future. In short, whatever the appearance of radical change in industrial relations that might be given by the repeated legislative changes of the period, there is no evidence that this was having a major influence on managerial policies.

2. STRUCTURAL INFLUENCES ON MANAGERIAL POLICIES

2.1. Size and Ownership Sector

What factors were most important in determining employer attitudes to the unions? A common argument in the literature is that a powerful determinant of employer attitudes to the unions is organizational size. As organizations become larger, it is suggested, it becomes increasingly difficult for employers to organize work and to maintain relations with the workforce on a personal basis. Instead, organizational life is based upon a complex web of rules and a major problem confronting the employer is how to ensure employee commitment to such rules. A solution to this is to expand the scope of joint regulation, on the grounds that where rules have been elaborated with the unions they are likely to be better adapted to the needs of the workforce and to receive legitimation through the process of negotiation. A frequent assumption in the past has been that the general trend in the first part of the century towards larger establishments would continue, thereby providing an important foundation for union growth. In the 1980s, however, this trend would appear to have been reversed, with a shift towards smaller establishments.

How does size of establishment relate in practice to employer attitudes to the union? Taking first the overall pattern of the data, there is, indeed, a very clear relationship between organizational size and employer favourability to trade union membership. In establishments with less than 25 employees, only 17 per cent of organizations were favourable to membership. The proportion rises to 29 per cent in establishments with between 50 and 200 employees (Table 2.3). Then there is a very marked rise to over 40 per cent in establishments with 200 or more employees. This appears to be the critical threshold; there is no further increase in favourability in the 500+ category.

However, the effects of size are heavily qualified by those of the ownership sector. Whether or not organizations were in the public or private sector had a major impact on attitudes to trade unionism. In the public sector, 47 per cent of organizations reported that they were favourable to trade union membership, whereas in the private sector the figure dropped as low as 12 per

TABLE 2.3. *Percentage encouraging trade union membership*

Establishment size	All	Private sector	Public sector
<25	17	9	44
25–49	22	7	51
50–99	29	17	45
100–199	29	16	37
200–499	47	26	58
500+	44	34	46

Source: Baseline Employers Survey.

cent. The private sector is by no means homogeneous: active support for union membership fell to a low point in chemicals and in retail (6 per cent), but rose to 24 per cent in construction and to 32 per cent in the finance industries. However, in no industrial sector were the figures for the private sector as high as in the public. This did not reflect strong anti-union feeling on the part of private sector employers; only 8 per cent reported that they disapproved of union membership. Rather, private sector employers were much more likely to be without any clear policy about trade unions, claiming that the issue had not arisen. The major difference between the sectors, then, lies in the prevalence of *active* employer support for trade unionism rather than in the frequency of negative attitudes.

The effect of size of establishment on policies to the unions is very different in the two sectors. It is only in the private sector that size of establishment has any marked effect. Whereas in the smallest private firms (25 employees or less) only 9 per cent of organizations were encouraging membership, in firms of 500 or more, the figure rose to 34 per cent. In contrast, in the public sector, there is very little difference at all between the smaller establishments and the large ones. It is notable that the smallest establishments in the public sector are more favourable to trade unionism than the largest establishments in the private sector.

The pattern of these results is confirmed by the logistic regression in Table 2.4. It is clear that the form of ownership is considerably more important than size as a determinant of policy. Overall, those in large establishments were more than seven times as likely as those in small ones to encourage trade unionism. However, if establishments are divided into private manufacturing,

TABLE 2.4. *Logistic regression on employer favourability to unionism*

Variable and level	Multiplicative estimates
Size	
<50	1.00
50–99	1.37
100–199	2.23
200–499	5.90
500+	7.39
Sector	
Private manufacturing	1.00
Private lower services	0.89
Private professional services	0.78
Public lower services	30.65
Public professional services	21.42
Pay comparability	
Other	1.00
Lower than average	2.33
Area	
Aberdeen	1.00
Swindon	0.60
Northampton	1.02
Coventry	2.28
Rochdale	1.61
Kirkcaldy	2.99

Source: Baseline Employers Survey.

routine and professional private services, and routine and professional public services, it is clear that whether or not organizations were in the public sector was a more powerful influence on employer attitudes to unionism. Organizations in the routine public services were thirty times more likely than those in private manufacturing to encourage unionism and those in the professional public services were twenty times more likely. Further, when the regressions were run for the public and private sectors separately, the size effect was found to be significant only in the private sector. In the public sector, the historical pressure of the state to extend and secure trade union rights has created a far more favourable environment for trade union organization, and this extends down into the smallest establishments.

2.2. The Impact of New Technology and Workforce Policies

If a major shift is taking place in management's attitudes to the unions, this is likely to be reflected most sharply in organizations that have been at the cutting edge of technological and organizational change. It seems plausible that it is when organizations seek to introduce change that they become most sensitive to the constraints that unions may impose on management's freedom of manœuvre. Were these organizations, in practice, particularly likely to have strong reservations about trade unions?

Employers were asked whether they had introduced technological change in the previous two years. The types of change were subdivided into four main categories: word processing; a new computer or computer applications; new plant, machinery, or equipment (other than a computer) which includes microelectronics technology; and new plant, machinery, or equipment without microelectronics. The picture this gave was of quite substantial technological change in the recent past: 38 per cent of organizations had introduced word processing, 56 per cent new computer systems, and 29 per cent new equipment with microelectronics. In addition, 33 per cent had introduced technical change of a more traditional type that did not involve new technology.

Our evidence, however, provides no support for the view that the organizations that had been at the forefront of introducing new technology were particularly unfavourable to trade union membership. If the analysis is confined to the two-way associations, organizations that had introduced new technology were more rather than less likely to say that their policy was to encourage membership (Table 2.5). It was only where traditional types of technical change had been introduced that there is a marginal decline in favourability to the unions. However, when added to a logistic regression controlling for size, sector, and labour market, none of the different forms of technical change emerged as statistically significant. A composite index representing the *number* of different types of technical change introduced also had no effect on the likelihood that management would encourage union membership.

Might it be that it was those organizations that were most concerned to rationalize and intensify working practices that were

TABLE 2.5(*a*). *Technical change and policies towards union membership*

| | Introduced in last 2 years | | | | | | | |
| | Word processing | | New computer systems | | New plant with micro-electronics | | Other new plant | |
	Yes	No	Yes	No	Yes	No	Yes	No
Encourages	34	25	31	25	36	25	27	29
Accepts	41	45	44	44	40	45	45	42
Disapproves	5	5	5	4	8	4	6	4
No policy	20	25	20	26	16	25	22	23
Other	1	1	1	1	—	1	—	1

Source: Baseline Employers Survey.

TABLE 2.5(*b*). *Policies towards union membership by proportion affected by new technology*

| Policy towards union membership | Proportion affected by new technology | | | | |
	None	1–12%	13–33%	34–65%	66% or more
Encourages	24	22	33	43	40
Accepts	45	47	44	31	45
Disapproves	4	7	3	3	5
No unionism	26	24	19	23	9
Other	1	—	1	—	1

Source: Baseline Employers Survey.

most favourable to the unions? As can be seen in Table 2.6, the two-way associations provide a little more support for the view that work reorganization was linked with less favourable attitudes to unions than was the case for technical change. Organizations that had increased the use they made of shift work, that had trained employees to cover jobs other than their own, that had made greater use of pay incentives and individual performance assessment, and that had replaced some of their regular employees with temporary workers were less likely to encourage union membership and more likely to express disap-

TABLE 2.6. *Rationalization of work and managerial policies*

Typed change increased	Percentage encouraging membership		Percentage disapproving of membership	
	Change introduced	Change not introduced	Change introduced	Change not introduced
Shift work	26	29	13	4
Training to cover other jobs	28	29	6	4
Use of pay incentives	24	29	6	5
Individual performance assessment	27	29	7	4
Work measurement/ method study	35	27	7	4
Replacement full-timers versus part-timers	39	27	8	4
Replacement regular by temporary workers	23	29	10	4
Reduction of surplus personnel	33	27	3	5

Source: Baseline Employers Survey.

proval of it. The differences, however, are very small. An index of work rationalization was constructed from a factor analysis of these items to give a stronger measure of the propensity of organizations to engage in the reorganization of working practices. Moreover, once size and sector were controlled for in a logistic regression, there was no relationship at all between the emphasis that management placed on work rationalization and its attitudes to unions.

This same picture emerged with respect to a range of other managerial labour force policies. Organizations that had developed internal labour market policies, that had extended the use of temporary or other types of 'peripheral' worker, or that had come to employ substantial proportions of part-time workers showed neither greater nor less favourability to the unions than other types of organization. In general, the innovativeness of organizations in terms of their approach to technical change, to the organization of work, and to the composition of their labour forces would appear to have no necessary implications for their policies to trade unions.

2.3. *Labour Market and Product Market Effects*

Rather more significant for management policies was the type of labour and product market in which they operated. Three of the areas in the study were traditional industrial areas with high current unemployment. One possibility is that where unemployment is higher, management would feel in a stronger position to undercut trade union power. It might, for instance, use the greater availability of labour to adopt a policy for recruiting those without union attachments. However, if the more prosperous labour markets are contrasted with those that had a more severe experience of recession, it is clear that there is no tendency for management to wish to weaken unions in the areas in which it had the greatest labour market power (Table 2.7). On the contrary, even when size and sector are controlled for, organizations in the high unemployment areas were more than twice as likely as those in the more prosperous areas to have a policy of encouraging trade union member-

TABLE 2.7. *Managerial policies to unions and labour market position*

	Encouraging (%)	Disapproving (%)
Higher unemployment		
Kirkcaldy	44	3
Rochdale	24	7
Coventry	27	5
Lower unemployment		
Aberdeen	28	3
Northampton	25	5
Swindon	28	6
Perception of pay compared with local average		
Somewhat above	18	8
Average	25	5
Do not compare	33	—
Somewhat below	44	1
Varies by job	49	1

Source: SCELI: Baseline Employers Survey.

ship. It seems likely that these traditional industrial areas have
developed distinctive cultures and patterns of industrial relations
characterized by a high degree of institutionalization of trade
union influence. The historically created commitment to such relationships makes them relatively immune even to labour market
conditions that might appear to be favourable to the development
of more aggressive managerial policies.

Another feature of an organization's labour market position
that might affect its attitudes to the unions is its relative position
within a particular labour market. Employers who were paying
above average rates might be expected to be less favourable to
the unions, either because they view them as responsible for their
comparatively high labour costs or because they anticipate that
the growth of union organization would exacerbate such costs.
Managers were asked whether their organization paid in line with
the local average, somewhat above the average, or somewhat
below it. The evidence in Table 2.7 suggests that there is indeed
an association with relative pay position. Where organizations
paid somewhat above the average, only 18 per cent encouraged
union membership, and, indeed, even among those that saw
themselves as being in line with the average the figure only rises
to 25 per cent. In sharp contrast, where pay was below average,
44 per cent encouraged union membership. Similarly, organizations that either did not compare their rates with local rates or
that found it difficult to compare in any simple way (because
some jobs were higher than average, others lower) were substantially more likely to encourage union membership than those that
paid average or above average rates. This relationship between
pay policy and attitudes to unions remains quite clearly significant even when size, sector, and locality are controlled for, with
the high and average payers only half as likely to encourage
union membership. The evidence does suggest, then, that the
greater the pressure on wage costs, the less favourable management becomes to union organization.

Finally, an important feature of the 1980s was the increased
pressure that organizations confronted in terms of expectations
from their customers and greater competition. Overall, 23 per cent
of establishments had been affected by increased foreign competition and 39 per cent by increased competition from other organizations in Britain. Heightened customer demand was even more

widespread: 90 per cent of establishments reported that their customers had become more selective about the price of goods or the
cost of services, 80 per cent that they had become more concerned
about quality, 78 per cent that they had become more demanding
about design or presentation, and 53 per cent that they attached
increased importance to delivery dates or speed of service.

Were those organizations that had been affected by such pressures significantly less likely to favour trade union organization? In
the first place, exposure to increased competition—whether foreign
or domestic—appeared to have no significant implications for
favourability to the unions. There was some evidence, however, of
an effect of heightened customer expectation. But different types
of customer pressure had rather different implications for managerial attitudes to the unions. Where establishments had been under
increased pressure in terms of price, quality, or design, they were
in general more favourable to union membership (Table 2.8). In
contrast, where establishments had been under pressure in terms of

TABLE 2.8. *Managerial policies to unions and customer pressure*

	Percentage favourable to union membership	
	When pressure increased	When pressure not increased
Pressure over		
Prices	30	15
Quality	28	25
Design	32	14
Delivery	23	35

delivery dates or the speed of service, they were less likely to be
favourable to trade unions. In general, then, increased customer
pressure was associated with a willingness by management to
encourage the position of the unions, although pressure on delivery dates constituted a major exception.

3. CHANGING PATTERNS OF UNION INFLUENCE

Managerial policies may have remained relatively stable over the
period but, in establishments where the unions had a presence,

the effective pattern of union influence over key decisions may have altered substantially, either because management was better able to implement its policies or because of factors outside management's direct control. To examine this, two questions were asked about whether or not trade union influence had changed over the past five years: the first focused on the issue of pay and the second on the way in which work was organized.

There was more marked fluctuation in union influence than in managerial policy preferences. However, there was no evidence of any general tendency for union influence to be undermined. The most frequent pattern was one of stability. With respect to pay, 51 per cent of establishments said that there had been no change in union influence and a very similar proportion reported the same for union influence over work organization (56 per cent). This left a substantial minority where the unions' position had changed, but it is notable this was more likely to have reflected an increase in union influence than a decline. Whereas 36 per cent of managers reported that union influence over pay had increased, only 13 per cent felt that it had decreased. For work organization, the pattern is virtually identical: 33 per cent considered that union influence had grown greater, 12 per cent that it had become weaker.

The intensive follow-up studies give an indication of the types of issues over which union influence over work organization had changed most significantly. The list of issues that was given for these more specific assessments was by no means exhaustive, but it covered a fairly wide range of potential bargaining areas. These included pay structures and job evaluation; the pace of work; the internal deployment of labour (manning and transfers); personnel policies such as recruitment, promotion, discipline, and redundancies; and labour force policies involving the use of part-time workers, contract staff, and temporary workers. In establishments where the unions had increased their influence, this was particularly marked with respect to pay structures, disciplinary procedures, and redundancy arrangements (Table 2.9). For unions representing manual workers, increased control over job evaluation was also important. Where influence had decreased, this was most marked with respect to the pace of work, the internal deployment of labour, and recruitment. Over the range of areas both the increase and the decrease of influence tended to be more marked for the manual than for the non-manual unions.

Duncan Gallie and Michael Rose

TABLE 2.9. *Areas of growth of union influence (%)*

	Unions representing manual workers	Unions representing non-manual workers
Pay structures	39	39
Pace of work	26	25
Manning	28	24
Job evaluation	35	24
Transfer	26	22
Recruitment	22	18
Promotions	22	24
Use of part-time work	28	22
Contracting out	25	21
Temporary workers	22	19
Redundancies	32	29
Discipline	40	33

Source: Baseline Employers Survey.

Despite their severe loss of power at national level, our evidence suggests that the unions retained their influence relatively well in those workplaces where they had a presence. Why should this have been the case? We asked managers what types of factors would make it difficult to reduce union influence. Quite consistently with the previous findings, the single most common response (38 per cent) was that there was no strong desire on the part of managers to do so. However, there was also an awareness that current arrangements reflected a balance of power that could only be altered at the risk of considerable cost to management. For instance, 24 per cent mentioned that it would lead to trouble in relations in the workplace and 17 per cent pointed to the strength of worker loyalty to the unions.

It was notable that very few managers (5 per cent) appeared to feel that existing legal arrangements were of much significance in affecting union workplace power. This might have reflected the fact that the most important changes had already been introduced in the legislation of the early 1980s. However, in response to a direct question about whether the employment legislation passed since 1980 had affected in any way the position of the unions in the establishment, only 14 per cent of managers thought that it had been influential, 43 per cent that it had little influence, and 43

per cent that it had had no influence at all. The points most frequently mentioned by those who thought the legal change had
been influential were that it had led to procedural changes in
union activity—for instance, increased use of ballots, that it had
made members more careful about taking strike action, and that it
had made unions less active or militant (Table 2.10). The major
reason given by the majority for why legislative change had had
little influence was that relations in the workplace were harmonious and therefore the issues addressed by the law had not arisen.

In general, then, the existing level of union influence was seen as
sustained by a mixture of managerial preference and the strength
of workers' support for the unions. Government legislation was

TABLE 2.10(*a*). *How 1980s Employment Acts have affected union
behaviour*

	Count (No.)	Proportion (%)
Use of secret ballots	7	32
Members more careful	8	36
Cut down on activism	5	23
Other	2	9
TOTAL	22	100

Notes: No. employers saying unions affected 'quite a lot/a lot' by Employment
Acts = 15. Low numbers, general replies.

Source: 30 Establishment Survey of Employers.

TABLE 2.10(*b*). *Reasons unions little affected by 1980s Employment Acts*

	Count (No.)	Proportion (%)
Harmonious relations already	29	30
Behaviour already orderly	21	22
Legitimate union action	5	5
Laws aimed at national level	21	22
'We ignore it'	8	8
Other	12	12
TOTAL	96	100

Note: No. employers giving reasons why unions little affected by Employment
Acts = 49.

Source: 30 Establishment Survey of Employers.

not thought to have played a major role in the past and the current state of the law was not considered to be an important factor accounting for union influence in the present.

4. SOURCES OF CHANGE IN UNION INFLUENCE

There were none the less important variations in the way in which union influence had changed. What were the major factors that affected this? The major potential factors are again the structural characteristics of the organization in terms of size, ownership, sector, and industry; the types of policies management were pursuing in attempting to increase productivity and efficiency, and the nature of the labour and product market position of the organization.

4.1. Size and Ownership

It was seen earlier that employer favourability to trade unions was greatest in larger establishments. In contrast, an immediately striking feature of the data with respect to union influence over both pay and work organization is that it tended to increase more in smaller-sized establishments, which are generally seen as unfavourable environments for the unions (Tables 2.11 and 2.12). In unionized establishments with less than 50 employees union influence over pay had increased in 44 per cent of cases and the figure was also over 40 per cent for establishments with between 50 and 199 employees. In contrast, it falls heavily to 19 per cent in medium-large establishments (200–499) and to a mere 8 per cent in the very large. A broadly similar pattern emerges for union influence over work organization, although the differences between the smallest and largest establishments are less sharp.

Ownership sector again had a major effect on union fortunes. In the public sector, union influence had increased over pay in 43 per cent of unionized establishments and over work organization in 41 per cent. In contrast, in the private sector, the respective figures were only 24 per cent and 17 per cent. Conversely, a higher proportion of establishments in the private sector had experienced a decline in union influence. Overall, whereas in the public sector union influence was four times more likely to have

Table 2.11. *Change in union influence over pay*

	Change in union influence (%)		
	Increased	Same	Decreased
All establishments	36	51	13
<25 employees	47	32	22
25–49	43	44	14
50–99	40	55	5
100–199	48	43	9
200–499	19	68	14
500+	8	72	20
Private sector	24	56	20
Public sector	43	48	9
Engineering	5	64	31
Other manufacturing	28	59	13
Retail	35	45	21
Finance	43	57	—
Private manufacturing	15	63	22
Private lower services	34	44	22
Private professional services	47	53	—
Public lower services	11	76	14
Public professional services	59	34	7

Source: Baseline Employers Survey.

increased than to have decreased, in the private sector there was a much more even balance between the proportion of organizations that had seen a strengthening and a weakening of union influence. As can be seen from the logistic regression reported in Table 2.13, it was above all in the public professional services that union influence was seen to have increased.

Within the private sector, industry made a very substantial difference to union fortunes. The most consistent evidence for an overall decline in the level of union influence was in the engineering industry. With regard to both pay and work organization, union influence was much more likely to have declined than to have increased. Whereas 31 per cent of engineering establishments reported that unions had become weaker over pay, and 29 per cent over work organization, the proportions saying that

TABLE 2.12. *Change in union influence over work organization*

	Change in union influence (%)		
	Increased	Same	Decreased
All establishments	33	56	12
<25 employees	47	45	8
25–49	32	55	13
50–99	36	56	9
100–199	38	59	3
200–499	18	62	20
500+	27	54	20
Engineering	7	63	29
Other manufacturing	16	76	8
Retail finance	30	56	14
Finance	9	91	—
Private sector	17	68	15
Public sector	41	49	10
Private manufacturing	10	71	19
Private lower services	30	57	12
Private professional services	10	90	—
Public lower services	25	60	14
Public professional services	49	44	7

Source: Baseline Employers Survey.

union influence had increased were only 5 per cent and 7 per cent respectively. The same general pattern was evident for transport and chemicals. In all other industrial sectors, union influence was more likely to have increased than to have decreased. The increase in union influence was particularly strong in the finance sector, but it was also marked in other manufacturing, and in the retail industry.

4.2. New Technology and Workforce Policies

The basic pattern whereby union influence was more likely to have increased than to have decreased was true both of establishments that had introduced new technology and those that had not. The frequency of increased union influence tended to be lower and the proportion of cases of decreased union influence higher in establishments that had introduced new technology

Source: Baseline Employers Survey.

TABLE 2.13. *Logistic regression on change in union influence*

Variable	Multiplicative estimates	
	Pay	Work organization
Constraint	0.08	0.12
<50 employees	1.00	1.00
50–99	1.56	1.06
100–199	0.91	0.80
200–499	0.39	0.68
500+	0.19	0.84
Private manufacturing	1.00	1.00
Private lower services	1.93	1.78
Private professional services	3.79	0.87
Public lower services	0.96	2.17
Public professional services	6.96	5.23
Employment of marginal workers (%)		
None	1.00	1.00
1–19	1.95	1.83
20–49	1.75	0.77
50+	1.62	1.36

(Table 2.14). However, the differences were very small and failed to reach statistical significance once size and sector were controlled for. Moreover, such effect as there was would not appear to be specifically a result of new technology. The differences produced by the introduction of more traditional types of technology were, if anything, more marked.

Turning to employer workforce policies, there was little relationship between the introduction by management of policies of work rationalization and changes in union influence. There were, however, two types of policy that were significantly related. The first was the employment of marginal workers. Establishments that employed marginal workers were markedly more likely to have seen an increase in union influence. This suggests that management may only have been able to achieve greater workforce flexibility at the cost of granting the unions additional controls over work organization and making greater concessions in terms

TABLE 2.14(*a*). *Change in union influence over pay by technical change and work rationalization*

	Increase (%)	
	Change introduced	Not introduced
Technical change		
Word processing	31	40
New computer system	29	46
Plant with microelectronics	33	37
Traditional technical change	25	42
Increased shift working	33	36
Training to cover other jobs	28	41
Work rationalization		
Increased pay incentives	29	37
Increased performance assessment	26	40
Increased work or method study	36	36
Replacement of full with part-timers	32	37
Replacement of regular with marginal workers	19	38
Reduction of surplus numbers	31	38

Source: Baseline Employers Survey.

of pay. Second, establishments employing part-time workers were somewhat less likely to have seen gains in union influence. However, once sector and size were controlled for in a logistic regression, the effect of part-time employment disappeared completely, while that of marginal employment only remained of borderline significance.

Finally, it should be noted that the labour market and product market factors, which had been relevant for the degree of employer favourability to the unions, were of no discernible importance for trade union influence. The level of unemployment in the local labour market, relative labour costs, and the extent to which customer pressure had increased all failed to reach statistical significance. It is particularly notable that there was no support for the view that high unemployment in the local labour market reduces union influence (Table 2.15). This may reflect the

TABLE 2.14(*b*). *Change in union influence over work organization*
(increase) by technical change and work rationalization

	Percentage of establishments	
	Change introduced	Change not introduced
Technical change		
Word processing	31	34
New computer system	33	32
Plant with microelectronics	29	35
Traditional technical change	28	36
Work rationalization		
Increased shift salary	38	32
Training to cover alien job	29	35
Increased pay incentives	25	34
Increased performance assessment	23	36
Increased work or method study	35	32
Replacement of full with part-timers	31	33
Replacement of regular with marginal workers	19	34
Reduction of surplus numbers	30	34

Source: Baseline Employers Survey.

fact that, despite having greater potential power in such labour
markets, employers have little inclination to use it. Alternatively,
labour markets may have a sufficiently high level of internal segmentation for the level of unemployment to have little relevance
for the leverage of workers in unionized establishments.

Overall, then, it would appear that the major factors associated
with the pattern of change in union influence were structural factors such as size, ownership, and industry. It was above all in the
public sector that union influence had been expanding. A particularly interesting finding, however, is the growth of union influence
in relatively small firms and in establishments that have resorted to
the use of various types of temporary labour. In contrast, the
introduction of new forms of technology, the rationalization of

TABLE 2.15. *Change in union influence by area*

	Pay (%)		Work organization (%)	
	Increase	Decrease	Increase	Decrease
Higher unemployment				
Kirkcaldy	40	30	30	10
Rochdale	31	18	31	8
Coventry	30	19	32	16
Lower unemployment				
Aberdeen	39	10	34	12
Northampton	41	9	38	10
Swindon	35	10	26	8

Source: Baseline Employers Survey.

work processes, relative pay position in the labour market, and changes in product market pressure neither favoured nor undermined union influence. Similarly, a high level of unemployment in the local labour market did not appear to weaken union influence. In short, where the unions were established, there is little evidence that their influence was being eroded either in general or in the establishments that were setting the pace in terms of technical and organizational change.

5. ALTERNATIVES TO TRADE UNIONISM

A significant feature of the 1980s was the growth of employer interest in the development of new forms of direct communication with employees. The motives underlying this have been a matter of some debate. For some, it represents a more or less conscious effort by employers to develop an alternative to trade unionism. Such a policy might not always be accompanied by an overtly anti-union ideology. Presentationally, the emphasis might be upon the need to remove any obstacle to the flow of communication between employers and employees in a modern organization. Whatever the nature of employer intentions, it could be argued that the introduction of procedures for direct communication might have the effect of reducing union influence. They might have a normative effect, weakening loyalty to the unions by increased employee identification with the company. They might also undercut the instrumental grounds for union support by removing employees' dependence on the unions for representation and bargaining.

There was certainly evidence from our surveys of the importance attached by management to the development of more direct relations with employees. Overall, 37 per cent of establishments reported that they had promoted some alternative means of involvement for employees apart from a union. Moreover, there was some sign that the introduction of such policies was successful in affecting employee behaviour. Managers were asked whether there had been any change over the previous five years in employees' readiness to get on with their work and to do it well. Whereas 46 per cent of establishments that had employee involvement schemes reported that effort had improved, this was the case for only 30 per cent of those without.

The intensive follow-up studies confirmed the importance in management's eyes of social factors in the workplace and the growing importance of good communication. The considerable increase in effort, quality, and work discipline reported by the majority of employees was seen primarily as an achievement reflecting the social competence of management. When asked to outline thinking in their organizations on the best ways to get work done, techniques for improving social relations constituted by far the largest general category of answers (Table 2.16), and the most often mentioned single method was social skill. Similarly, the most frequent explanation given for the improvement in employee discipline over the preceding years was the success of management's efforts to motivate workers (Table 2.17). Moreover, explanations in terms of the increased 'market-mindedness' of employees (the second most frequent type of answer given) might also be seen as reflecting a normative change produced partly by the increased effectiveness of management communications.

To what extent was this type of managerial emphasis on employee involvement associated with a desire to undercut union influence? If one looks at the relationship between management's favourability to union membership and the existence of employee involvement schemes (Table 2.18), it is clear that direct communication was not seen as a substitute for union representation.

TABLE 2.16. *Prevailing view on ways to get work done[a]*

	No.	Proportion (%)	Category (%)
Social relations theme			
Social skills	64	30	
Supervision	16	8	
Acting fairly	15	7	
'Cliché' reasons[b]	14	7	
Participation theory	11	5	
All social relations			57
Technical theme			
Increased responsibility	26	12	
Training	18	8	
Appeal for efficiency	8	4	
Flexibility of unit	2	1	
All technical			25
Other themes			
Financial means	18	8	
Coercion ('macho management')	9	4	
Stability	5	2	
Unclear definition	1	0.5	
Other	6	3	
All other			18
TOTAL	213	100	100

Note: The number of employers reporting they had a view was 142 (74%). Coding allowed for each employer to refer to up to four features of the prevailing view, in order of priority. Very few employers did in fact mention more than two, and no allowance has been made for the relative importance of features, where more than one was recorded.

[a] Means of achieving or incentives to effort: 'Is there a particular view about how to get work done?'

[b] 'Cultivating good human relations', 'Treating people as people', etc.

Source: 30 Establishment Survey of Employers.

Indeed, the notable point is that organizations that had introduced employee involvement schemes were more, rather than less, likely to encourage membership (33 per cent compared with 26 per cent). It still might be the case that, within unionized firms, the objective effect of such policies might be to weaken the unions. But even this hypothesis receives little support from the

TABLE 2.17. *Reasons for better employee relations*

	No.	Proportion (%)	Category (%)
Normative changes			
Success of effort to motivate	34	23	
Employees more market-minded	21	14	
Pay incentives abandoned	3	2	
Fall in morale of unionists	2	1	
All normative changes			40
Technical changes			
Reorganization	15	10	
Flexibility	12	8	
Internal change	8	5	
Drive to reduce costs	7	5	
Decentralization	3	2	
All technical			30
Economic factors			
Fear of redundancy	19	12	
Money incentives	7	5	
Outside threat	8	5	
Loss of personnel	1	1	
All economic factors			23
Other	10	7	7
TOTAL	150	100	100

Note: The number of employers giving one or more reason was 105 (55%). More than one reason could be cited, in order of priority, but relatively few employers gave such multiple reasons. No allowance has been made in scoring for the relative importance of reasons, where more than one was recorded.

Source: 30 Establishment Survey of Employers.

data. Although union influence over pay had increased less in establishments that had introduced employee involvement (in 33 per cent of cases compared with 38 per cent in other establishments), it was still much more likely to have increased than to have decreased. Most crucially, union influence over work organization (the area that one might have expected to be most affected by such schemes) was more likely to have *increased* where direct employee participation had been encouraged (38 per cent compared with 30 per cent).

TABLE 2.18. *Employer favourability to unionism by employee involvement schemes*

Attitudes to membership	Employee involvement scheme	
	Introduced	Not introduced
Encourage	33	26
Accept	41	45
Disapprove	3	6
No policy	22	23
Other	2	1

Source: Baseline Employers Survey.

What factors then, did underlie the adoption of employee involvement schemes and how did they compare with those that affected employer policies to trade unions? Employer policies to trade unions were most heavily influenced by the size of the organization and by whether or not it was in the public sector. The picture with respect to employee involvement schemes is rather different. Although size of establishment was significant, the pattern was not a linear one. The organizations that were the most likely to have employee involvement schemes were either medium-small (50–100) or very large (500+). More fundamentally, ownership sector, which had been such an important factor in accounting for attitudes to trade unions, was of no discernible importance for employee involvement procedures (Table 2.19(*a*)).

Another striking difference lay in the connection between such policies and other organizational policies. Employer attitudes to trade unionism appeared to have little to do with either the concern to introduce technical change or the nature of their workforce policies. The emphasis on the development of employee involvement, in contrast, was closely related to both of these (Table 2.19(*b*)). As can be seen from the logistic regression reported in Table 2.20, employers who had introduced new technology were considerably more likely to have taken steps to improve communications. Further, those employers who had internal development policies for training and promotion were particularly likely to have set up such schemes. Finally, organizations where part of the workforce consisted of 'peripheral' workers, for instance workers hired on short-term contracts or from agencies, also placed a greater emphasis on

TABLE 2.19(*a*). *Establishments and employee involvement scheme*

	Establishments with schemes (%)
<25 employees	21
25–49	29
50–99	49
100–199	46
200–499	47
500+	41
Private manufacturing	38
Private lower services	29
Private professional services	17
Public lower services	49
Public professional services	38

Source: Baseline Employers Survey.

TABLE 2.19(*b*). *Percentage with employee involvement schemes by technical change*

	Introduced	Not introduced
Word processing	44	32
New computer systems	43	29
Plant with microelectronics	47	32
Traditional technical change	43	33

Source: Baseline Employers Survey.

employee relations. Such policies might be seen as a way in which employers seek to obtain the stability and commitment of their core workforce, by passing the costs of market fluctuations on to their peripheral workers. In short, employee involvement schemes appeared to be linked to the demands of technical change and to the adoption of more strategic types of overall workforce policy.

Overall, then, employee involvement schemes would appear to be closely linked to management's perceptions of motivational needs generated by technical change and to their broader orientation towards building up the level of skill and commitment in the workforce. There is no evidence that they were associated with managerial hostility to the unions or that they in practice led to any overall weakening of union influence.

TABLE 2.20. *Logistic regression on whether employer has an employee involvement scheme*

Variable and level	Multiplicative estimates
Size	
<50	1.00
50–99	2.00
100–199	1.42
200–499	1.28
500+	1.58
New technology	
None	1.00
1 Type	1.76
2 Types	1.09
3 Types	1.60
Internal development policies	
None	1.00
Production or training	1.21
Production and training	1.69
Employment of marginal workers (%)	
None	1.00
1–19	1.64
20–49	2.25
50+	1.85
Increased foreign competition	
No	1.00
Yes	1.07

Source: Baseline Employers Survey.

6. CONCLUSION

Our evidence points against the view that the 1980s saw a widespread growth among employers of more hostile attitudes to trade unions. Strong forms of anti-unionism among employers remained relatively rare. Where unions were present, few employers reported any change in policy towards the unions during the preceding five years and only a very small minority wanted a change in policy in the future. There was also little evidence of a loss of union influence within the workplace. The most prevalent pattern was one in which union influence had remained unchanged. The exceptional case was the engineering industry where there had been a very clear tendency for union influence in the workplace to decline.

These findings are broadly consistent with others obtained from survey work carried out at the same period. In particular, the Workplace Industrial Relations surveys (Daniel and Millward, 1983; Millward and Stevens, 1986; Millward *et al.*, 1992) show the considerable resilience of existing forms of British industrial relations arrangements in the 1980s, at least in those workplaces where they were long-standing. There does appear to have been some decline in union influence towards the end of the decade (Millward *et al.*, 1992), but this was mainly linked to factors such as changes in the size and occupational mix of workplaces, and to the decline of public sector employment. It was *not* found to be linked to any general hardening of employer attitudes towards union representation. Moreover, even at the end of the decade, there was still no sign of the emergence of any novel, non-union arrangements distinct and coherent enough to be called a new system. While a number of *ad hoc* experiments were in progress by the end of the 1980s, these were local improvisations and not an attempt to implement some more general blueprint for a new system of employee relations (see Marginson *et al.*, 1988, ch. 4; and the case-study evidence in Chapter 3 of this volume).

What accounts for the persistence of traditional patterns of industrial relations? First, our evidence suggested that employers saw some positive advantages to such arrangements. They reflected a belief that the unions helped to improve communications with employees and to heighten social integration. Second, some of the factors that might have been thought to weaken the position of the unions turned out to be of little significance. There appeared to be no contradiction between the drive for technical and organizational change and employer favourability to trade unionism. Further, new employer policies for improving direct communications with employees were conceived as complementary to, rather than as substitutes for, more conventional union channels. Finally, a high level of local unemployment was associated neither with more anti-union employer attitudes nor with a weakening of effective trade union influence in the workplace. This may have been due to a high degree of segmentation in the labour market, such that the unemployed did not represent any serious threat to the jobs of those in employment. Alternatively, employers may have been reluctant to sacrifice the long-term advantage of good established relations with their employees for any short-term benefits that could be gained from trying to undermine the unions in temporarily favourable economic conditions. Certainly, our data suggest that employers decided on their policies in the light of the logic of their local situations and that the legislative programme of union reform introduced by the Conservative Governments had remarkably little impact upon the everyday pattern of industrial relations in these localities.

There were, however, two factors that did appear to affect substantially the position of the unions and that might, in the longer term, have serious implications for union strength. These were size of establishment and ownership. Employer attitudes to the unions were less favourable in smaller-sized establishments, and, if the current tendency for an increase in the relative proportion of smaller-sized establishments accelerates, this might weaken the unions in the longer run. Yet, the implications of the growth in the number of small establishments were less clear-cut than is sometimes assumed. First, our data suggested that there was no *necessary* effect of establishment size, as was shown by the fact that it made little difference at all in the public sector. Second, the tendency for unions to *increase* their influence was also most marked in smaller establishments, perhaps indicating that the unions may be developing more effective ways of building up their presence in this sector.

There can be less doubt about the importance of the public sector for union fortunes. Management was more likely to encourage union membership, and union influence was more likely to have increased in public than in the private sector workplaces. The Government's privatization programme, then, may have constituted a greater threat to the unions' longer-term influence than its specific legislative programme for industrial relations reform.

3

Still Life in Swindon: Case-Studies in Union Survival and Employer Policy in a 'Sunrise' Labour Market

MICHAEL ROSE

1. SWINDON AND THE DE-UNIONIZATION HYPOTHESIS

The findings discussed in this chapter are based upon a set of case-studies of workplace level industrial relations, employee involvement in trade unionism, and the development of employer policies towards unions, undertaken by the Bath team in a Related Study[1] of the SCELI programme. (The scope of related studies is discussed in the section on the SCELI data on trade unionism in Chapter 1, and in the Methodological Appendix at the end of the book; further related studies of trade unionism are presented by Penn and Scattergood in Chapter 7, and by Sewel and Penn in Chapter 8.)

The present Related Study was carried out in the southern English town of Swindon. Swindon is situated in the middle of a corridor of new industrial development stretching from the London Heathrow airport westwards along the M4 motorway into South Wales. The Swindon travel-to-work area[2] includes many prosperous small towns and outlying commuter villages, besides its core town, which until recently has often been regarded as something of a geographical curiosity—a 'Northern town that slipped two hundred miles South'. On several grounds, the Swindon locality seemed to offer an appropriate context for case-studies of the survival power of unionism in the 1980s.

Though well-established, and at times a serious force for local employers to reckon with, trade unionism in Swindon had never been known either for its industrial militancy or for any strong ideological content. By the mid-1980s, the problems of local engineering industries had left it much weaker in terms of membership and influence in local politics. At the same time, the local authority had long been projecting Swindon—with considerable success—as a 'sunrise' town ready to grasp a new future in electronics, financial services, administration, and research. (Firms in such branches were even moving to the town in the depths of the recession of 1981–3.) Employers in such growing industries were considered by many observers to be inimical to trade unionism, partly because fewer blue-collar workers would be required, and partly because the new employers were thought more likely to avoid, or openly oppose, recognition of trade unions. Some at least of these incoming employers were indeed non-union firms and intended to stay so. Social scientists (SAUS, 1985) as well as local unionists began to ask whether Swindon unionism might not weaken still further, thanks to the growing number of these 'sunrise' firms. Arguably, such incoming firms might also have a 'demonstration effect' on those firms that did recognize unions, by showing how existing union channels could be superseded, or bypassed, by new, non-union forms of representation.

From the beginning of the 1980s the drive to extend the flexibility of employment practices and work-rules (Atkinson, 1985) had implied a growth of temporary, part-time, or other 'precarious' work for less well-qualified workers. If this trend was accompanied by efforts to increase the commitment of more valued or 'core' workers through improving their security of employment, by awarding them staff status, or by extending fringe benefits such as private health insurance, traditional union organization seemed likely to be weakened. In the workplace, managers would have a far freer hand in adopting novel methods of communication designed to increase a sense of involvement and identification with the employer's aims and outlook. If such a process was indeed occurring on any scale, Swindon—with its growing number of new firms, and its traditional craft unionism in rapid decline—seemed a likely place to find it.

The wider political context seemed to make for a widespread, and more or less inevitable, rejection by employers of traditional workplace industrial relations and trade union influence has been discussed in Chapter 1. As noted there, the hypothesis of a resolute, well-organized Employers' Offensive (Hyman and Elger,

1982), was not an unreasonable one in the light of the abrupt rejection of corporatist economic management, the hostility to unionism on ideological grounds of many government figures, the widening scope of restrictive legislation, and the fall of union membership as the early 1980s recession stripped two million employees from the payroll of British manufacturing industry. Early speculation (*Personnel Management*, 1981) that parallel attempts would occur to 'Japanize' the employment relationship and British industrial relations were perhaps less well-argued; but the notion that local union officials were being transformed into compliant 'sweethearts' of newly confident 'muscular managers' was based upon at least some, albeit less substantial, evidence.

There can be no doubt that most employers were content to see the influence of unions fall sharply in the years after 1979. But by the middle of the decade it was already questionable how far most managers in unionized workplaces had adopted the view that higher productivity, greater flexibility in working practices, and increased worker commitment could only be achieved by a much more intense anti-union campaign at the workplace level, let alone that they necessarily demanded a non-union workplace. Equally important, it had been far too readily assumed that managers would have the resolution, skills, and resources required to devise sophisticated, non-union employee relations regimes and operate them competently. There are costs in carrying out de-unionization in any case, and these were repeatedly discounted if not disregarded. Especially in larger firms, unions can simplify bargaining processes, grievance handling, and the flow of communication. To devise and operate alternative arrangements requires high motivation, adequate training, much effort, and strong backing from senior management. The existence of such conditions should never be lightly assumed by social scientists concerned with the British workplace.

From an early date, case-studies of workplace employee relations (Rose and Jones, 1985) were showing that some caution was justified on the foregoing grounds. True enough, this research did show that significant changes in the position of union representatives within workplaces had often taken place, and suggested that others could well follow in due course. Union authority among employees seemed to be weakening, but marginally rather than dramatically, thanks to such factors as high unemployment, the disappearance of nationally negotiated incomes policies, and new employment legislation, not to anti-union policies and action on the part of local management. Loss of influence by unions over work organization, for example, could be offset by closer involvement in training or in planning technical change. (Results from the Employer 30 survey discussed in the previous chapter were to confirm this finding.) In many cases, other research of the mid-1980s suggested, shop stewards were even continuing to influence the definition of work tasks, setting of piece rates, and award of overtime much as they had done in the earlier period (Batstone, 1985).

Observers who predicted an anti-union Employers' Offensive, as noted in Chapter 1, had too readily assumed the collapse of union power at a national level must be followed by its collapse at the level of the workplace. They may also have misinterpreted (and as a result overstated) support for unions during the 1960s and 1970s, during a period when shop-floor militancy was rising. If the 1950s had been taken as the basis of comparison, the situation in the average workplace in the mid-1980s would have seemed more familiar, and in that sense more 'normal'. Some union leaders were to make a similar mistake in organizing resistance to government policy or conducting industrial action in the 1980s, with disastrous results for their organizations.

Perhaps there was some reluctance also to acknowledge how far employee attitudes towards unions have always been affected by calculation and personal self-interest: such economic instrumentalism (Goldthorpe *et al.*, 1969) helped boost union strength during the corporatist 1970s, when it became essential for many employees to belong to a large wage-bargaining group and pro-union legislation encouraged union membership (for example, through the spread of the closed shop). With the disappearance of corporatism in the 1980s, many employees felt they no longer had a need (or, to put it more brutally, even less use) for union membership and involvement. However, such an instrumental, conditional attitude to union membership also threw doubt on the real scope for employers to 'Japanize' the employment relationship. Plans for integrating employees more closely in the firm, when they are inspired by a strong unitarist ideology (Fox, 1971), generally presume a need on the part of employees for moral involvement (Etzioni, 1975) with the employing organization. Hardly any research is available to demonstrate that such a need is felt by most British employees, in more than the most superficial sense. Theories of Japanization were especially likely to overlook this awkward feature of British workplace culture.

Despite the logical weaknesses of these theories of de-unionization and incorporation in the enterprise, and their lack of strong supporting evidence from the field by the mid-1980s, their importance for organizing debate was recognized during the planning of the SCELI research on trade unionism. If there were any important trends of this kind it was important to make an attempt to detect them. It seemed reasonable to suppose that a non-union work culture might have a better chance of growing in a rapidly changing town like Swindon than in still largely traditional industrial localities. This reasoning would apply equally in the case that unionism was surviving, although in an often heavily modified form.

First, as noted above, there was the nature of the town as a changing industrial centre; the kinds of employment Swindon was attracting might matter as much as the employee relations philosophy of employers themselves. Second, as the findings from the Work Histories/Attitudes survey reported by Duncan Gallie in Chapter 4 show, the Swindon employee sample expressed less overall commitment to unionism than the samples in the 'smoke-stack' localities represented by Kirkcaldy and Rochdale. For example, fewer Swindon employees, 32 per cent against a sample total of 40 per cent, were current union members, and the gap in support among women employees was even more marked. Swindon (with Northampton) had the fewest employees (31 per cent against 38 per cent for the whole Work Histories/Attitudes sample) positively favourable to unionism. It had the smallest proportion of those who were 'very favourable' and the highest proportion of those 'not at all' favourable to unionism. Swindon also had by far the largest proportion (23 per cent against 15 per cent) saying that union membership had grown less important in the last five years.

It is important to note that these findings do not necessarily result from some unique 'Swindon factor'. Again as Gallie points out in Chapter 4 (see Table 4.15), the findings on current union membership do not seem to show any strongly independent effect for locality *per se*. When structural factors (in particular, social class, size of establishment, industry, sector, and gender) are

introduced as controls in Gallie's model, the statistically measured importance of the locality variable falls considerably. The
influence of the locality falls further still when a control for
favourability to unions is added.

However, it can be argued that the relative favourability of the
locality samples to unionism was itself a feature of the locality,
and one which is not further reducible to other structural factors
or individual characteristics. Yet Gallie (Table 4.13) also shows
favourability to unions to have itself been affected by at least
some factors which themselves are structural and individual:
gender, sector, and size again; but also by the length of union
membership, and employer policy towards union membership.
Kirkcaldy employees have higher commitment to unionism. This
may reflect a strong pro-union local culture and tradition, similar
to a Labour voting tradition. In all probability, it also reflects the
structural fact that Kirkcaldy was until recently a town with a
high proportion of male, public sector workers employed in mining and ancillary industries where union membership was encouraged or required by employers. When normative factors are thus
replaced by structural variables, much of an apparent locality
effect disappears. It is important to note this at the outset. The
question of a 'locality effect' will be raised again briefly in the
conclusion to this chapter.

In any case, the main aim of this chapter is not that of determining how far Swindon can be thought of as a locality already
relatively unfavourable to unions. While the chapters by Gallie,
by Elias, and by Main weigh the effect of sets of major structural
variables on, in turn, attitudes to unionism among employees, the
propensity over time to become a union member, and the scale
of the union wage mark-up, referring to the Work Attitudes/
Histories sample, the present chapter tries to provide a more
qualitative understanding of processes of personal involvement in
unionism, and their relation to the employee relations regime and
policies of the employing organization. In so far as it enables a
'test' of locality effects, it is one aided, as well as limited, by a
more ethnographic methodology.

In the Work History/Attitudes survey, employer policy towards
trade unionism had to be reduced to a simple assessment from
the employee of an employer's favourability to union membership. The Swindon related study was able to look at and assess

employer policies in some depth—their degree of coherence, or how far ahead they were planned—as well as to examine their effect on employee attitudes through observation as well as close questioning of individuals. Above all, the attitudes towards trade unions of managers and employees were recorded largely in their own words and could be probed or even, on occasion, challenged. The consistency and intensity of attitudes could be gauged. Complex feelings or judgements could be summarized or illustrated in sometimes graphic comments. These were to be valuable advantages. But making best use of them depended on choosing appropriate case-study employers.

2. CHOOSING THE CASE-STUDY EMPLOYERS

A constraint of a case-study approach is that only a small set of workplaces can be examined. It was important to ensure that the cases chosen were appropriate for examining the theoretical and policy issues outlined above. Employers were selected in order to meet four main conditions: (1) they should be in vanguard industries; (2) the size of establishments should be small to medium; (3) most should be new firms or have experienced relocation to Swindon; and (4) in all there should be high proportions of women employees. In addition, for reasons given below, it was thought essential to include at least one public sector employer.

Theories of the 1980s predicting union decline often stressed the replacement of old, heavy industries by new ones such as electronics, research, or administration. In such activities, it was argued, the skill mix was altering towards white-collar work, the average workforce would usually be smaller in 'start-up' firms (facilitating close-knit relations between staff and managers), and it would be easier to experiment with new employment regimes on green-field sites near growing towns lacking a tradition of active trade unionism (Lane, 1984). Finally, the higher proportion of women workers in the new industries was to be seen as an obstacle to unionization, for example because turnover among women employees was often higher, their attachment to paid work generally lacked a longer-term or career perspective; while it was widely accepted that women are much less conscious of conflicts of interest with an employer or prepared to become part

of a workplace community. In public sector workplaces, especially those likely to be privatized or 'hived off', established trade
unions were having to face the prospect of exposure to market
pressures and possibly abrasive new management partners.

In seeking establishments for case-study the aim was, then, to
ensure the selection of workplaces that seemed more favourable
than others for the creation of new regimes of control of the kind
specified in the de-unionization scenario. Weighting the panel of
cases in this way followed much the same logic as that of
Cressey, Eldridge, and MacInnes (1985: 9), in their case-studies
of employee participation schemes: when seeking signs of novel
developments in employment relations it is important to choose
the best—the ostensibly most promising—rather than the worst,
cases.

The main features of the case-study workplaces are set out in
Table 3.1. The employers all belonged to new, expanding
branches—electronics, scientific research, financial and technical
administration. All employed under 500 full-time staff. Even in
the two manufacturing plants a high proportion of staff worked
in white-collar, technical, or professional positions. In all workplaces, there was a high proportion of women employees. Two of
the cases had been set up in Swindon (one very recently) by outside firms, and two had relocated (again, one very recently) from
London. Ownership also differed in important ways. One electronics firm was the subsidiary of an American multinational, the
other a semi-independent off-shoot of a large British federated
firm. The corporate headquarters was that of a British multinational. The research establishment was a public sector
employer fitting the specification given above.

It also seemed important to include such a public sector workplace for control purposes. Unions in the public sector in the
1980s often faced a hostile, openly antagonistic 'real' employer—
the government—though workplace managers might well be willing to keep established institutions and procedures alive. But
public sector unions had held on to their membership more successfully than most private sector unions (MacInnes, 1987;
Millward and Stevens, 1986). Beyond the importance of examining such tensions, there were two additional reasons for including
a public sector workplace. First, there was the effect, noted
already, of possible privatization on attitudes to unionism. Plans

---

TABLE 3.1. *Main features of case-study workplaces*

Employer	Unionized subsidiary	Non-union subsidiary	Unionized head office	Unionized research centre
Sector	Private	Private	Private	Public
Product/service	Electronic components	Consumer electronics	Corporate headquarters	Scientific research
Ownership	American multi-national	British multi-national	British multi-national	British Government
Years in Swindon	30	2	15	5
Employees	350	250	650	400
Ratio men : women	1 : 3	2 : 1	2 : 1	5 : 2
Ratio non-manual : manual	1 : 3	2 : 3	19 : 1	10 : 1
Employees with career outlook	Very low	Low/moderate	High	Very high
Unions present at site	1	None	1	5
Union membership	Low	Very low	Moderate	High
Model of employment relationship	Pseudo-parental	Populist egalitarian	Corporate formalism	Public service
Dominant management style	Directive	Explanatory	Mixed	Consultative
Pay determined/bargained	On site	On site	On site	Off-site

Source: SCELI, Swindon Related Study.

had been aired to privatize some of the activities of the public sector workplace chosen for the study. These would, in all probability, radically alter its control regime if pushed through. Second, the traditional Civil Service representation system, known as 'Whitleyism', was in any case being eroded. Both changes obliged its employees to think carefully not only about the value they placed on union representation in general but also that ascribed to the long-established, highly institutionalized Whitley system.

It was essential to include at least one non-union private employer, although such firms are often unsympathetic towards social research concerned with their employee relations policies. The firm that agreed had been established a year or two earlier. It did not want to recognize unions if it could avoid doing so because it believed 'newer' forms of representation were more valid and effective, for staff as well as management. So far as could be ascertained, it had not adopted its non-union policy for ideological reasons. Indeed, it had balloted its staff on the option of union representation, though it appeared not to have maintained a publicly neutral stance in so doing. Quite probably, the main reason for holding the ballot was to add legitimacy to the policy. It was alleged by pro-union employees to have been held at a moment particularly favourable for producing a 'no' vote, with questions so worded as to steer voters towards the decision it hoped for. The non-union firm certainly wished to develop an organizational culture stressing a direct bond between employer and employees. But it has to be said that its managers did not have the air of anti-union warriors interested in making doctrinal points.

Its longer-term employee relations objectives were the most clearly spelled out of the four employers. In this sense at least, it can be said to have possessed a strategy of control, and one which reflected a definite set of objectives as well as an ethos of human relations. Yet some of the practical implications of this strategy seemed to the researchers rather incompletely thought-out. (Above all, it seemed to underestimate the management skill the strategy would require as business expanded, and the need to earmark sufficient resources to provide it.)

The other three employers defined their employee relations aims (and principles) in far less explicit terms. None the less, all of them claimed to have policies to develop or maintain them which had been arrived at in a rational way. It is hard to avoid using the term 'strategy' to refer to these policies as a whole and to the results attributed to them, as some managers in these establishments themselves habitually did. But in doing so, some caution is called for. The term 'strategy' has too often been applied to a set of events that happen to fit a pattern, or can be rationalized into a pattern, although they cannot be shown to be the outcome of earlier decisions made in line with an unfolding plan (Storey, 1985). Properly speaking, the concept of strategy should refer only to a consciously prepared, well-defined plan. But its use in some looser sense is very common, and this wish to impose coherence at times almost by fiat is an interesting and important feature both of the British employment relations scene and of academics concerned with it. The question of how far strategies properly speaking did exist will be raised after examining each case, with some further comment in the conclusion.

However, there did in all cases appear to exist a more definite set of understandings about the essential nature of the dominant regime of control in operation. These implied regimes could be characterized and labelled with some confidence as fieldwork progressed. Each of these regimes will be examined in turn below.

3. ESTABLISHED FAMILISM: THE UNIONIZED SUBSIDIARY

The subsidiary of a large, American-owned electronics company, this employer manufactured a standardized electronic control component in various models and types. The plant on the site dated from the mid-1960s, and at the time of the fieldwork it employed around 350 staff. Apart from some redundancy at another, smaller site in the locality, the unionized subsidiary seems to have had an uneventful past, and local management was confident the American parent company would keep an operation of some sort going in Swindon for the foreseeable future.

Around 75 per cent of the firm's main-site staff were women, two-thirds in manual grades. Outside the office, levels of general education were average to low, technical training was poor, and other work experience often limited. Around one-third of production workers, we were told, were unionized (in the AEUW). However—and significantly—both managers and union representatives were unclear on this point. Employee informants claimed that the real figure for currently paid-up members was more like 25 per cent among production workers and 15 per cent overall. The union was not formally recognized for pay negotiation, but it routinely put in a (somewhat unrealistic) annual claim nevertheless. Managers, by their own admission, would then 'go through a ritual process' of informal consultation, appearing to give some way when union representatives were persistent, but in fact 'always doing exactly what we would have done anyway'. The only industrial dispute anyone could recall had occurred many years earlier and had involved office and technical staff, not the factory. If the unionized subsidiary had wished to experiment with its personnel policies, or become a non-union employer, it could have done so without hindrance.

Local managers saw no point in altering the existing employee relations regime, with which they claimed the staff were as happy as they were themselves. The main feature of the regime of control was a style of management which blended paternalism with what seemed to the fieldworkers a sometimes rather forced informality. This 'culture' was to be seen most clearly in the manufacturing area. Its fundamental character was conveyed in everyday nomenclature. This firm had a full set of official job-titles and grades that applied to the factory operations. But all women employees in the works in practice shared the same status: that of 'girl'. This term for a woman factory worker is still in use in the 1990s, in some workplaces. It was far more widespread at the time of the research. It was, then, perhaps not the term itself so much as the way it was used, and the assumptions that were packed into it in this particular workplace, that are important. Some 'girls' were indeed teenagers, though most were in their twenties or thirties. Senior women employees were also referred to as 'ladies'. But in general women operatives of any age were referred to, and very largely thought of themselves, as 'girls' in the special sense implied in the firm's culture.

It is essential to draw attention to this terminology not because use of the word 'girl' at the site was already old-fashioned or sexist—though it evidently was both. It also involved the attribution of a pseudo-familial status. 'Girls' were in some sense 'nieces' if not 'daughters' in the eyes of managers. One senior manager candidly spelled out for us the large measure of open paternalism ('I'm not afraid to use the word') in this way of treating the female production staff. He regarded his own 'folksy' familism as a well-tried and dependable method for giving women manual staff a sense of personal involvement in the firm, and even some emotional uplift.

The ideology was familial in a second and more direct sense too. In recruitment, potential as a 'family member' was said to be far more important than formal education, 'brain-power', or qualifications. A good recruit for production work was a young woman who could work quickly and put up with intensely boring work. Existing staff, it was pointed out, could screen out sisters, cousins, nieces, or daughters who lacked the right aptitudes (punctuality, deference, family spirit). New entrants coming through this kinship sieve would also have heard, some managers told us, very complimentary reports about the firm's 'cosy family atmosphere'. If need be, an older relative could help apply work discipline 'in every way from, at one end of the scale, being tipped off by us to give her [younger relative] a discreet prod, to, at the other end, pulling her out of bed on cold winter mornings'.

This familist philosophy, fieldworkers were told, partly reflected the ethnic composition of the market for lower-grade labour when the firm had set up in Swindon two decades previously. Substantial Polish and Italian communities, composed of former displaced persons and war-time refugees, had become established in Swindon at the end of the Second World War. In both, female subordination and 'good habits' were supported by religious beliefs and the extended family. The unionized subsidiary strongly favoured recruits from both these communities. By the 1980s, however, collective upward mobility and out-marriage were rapidly drying up these formerly well-stocked pools of family-minded, deferential women workers.

The firm had also noted a growing impatience with repetitive production work. To counter this it had experimented with new types of work organization. All assemblers were now organized in small (5–8 women) teams. Though these did not quite amount to the autonomous work groups advocated since the 1970s as a means of rebuilding meaning in work, they were acknowledged to have given more control over rates of working. Each group was given a production target for the day and could watch its output accumulate at its side. Each group was also self-regulating to the extent of deciding the timing of its own members' lunch breaks, rest pauses, and changes of work operation. The firm mixed younger and older women in each team, with the latter generally setting the pace, although it was claimed that the younger women could always outpace the older women whenever they wished to. Managers claimed that jobs were tailored to individual abilities. However, no concrete examples of how this was done were provided by managers or put forward in the employee interviews.

Such work re-design may indeed form part of relatively advanced management control philosophies, reflecting the existence of genuine strategies for altering employee relations (Knights *et al.*, 1985: ch. 1). At the unionized subsidiary, the aim was clearly much less ambitious. Group-working, fieldworkers were told, was designed to appeal primarily 'to the "knitting syndrome" '. The girls would find it possible to talk and listen to the radio at the same time as working, thanks to the positioning of operatives around the (relatively quiet) equipment and machinery. This reduced any sense of isolation and boredom, cutting turnover and improving morale. In fact, production workers still reported considerable boredom with assembly tasks.

There's no satisfaction whatever in the actual work. We need to be able to swap around properly every week or so. . . . It'd not be so boring then.

Skilled production and maintenance work was done by men, but some women were employed in the stores and packing area. In the office, there was greater overlap between the sexes, and women held some of the small number of local management positions. It was almost impossible to move between these echelons. One assembler with experience of office work had recently been appointed to a clerical job on the site. This was cited as a major exception to the rule. For women production workers the maximum possible promotion in practice amounted to an upward move of two grades, to supervisor. The firm had a very strong preference for supervisors with such works experience, but claimed that girls generally feared losing their close social contacts by accepting supervisory responsibility. There was no systematic training for any of the work tasks, or for promotion, and it seemed to strike management as a curious idea that there should be any need for it.

The firm thus had no policy of creating employee commitment through offering possible career ladders or by encouraging firm-specific training. Managers seemed unsure whether it would pay to adopt these policies. They pointed out that the firm's productivity had risen in the 1980s thanks to straightforward work intensification rather than to greater training or skill enhancement. Operatives and white-collar staff also remarked on the greater pressure for output. Yet extra effort, they complained, went unrewarded and unnoticed:

They do a sample check, and they're checking up more now. If a [given] lot are faulty they send all the work back and you have to go through it, checking every single item one by one. It could be a whole week's work.

The firm had not considered adopting more modern supervisory styles to increase motivation and involvement. Staff in the works were especially likely to say that it was very important to them that someone noticed how hard they worked and showed some appreciation. They were also the most likely to claim they worked hard but that nobody appreciated their effort. It was easy to check up on how well a job was done, and both workers and managers knew when a target was met or missed: it was 'obvious' to everyone. However, supervisors in a more considerate—or more manipulative—firm might have been told never to overlook 'obvious' achievements by employees, however minor.

The production director considered that supervisors spent sufficient time on informal communication, and were skilled at it. Asked what such skilled supervision involved, he promptly gave a practical demonstration of what he considered good technique. This rapidly reduced several operatives to blushing hilarity at what seemed to the fieldworkers his somewhat over-familiar 'Uncle Alex Act'. (This was not his real name.) Interviews suggest he badly misjudged the views of production staff about managers' inter-personal skills:

You're just a number here. Management are all right in themselves, but we don't have a lot to do with them. It's so hard to make an impression. They could get more involved in our situation.

The American parent company, we were told, had a world-wide 'Communications Program' operated from the United States. This was allegedly inspired by Japanese models. Personnel staff implied that it was not to be taken very seriously by us, or had been by them, partly because it was sent 'like a kit'. The material (especially the videos) available under the Communications Program, these sources staff considered, would strike a British audience as insincere or—*pace* the 'Uncle Alex' approach—patronizing. They made as little use of it as they could, though the videos were stored 'somewhere round here'. Nor had there been any attempt to set up 'one of those quality cults', with quality circles in the Japanese style. The production manager saw no need whatsoever for such changes, or any others, while there was no pressure from the parent company to push change any further. As he saw it: 'Why should there be, provided production figures stay good?'

The firm had even been cutting down on its own formal workplace briefings, not realizing how much some employees actually valued them:

You could contribute to the discussion. . . . But over the last year interest has dried up. All you expect [nowadays] is a notice on the board, even for redundancies. The company's attitude is more distant. Its attitude is 'take it or leave it'.

As suggested at several points, managers felt they already had a successful policy of employee involvement. But only one policy, the recent extension of staff status to all employees, which had made every employee eligible for the company's private health scheme and private pension plan, was widely cited by staff themselves as having recently increased their sense of identification with the firm. Award of staff status was, to all appearances, appreciated not just for its material benefits but because it implied a higher underlying level of trust. Employees had themselves become responsible for reporting the reasons for their absence from work, and this helped them to feel they were being 'for once' treated as adults. Yet astonishingly, the employer seemed little aware of, or interested in, these positive effects.

In other respects, the impression gained from interviews with staff was one of slowly deteriorating relations and mutual trust. Few informants thought employers in general had been attempting to build closer relations with their employees as union support declined in the 1980s, or had succeeded in doing so. Most employees reported that relations between management and employees had been harmonious for the period since they had joined the firm. Yet only half thought the workplace atmosphere was relaxed. In theory, everyone was on first-name terms with everyone else. In practice, this 'friendliness' sometimes caused embarrassment. (Having witnessed the 'Uncle Alex Act', the fieldworkers understood what these employees were driving at.)

Overall, then, there was a clear gap between the ways workers experienced control and the ways management believed workers experienced it.

Managers believed the prevailing supervisory style was consultative, even democratic. Employees sometimes found it 'bossy', though lacking in conviction. Managers, it was asserted, would give orders through supervisors, but were 'too frightened to tell us directly'. Unlike staff at the other three workplaces, very few informants mentioned factors such as managers' readiness to communicate, or high levels of trust in employees, as the best thing about the way the organization was run. In sum, there was a striking contrast between what managers believed to be the informal, easy-going, trustful, 'parent–child' tone of employee relations, and employees' own accounts of muddled, insincere, and occasionally arbitrary forms of treatment.

As noted earlier, there were three main themes in employee criticism. One was remoteness. Managers allegedly 'hid themselves away in their offices'. Older workers compared them unfavourably with the personally approachable American managers who had run the firm in its early days, and were always to be seen touring the plant. The present managers were often described as inaccessible, hiding behind a screen of 'big-headed whitecoats' (technicians and supervisors).

A second complaint was of a *reduction* in trust. If someone was found not working, or was going to the toilet often, managers were likely to assume without further thought that they were time-wasting rather than unwell. Although the firm was thought to be rather understanding about granting time off to deal with emergencies, it had cracked down hard on anyone suspected of absenteeism or malingering. As noted, there was resentment of the perceived failure of managers to provide positive feedback about performance, while failures were quickly noticed. Successes such as a gain in quality might or might not be acknowledged.

Finally, although the parental approach of this employer had been moderated, at least in formal terms, by the award of staff status, the firm had failed to follow it up. As noted earlier, monthly payment by cheque, private health benefits, and membership of the company pension scheme had brought a temporary fillip to the self-esteem of many staff. In other respects, the 'family atmosphere' had been soured by the drive for higher output and better quality. This drive was backed by the increasing authority given to—or assumed by—technician-grade staff (the 'whitecoats'). The latter seemed to have become unpopular in part because they were ill-trained for their growing supervisory role. In order to take best advantage of the favourable climate for change that existed in the mid to late 1980s, the firm would have needed to import ideas and managerial skill to alter its employee relations regime. It had seen no need to do so. This complacency also marked its treatment of trade unionism.

There had been recent falls in work satisfaction in the unionized subsidiary, and this demand for extra effort had reduced any sense of employee involvement. In other circumstances, such changes might have bred a wider sense of grievance, providing some of the conditions in which employees might have become more involved in trade unionism. Yet there were no signs of this having happened, or being likely to. For its part, the firm seemed to discount completely such a revival of union support. Its policy towards union representation and recognition seemed not to have altered in any significant way throughout the 1980s. It recognized the AEUW's right to organize the workforce, and provided it with modest facilities, remaining certain that it would never become a power to be reckoned with.

Employee views of the union were coloured by apathy, resignation at its weakness, and indifference towards any change of its role, whether this might be towards still greater marginalization or towards greater strength and influence. Although a minority (one in four of our two dozen employee informants) said it mattered a great deal to them that a union was present for employees to join, three of these people had not personally joined the union, or had let their membership lapse. Compared to other case-study employers, rather more people at this firm said it did not matter to them that a union was present (or absent). As in the next case-study—another private sector manufacturing firm— many employees seemed to think it hardly mattered one way or the other. They explained to the fieldworkers that, personally, they were neither for nor against unions, but that the subject was without importance for them and that they thus had few opinions to express.

For the minority which did take at least some interest in trade unionism as a whole, the main problem was to be defined as one of insufficient local bargaining strength. The problem was circular: the union could not bargain effectively because it lacked members; it lacked members because it could deliver no extra benefits. Nothing seemed likely to offer an escape from this impasse.

Management does listen, but numbers of paid-up union members are so small sometimes they don't even listen. Our previous pay-rise, they just informed us what it was. That was that.

Once the union was strong here. But it's not got much power now, that's why I've not joined. They just accept management's decision.

When it was pointed out that they could personally reduce the problem of numbers by signing up, they responded in such a way as to show that they considered such an action futile. One or two informants also referred to their residue of trust in management, or to the unions' record at national level, especially in the pre-1979 years, as reasons not to become members. But detailed knowledge of union affairs was poor. Even a union representative ('I'm terrible, aren't I?' she said with open embarrassment) could not name any national leaders of her union, present or recent. Among those having an opinion, it was felt that the Employment Acts of the 1980s were a 'good thing' if they curbed union power at a national level. There was less agreement over the effects of the legislation in the workplace:

I think [the new workplace legislation] undercuts the need for a union. Nowadays people know it's against the law to work when the lights go off or the temperature gets too high.

Unions are more important now. People here aren't *against* unions, but they don't want to pay a sub every month—it's £2.80 now—especially the younger ones.

A feeling—though it was often poorly explained—that trade unions had generally grown less important was widespread, but as already noted a large minority declared that they had no real opinions on this or other trade union issues because they had too little information, or had never thought it worth considering them. Yet it should be clear that this weak support for unions was in no sense a product of any policy of employee involvement by the firm—and still less of its paternalism. For its part, the firm seemed to treat the subject of trade unionism with no greater interest, and with not much greater knowledge, than did employees themselves.

Management would very probably have increased union authority by recognizing it as a bargaining partner, especially for pay-bargaining. On the other hand, it could almost just as easily have withdrawn its recognition, and the provision of facilities, if it had wished to do so. When asked why the firm had not taken such steps, the personnel officer pointed out that she already spent 'far too much' time trying to recruit the employee members of the firm's Social Panel, and representatives for the Health and Safety committee, even though staff could get time off work without loss of pay to go to their meetings. She only half-jokingly suggested that, from her viewpoint, it would be 'a damn good thing for the firm' for the union to develop more real influence—at least more employees would have a better overview of the firm's current position, and thus develop an interest beyond their immediate work tasks and work group. She was surely correct in making this point.

In terms of paid-up membership the union had declined to a weakened, almost terminal condition, but the unionized subsidiary 'kept the union on a life-support machine'. In terms of the objectives for management apparently implied in some government utterances of the 1980s, this 'rescue' would have to be seen as a serious management 'failure'. Much in official policy statements, in the employment legislation, in the public utterances of ministers, and in what was widely accepted as some vaguer logic of change, implied that the reduction or removal of union influence at all levels of economic life was worth a positive effort on the part of management. There was the strong suggestion in this that management would generally take, or at least wish to take, the opportunity to do away with any involvement with unions. According to this line of thinking, the firm ought to have been 'helping the union on its way out', rather than to survive. Though such institutional euthanasia would have been simple and undetectable, the firm was holding back from it. It may have done so because, from its point of view, a weak union seemed better to it than no union at all. It may have been unwilling to develop its own, company controlled representative system. (Both possibilities seem likely.) What is certain is that the issue did not matter very much for it.

Managers of the unionized subsidiary were not atypical in their reluctance to alter a convenient *status quo*. As the chapter by Gallie and Rose in this volume points out, only a small minority of unionized firms in the Employers 30 survey had even considered derecognition in the 1980s, let alone attempted it. In many unionized firms, and the unionized subsidiary may provide a good instance of such employers, no change at all in policy towards unions was reported. It seems likely that such employers did not consider change necessary because existing arrangements seemed convenient and untroublesome to them, with the 'union question' being given a very low priority on their agenda compared to other kinds of change.

It has to be added that, at first, the difficulty in determining what the policy towards the union of the unionized subsidiary actually was caused some frustration. The mistake of the fieldworkers was to assume, as many researchers were wont to do at the time, that some definite policy—even a 'strategy'—must exist. The fact had to be accepted that, apart from continuing along established lines, and helping the union to maintain a presence, no carefully considered policy existed. Pragmatism and inertia, rather than fashionable management theory or doctrinaire values, account for the firm's approach to trade unionism. To call what policy there was a 'strategy' would seem in this case to be unwarranted. A quite different case—an employer with an explicit, calculated, non-union strategy for employee relations—will be examined in the next section.

4. POPULIST PARTICIPATION: THE NON-UNION SUBSIDIARY

The non-union subsidiary was a medium-sized electronics firm. Its market situation differed in two essential ways from that of the unionized subsidiary. First, its products sold in increasing volume in a rapidly expanding consumer market with high profit margins. Second, it had been expanding dynamically and was confident of its future growth. It was less than four years old and had the backing of a large British-owned electronics group. Senior managers from the parent company made periodic visits to the site. Apart from passing this inspection and providing

financial information to the London office, local management
was left to get on with its job as it saw fit. This autonomy was in
part *de facto*, due to 'this site being the furthest from London',
according to the Swindon managers, not because the parent
regarded it as an experiment. The young local management
group were set targets for output, cost, and profit. They said they
had a largely free hand over how to meet them and had 'made
space' to develop local employee relations as they wished.

This semi-detached relationship was probably important for
the future of employee relations at the Swindon site. Site management had an image of the employee relations regime it
intended to build. Its two chief features were close communication with employees and the exclusion of unions. It had backing
for this programme from its London head office. But to develop
the system it might later need to invest heavily in management
training and skill, which would cut into the operating profits it
turned in to the main company. How far it would succeed in
securing these resources was not clear.

The non-union subsidiary was a production-led operation.
Manufacture of the product was partly automated, but it called
for constant attention to quality during fabrication, and care in
handling products during all stages of production and dispatch.
Rising sales, as well as its high fixed costs, required shiftwork.
While many production-area jobs were stressful or boring because products were standardized and produced in large batches,
maintenance tasks usually needed high skill. With the help of the
Advisory, Conciliation, and Arbitration Service (ACAS) the firm
was trying to evaluate jobs, produce gradings and possible career
paths, and define training and education profiles for each main
job. (It lacked the management skill to do this itself and could
not obtain it from the parent company.) Training in other skills
was acknowledged already to be falling behind needs because the
firm could not release personnel for long periods and lacked
internal training resources.

The firm was suffering other growth problems. Its production
management skill had been stretched to the limit. Some inter-
viewees claimed that organization of production was going
through a 'stage of chaos'. Others thought the real problem was
'upstream', in the translation of customer orders into production
schedules, rather than in the factory itself. (Rapid response to

orders was essential for many lines.) Whatever the truth, production planning decisions were acknowledged to be resulting in some 'very erratic' patterns of work. This demanded constant alterations in shiftworking duties. Functional flexibility was demanded of all employees, virtually as a condition of service. But shiftwork, especially nightwork, was disliked by nearly all employees doing it. It was an issue upon which, some employees thought, the firm's non-union policy might eventually founder if it was mishandled.

Managers repeatedly agreed that training had to be improved for many management, supervisory, or planning jobs. But they pointed out that average levels of skill, work experience, and other forms of human capital were already much higher than might be expected in what had been until then a small batch-production operation. This point was a valid one; it is worth noting that the firm's attitude towards training, especially for routine workers, was quite different from that of the unionized subsidiary. It had warmly welcomed recruits, even for production tasks, with higher than basic levels of education, training, or experience. A sizeable minority of its staff had indeed gone through redundancies from work requiring traditional craft qualifications. The selection process had, managers believed, produced recruits with above-average reliability and commitment. Operatives thus might be made responsible for some maintenance tasks and quality control checks as soon as they joined the firm. Personnel staff thought most of them had 'the potential to grow with the firm'.

Some informants had indeed been promoted rapidly as the firm expanded. Their previous skills, they said, had been rewarded after a period spent 'proving themselves'. Doubts were expressed over two main points. First, would later recruits have so many opportunities? Second, would the skill used in previous work always be relevant to the technical or supervisory work these well-qualified operatives moved into? But nobody pressed these questions.

A second means of building personal commitment to the firm was through a cellular structure of production teams in each department. The teams were generally small, five to eight people, though sometimes up to twenty in production areas, with a very clear 'core' role for each member. Management encouraged a

view of the site as an egalitarian—or at least 'matey'—extended
group or 'community' that had abolished the snobbish distinction
between works and office, and likewise seemed genuinely
unhappy with a sharp division between skilled and non-skilled
work. The firm expected high levels of commitment to this populist philosophy and to 'The Team'. One result that was claimed
to reflect its success in doing so had been very high attendance
rates. The absence figures cited to the researchers were the lowest
among the case-study employers. (Matched teams from the three
daily shifts in the production area were pitted against each other
on absence figures and quality. Graphs of absence figures were
put up publicly.)

Management had set out to build a 'culture of communication'. This effort faced a severe problem. Contact with some
employees was difficult because they were tied to a shift or iso-
lated in 'clean rooms' (where the most delicate operations were
carried out) throughout their shift. One way of handling this
problem was to issue briefing sheets promptly. For example, a
management team meeting was held every Monday morning. It
was conducted half-informally—no minutes were produced—and
could make no decisions in its own right. But it was regarded as
a pointer to all important current events. The meeting agreed a
briefing sheet of 'everything important' that had been said. This
was circulated to all employees, and managers attending the
meeting were expected to comment on items when asked to do so
by their subordinates.

Communication took a second, more diffuse form. This was
aimed at creating an atmosphere in which employees would accept
that 'there's none of that awful Them-and-Us stuff in this firm'.
The site management thus favoured a definite house-style in personal behaviour, stressing informality, personal openness, and
camaraderie. This bore little resemblance to the threadbare 'happy
family' ideology of the unionized subsidiary. It was somehow
curiously reminiscent of Australian television 'soaps' such as
Neighbours. The model relationship was not parental so much as
fraternal. Far from embodying the openly sexist social models,
imagery, and language current in the unionized subsidiary, the cultural ideal seems to have been a 'post-sexist mateship' in which
women were to be included naturally and automatically. Women
employees themselves approved of it as warmly as the men.

The non-union subsidiary had a high proportion of non-manual, technical, and supervisory employees, many of whom had long and diverse work experience. It needed to integrate a far greater variety of individuals and types of outlook than the unionized subsidiary. The strongly populist and egalitarian site ethic had so far been an effective solvent for these differences. Possessing a ready friendliness, an affably egalitarian manner in treating others—and a readiness to accept such treatment from them—was seen as an integral part of productive work behaviour itself, since it increased functional flexibility ('readiness to muck in'). Managers also believed a 'matey' human relations atmosphere was treated as an important non-money reward by most staff, and much comment in the interviews with staff suggests they were correct.

Managers and supervisors were expected to pay careful attention to their own way of approaching subordinates. The prevailing style of supervision was most often seen by employees as 'explanatory' (Hofstede, 1983), with managers arriving quickly at decisions without taking extensive soundings among employees; but, once having taken the decision, taking pains to explain it and answer queries in full. One or two employees who thought their managers exercised control in a more directive way said they actually preferred this pattern. On all sides there was high approval for managers' availability and egalitarianism:

Managers don't segregate themselves with that 'I am the Manager and you are the Employee' stuff—there's none of that.

Employees approved of the policy of timely communication, but some pointed out weaknesses in it. Information provided after the Monday morning meetings, they said, was sometimes taken with a pinch of salt. Several informants argued that site managers knew less than they seemed to about how the parent company might be planning to develop the product range, or what new investment in plant or training it would authorize. Nor did meetings put a stop to numerous rumours about threats to the firm's future. (The theme of the rumour often featured the independence of local management—would the parent continue to give it such a free rein?) But the good intentions behind the meetings were accepted—the meeting showed that the readiness to communicate was 'genuine, and managers do react to points raised the previous week'.

Most informants thought the firm expressed high levels of personal trust through its supervisory and communications practices: management trusted employees almost completely, it was said, to get on with their work in a conscientious way, 'without hassle', and observation bore this out. (Once admitted to the site, the fieldworkers were themselves left to get on with their own work without interference.) Only security checks occasionally marred this feeling of being trusted, but some inspection was regarded as unavoidable. (Products were high value-added items, highly portable, and would no doubt find a ready market at local car-boot sales.)

From a production point of view they have 100 per cent confidence in us, and plus. But did you know they search our cars?

Several employees (including one who said he had had 'over 30' previous jobs) said that the atmosphere, at the personal level, or in terms of manager–employee relations, was the most relaxed they had ever known:

The friendliness of the atmosphere is remarkable. It's not a daily piss-off to come to work. Honestly, in that area, I can't think of any way of improving on what we have, none at all.

Some former craft-worker employees, who had previously worked in large local engineering firms, had found the all-pervasive 'mateyness' unnerving at first because they were unused to thinking of unskilled workers or women as 'real mates'. One or two continued to distrust the motives behind the open management style, or to question whether it could be maintained. The change in workplace culture was especially difficult for some former employees of the (recently closed) Rail Workshops (BREL), for whom deference had been a way of life:[3]

In BREL [former railway workshops], it was totally different. There was, like, pictures of Isambard Kingdom Brunel everywhere—Isambard Kingdom Brunel on the carpets, Isambard Kingdom Brunel up on a cloud in the sky looking down, no doubt—though that did teach you a bit of respect for your superiors at work, that was the theory. Here I even call my own boss 'Robert', his first name. At BREL you'd never dream of calling even a foreman anything but 'Mister' something. In a manner of speaking, they all but wore bowler hats still.

There was a degree of nostalgia in these reminiscences, and the former BREL staff had at first undoubtedly experienced some severe culture shock. But key elements of the firm's employee relations strategy—recruitment of higher-skilled workers, good communication, management accessibility, the propagation of an egalitarian populist atmosphere at the site—had unquestionably helped to generate high levels of personal identification even among these former 'labour aristocrats'. Many informants commented at length on their own satisfaction with the social contacts work provided, resulting in high levels of work commitment on their own part. Some added that this also produced commitment to high levels of effort:

People work really hard here. Everyone's a go-getter. There's a sense that here's an up-and-coming place, somewhere to get in on, on the ground floor. Where I worked before, there were such negative attitudes, they were all skiving. There's very little of that [skiving] here.

Here, though, there was a possible problem for the future. The non-union subsidiary could combine individualistic 'go-getting' with a matey 'site collectivist' ethos because it was still a small firm which was rapidly expanding on the success of its high-margin main product. But even some managers wondered how soon growth would make it harder to reconcile commitment and productivity with close-knit, 'matey' workplace relations. Personnel and supervision practices were built on the assumption that the firm would remain a non-union employer, and were intended to remove the grounds on which any reasonable call for unionization could be made for the foreseeable future. Growth in the size of the operation, it was recognized, might in due course make the 'matey' workplace culture much harder, perhaps impossible, to maintain. Thus some managers themselves admitted to the fieldworkers that they believed demand for a union could grow strongly in the future.

This firm, it should be stressed, was not an *anti*-union employer either along traditional paternalist lines or in the then topical, Thatcherite sense. It saw the decision not to recognize a union as a rational policy choice by management (one which, most happily from the firm's point of view, had later received democratic endorsement), not one imposed for narrowly ideological reasons. Though there was some question whether its procedure had followed very best practice, it had indeed balloted employees on union representation, resulting in rejection. Nor

did it put pressure on individuals to renounce union membership
on an individual basis: the small number of its employees who
had kept up previous union membership made no secret of their
continuing involvement. (Two were interviewed during the fieldwork.) It had been confident that its policies of open management and egalitarianism, given wider public hostility to unions,
would end any lingering commitment to unionism among its
employees. Still, the ballot on membership had created an important precedent. (If employees' attitudes changed because of further growth, and unions regained public approval, would the firm
be able to refuse to hold another ballot?)

It is not known how far the non-union subsidiary attempted to
screen out potential union organizers. One or two informants
alleged that it did so and preferred vocal anti-union recruits. The
research produced no reliable evidence either of such vetting, or of
positive discrimination in favour of people with strong anti-union
views. However, the minority of the manual staff that did sub-
scribe to anti-union views was larger than in other case-study
firms, or in the Swindon sample of the Work Histories/Attitudes
survey. On a rough estimate over half the workforce had at some
time been union members, and a few were known to have had
extensive experience of union affairs and industrial action. A very
high proportion (perhaps around four out of five) had fathers who
had been union members. On the other hand, very few indeed of
its younger workers had first-hand experience of unionism.

Nearly all employees interviewed at the non-union subsidiary
said that it had grown less important to belong to a union in the
1980s, that unions made no worthwhile contribution to the life of
the country and could in fact be harmful to it, and that the
restrictive legislation of the 1980s mattered a great deal and
would be effective in curbing union influence (which, many commented, would be no bad thing). Still, anti-union commentary
was mostly of a relatively mild nature, while fervent anti-unionism was rare:

This firm's all the better for there being no union here. If you've got a
problem you should go directly to your boss to sort it out, and you can
do that here.

I don't miss them—I don't go a lot for unions. . . . At [previous
employer] they just caused problems.

In some cases, this coolness reflected earlier disappointment with unions as bargainers and defenders of employee rights:

But when it came to major problems, redundancy in particular, there was no fight in them at all; they just accepted management's proposals.

When it gets too hot they're gone, they're no longer there to help you, are they?

Even such 'condemnations' of unions put ideological objections in second place or did not mention them at all. The real problem for trade unionism that emerged at this firm boiled down to a question of perceived relevance. Informants at the non-union subsidiary, more so than at other sites, sometimes grew impatient when the researchers asked for explanations of their attitudes to unions. This reaction took a quite different form from that of traditional anti-unionism based on social or political principles. Rather than objecting to a possible interference with individual freedom, or to the risk of souring employer–worker relations, some younger informants in particular stated that their interest in unions was low because they were members of a new generation which simply had different interests and values from older workers:

I'm not interested in a union, and that's all there is to it.

People in my age-group or younger just aren't interested in unions. It's not a question of 'for' or 'against'. Older people here or anywhere might still be ardent supporters of unions. Older people simply believe in it a lot more. What's *my* view? I'll tell you straight: I just don't care.

In itself, a lack of involvement in trade unionism among younger people is not a recent development. For example, Peter Elias's review of the Work Histories/Attitudes data on union memberships in Chapter 5 suggests that the readiness to become a union member (voluntarily) was closely linked to the number of years employees had spent in the labour-force throughout the post-war period. Possibly, the *degree* of apathy found among these younger employees was amplified in some way by the site ethos. But there is no good reason to believe that their indifference to unionism resulted mainly from indoctrination by local management. In fact, the often rather assertively voiced indifference of these younger informants was sometimes hedged with qualifications. For example, some younger informants acknowledged that there might be times when it would be useful to have a union spokesman in a workplace dispute, or because 'in time, bosses might go back to their bad old ways'. Perhaps significantly, it was noted that a firm that grew larger might be forced to accept a union as a 'necessary evil' of its own growth.

In other words, while the attitudes to trade unionism these younger employees expressed to fieldworkers were characterized above all by lack of any serious concern with, or interest in, the whole question, there was at times a suggestion that such an attitude might be conditional upon the continuation of their present, largely favourable experience of the employment relationship. Former union members, it should be noted, were far more likely to have an attitude towards trade unionism that was pragmatic, not ideological. Technicians from the former railway workshops were an especially interesting group of informants in this respect. These men had known traditional, fully unionized plants and the culture of British craft unionism, but claimed to have made the adjustment to a non-union environment without trouble. Indeed, they could be sharply critical of traditional craft unionism:

What I could never stomach was having a *second* set of managers. The union figureheads were always telling you what to do, what not to do. There was one occasion at [previous firm]. The union bosses said: 'You're all going on strike!' 'Oh *are* we?', we said, 'Well, no we're not!' At first they just couldn't believe this, but we made them step down.

Not having a union is in certain respects a good thing—it removes that 'you versus them' thing.

None the less, these last two comments were made by men who had kept up their union membership (in the AEUW, and EETPU). Why had they done so when they personally seemed to so critical of unions?

I'm not the only one who keeps up a membership. Every man in [his department] is an ex-craftsman, there's even ex-vehicle builders and they were a sort of cream. Craft may not count for much here, but they still have it. I'm still in it [his union] because I suppose they're a rallying-point to fall back on. Unions were started for good reasons. But the companies that don't have unions today, like [this firm], are the companies that've learned a lesson. They want to keep the union out, so they have to try that little bit harder. The question is: Can they keep it up? Because once they stop . . .

The firm's not against people being in a union. The real
have no negotiating rights. I'm not so worried about r
worry over handling possible grievances, having some l
tion].

These statements suggest that the 'experienced unionists'
regarded it as a serious possibility that their new employer might
at some future date 'forget the lesson' it had learned, or stop
'trying that little bit harder'. Such informants certainly appreciated the firm's friendly atmosphere and the way they were at present managed, but believed it was quite possible that these
methods would later be abandoned. Even more clearly they held
back from commitment to any ideology of employee incorporation implied in the policies. Their questioning attitudes to unionism were thus balanced by mental reservations about the ultimate
good intentions of employers, and a mild impatience with a unitarist vision of the employment relationship.

What change of conditions, then, might bring the non-union
policies under serious pressure? Most of the potential support for
unionization was to be found among the firm's higher-skilled
employees, but this group had little sympathy for commitment to
trade unionism along traditional craft lines. It was apparent that
any readiness to support trade unionism in future would be
based squarely upon workplace instrumentalism:

I'd like to see a union in here, and so would other parties here. But
management is very against this—it's aghast at the thought that we'd be
organized. A union coming in here would result in having it recognized
what it's really like—the hi-tech industrial situation and its management.
By that I mean the conditions, and the shifts especially, not so much the
pay. You'd have that backing here if you had a case against the company. And that's where I want my union—in here. You'd be in a position of when you're on the shop-floor you have a voice to answer back,
making it a happier place for the workforce, not being under the thumb
of managers.

The type of union involvement envisaged here is essentially limited and moderate. But would some of the young, 'assertively
apathetic' workers come to support this type of unionism if they
were ever to lose trust in the firm, or its culture was forced to
change? At the time of the fieldwork, the positive wish for union
representation at the non-union subsidiary was held by very few

employees. It would be unwarranted to conclude that the weakness of this potential support can be attributed to the firm's non-union strategy of employee involvement. (For once, the term 'strategy' seems justified.) The policies had probably had some effect, but by reinforcing attitudes that already existed, rather than by implanting new attitudes and values. The possibility of eventual unionization will be discussed further in the conclusion, but three remarks can be made at this point.

First, for the time being, the younger workers, with what might be called their assertively apathetic attitudes towards the whole subject of trade unionism, rendered the firm virtually 'union-proof'. But their assertive indifference to trade unionism was not created by, or in most cases accompanied by, active commitment to the employer. Commitment certainly existed in the non-union subsidiary, but it was to a work-group, more broadly to the people who worked on the site, not to the company as a social or economic unit. The firm had built up considerable expectations in these young employees thanks to its rapid expansion. If it could successfully maintain regular improvements in their rewards, their prospects, and the quality of their work life, they would most probably continue to accept the employment relationship as it stood. But doing so depended, in large degree, upon further expansion and an easy product-market.[4]

Second, the firm's populist message was based, in large measure, upon acceptance of the idea that openness, egalitarianism, and camaraderie in face-to-face relations between managers and subordinates symbolized an identity of interests between employer and employees. There may be a great overlap of such interests, of course, even though there may not be full identity. But it evidently becomes harder to maintain such an idea mainly through face-to-face relations as a firm grows larger and older. These changes result in strong pressures towards institutionalization or formal procedures. One result can be a demand for institutionalized representation, and the form of the latter is most often a union.

The third comment worth making at this point also centres upon contingent factors. In some respects, the firm's human resources planning was inadequate, not to say sketchy. Over the longer term, the present employee relations policies depended upon steadily increasing the quality and level of training, especially of younger supervisors and managers. It remained very uncertain whether the parent company would allow the firm to allocate the resources necessary for this expanding programme, or would continue to treat its subsidiary almost exclusively as a 'cash cow' to be milked hard until, perhaps within ten years, the market for its product suddenly collapsed—as well it might.

The existing friendly and purposeful atmosphere at the site reflected the enthusiasm, energy, and charisma of a young, personally committed management team, which had always been quick to plug operational gaps with energetic improvisation. But an enthusiastic young management team is by its nature a wasting asset, and may rapidly disappear altogether, as its members are bought up by other firms, or burned out in overwork. If new, personally less highly motivated managers took over, the pressures for formalized bargaining would probably increase, bringing closer the possibility of union recognition.

At the time the fieldwork was undertaken the firm's strategy of employee involvement and non-unionism was working according to plan, certainly in the sense that no strong support for unionization existed, or showed signs of appearing. How far the firm's employee relations practices can actually account for the attitudes towards trade unionism found among the workforce during the fieldwork is more questionable. There is no evidence that these policies had much affected the view of unions held by those of its employees who had experienced union involvement in previous posts: the critical attitudes to unions they held had developed from those experiences, not from the firm's non-union ethos. (This atmosphere may, however, have made it easier to voice their negative feelings.) At the same time, their cautious support for a limited, instrumental type of unionism remained in place.

On the other hand, the accessibility of managers and their populist rhetoric may indeed have helped to harden the sheer indifference towards trade unionism of the younger employees. Whether this regime and its ideology had, as it were, inoculated these employees permanently against trade unionism is far more doubtful. Growth in the size of the firm could well threaten its previously 'matey' atmosphere, while the greater employee relations skill a larger and more varied workforce would demand from supervisors and managers called for a much higher expenditure on training than might be forthcoming. In such an eventuality, the assertive apathy of some younger employees might give way to other, perhaps more thoughtful attitudes about the relevance of trade unions.

5. MICRO-CORPORATIST FORMALISM: THE UNIONIZED HEAD OFFICE

The head office employer acted as the management company for a large, diversified British-owned multinational company. It shared its Swindon site with the UK base of some of its operating companies, but was managed separately. The head office had moved to Swindon in the 1970s, to escape central London rents. Its enviable site ten minutes from the M4 motorway commanded a panoramic view of the Berkshire Downs. The offices, set in their own extensive and carefully landscaped grounds, brought to mind well-funded international agencies. Some management informants referred to the site as 'this campus'.

The head office had largely escaped the early 1980s recession thanks to its financial strength and mix of products, and it was confident about its future. But the regime of control at the head office was undergoing change thanks to the knock-on effects of tougher markets, and to internal pressures for better use of resources. The company as a whole had resulted from a merger over ten years earlier. The dominant partner, in the words of one of its manager employees at the time, had been 'rich, traditional, laid-back, and very British', the member of an international cartel. It was generally considered to have operated a decidedly— though benevolently—paternalist employee relations policy at that time. This system seems to have prevailed, at first, in the merged company. Since the onset of the early 1980s recession, however, the head office had set out to modify it, albeit in what appears to have been a rather desultory way. Thus at the time of the fieldwork the head office was still considered a generous employer, with a comparatively indulgent regime of control; but it had grown relatively more demanding in terms of personal work discipline, quality of output, and overall efficiency.

The 1970s merger had almost coincided with a successful unionization drive that left all but top management grades covered by collective agreements. Once the employee ballot in favour of trade union representation went against it, the head office had accepted the decision with good grace, but henceforward made efforts to incorporate the union. For a time, some informants alleged, this policy of incorporation had resulted in relations between union representatives and personnel staff that were almost collusive. This could not be substantiated. In the formal sense, certainly, the firm supported the union to the extent of providing facilities for meetings in working time, and treated it as a serious bargaining partner on the understanding that the union would help management maintain discipline and back the firm's drive for higher productivity. It will be seen below that relations between the employer and the trade union approximated in many ways to the pattern Warner (1983, 1984: 64–5) has termed micro-corporatist.

The head office workforce was overwhelmingly (around 90 per cent) a non-manual one. A large proportion of its employees had both high levels of education, and at least some professional training, and looked on their work very much as part of an evolving career. Around 40 per cent of the staff were women. Though most women employees worked in routine secretarial, clerical, or documentation areas, they were beginning to appear in executive posts in areas such as sales, computing, personnel, and public relations.

Head office managers expected this change to continue in areas such as customer relations, where the work involved dealing with enquiries or complaints from clients of the operating companies. Almost half head office informants, far more than at other case-study sites, said contacts with clients or customers were the main determinant of their work-effort, and of the structure of their work itself. At times they could make their working day sound a little like the model of the work process in a post-industrial society as described by Bell (1974). The head office thought women were more adept at such work, or at supervising those who did it. Those women with the right aptitudes were said to enjoy 'the sense of being in control' it could bring. An informant who had joined the firm after selling her own small business and who seemed destined for higher things in the firm declared:

Nothing is more satisfying to me than handling difficult clients.

There was a more sceptical view of this 'charm-work':

Angry clients phoning from northern towns are disarmed by a half-posh female voice with a southern accent. They're the head office charm-barrier.

Much of the other work at the head office, however, called for technical or professional skills rather than (or in addition to) social ones. In this respect the head office resembled the research centre discussed in the next section. Over a third of informants said that high-level qualifications were necessary for the work they did. Over four-fifths had training specifically for their present work. (This was the highest proportion at any of the sites.) In over two out of five cases their training had lasted over two years. All these proportions are far higher than those in the Work Histories/Attitudes sample. Only the research centre (see next section) had more professionally trained employees.

The work was covered by formal job descriptions and in theory tasks had been designed after work-study. But it was widely believed that the company had 'carried a lot of fat' in the past. A personnel manager explained that the head office had not merely escaped the economic depression following the 1973 worldwide oil crisis: the rise in the world price for oil and oil-products had dramatically increased its cash-flow and profit-margins. In the 1980s, however, the price of oil had fallen while consumers were growing more 'green-minded'. The company had been forced to cut staff in the early 1980s when it moved to Swindon. Though modest beside the cuts in manufacturing of the early 1980s, these came as a severe shock because the company was thought to offer a job for life. (Likewise, it was pointed out, managers had developed unreal expectations about the 'correct' minimum size of their 'empires'.)

The shake-out (or 'cull', as some managers referred to it) was followed by an efficiency drive. As with other case-study employers, large majorities of employees reported a recent increase in their own work effort, as well as in the quality of the work or service they produced, and the flexibility of their task structures. However, the proportions reporting a large increase in these aspects of work were lower than at all three other sites or in the Swindon sample of the Work Attitudes/Histories survey.

The efficiency drive required an all-round expansion and upgrading of skills, particularly in handling computers, word processors, or other information technology. But it was widely felt that the company had seriously bungled some parts of this change, especially for semi-professional employees:

The computer was the biggest change. Everything went on large sheets of paper and these and the print-outs were much easier to read. That was positive. I liked that part of the change. The bad side was the lack of any real training for doing the new work, or getting an understanding of how the new systems worked.

They just gave us the terminals and a tutorial book and it was up to us to teach ourselves. No one can tell me we didn't need proper training. The secretaries on word processors get that. We don't merit it. Why ever not? Of course it's possible this firm simply forgot.

Besides complaints of this kind, there was widespread agreement that everyday life at the head office was marked by—and suffered from—intense workplace politicking, and tantrums brought on by status sensitivity. But most informants were satisfied with their own jobs and on the whole felt that the firm had been making a more determined effort to build a closer relationship with its staff, partly by encouraging a less formal personal manner. A personnel manager commented:

It's broadly true—they've been trying to change this firm for almost ten years, to build this closer relationship with staff. But the results are patchy. Taking up the question of trust, there's no general answer. It varies greatly with which grades and what department we're talking about. They maybe want to trust people more, but they have a terrible job bringing themselves to do it.

Informants were far from being agreed on what new kind of control patterns the change might be producing. About a third of informants thought the style of management at the head office was one of the best points about the firm as an employer. But their descriptions of it were very diverse:

It's largely a personal thing—my own manager wants to get on well with people, and it's the kind of department which tends to be more sociable than most, so maybe it's not typical. At department level managers have a *great deal* of trust in employees, I have recent direct experience of that.

This firm isn't monolithic. It's a mixed bag. There may be a common policy. But it can be distorted or ignored at department level. We go in for lots of consultation in my department. Down the corridor, I don't know, some can be more dictatorial.

As few as one in four informants thought the best feature of the control system at the head office was an atmosphere of individual trust—far fewer than at some other case-study sites; but absence of trust was not, apparently, the cause of much ill-feeling. In any case, the deficit of trust was only a relative one:

Unless they did have a great deal of confidence in employees they'd never get anything done. What they still need to do is to explain their objectives to us better, take us *into* their confidence.

They do [have confidence in employees], but you're talking about different degrees of it. Some employees care, others don't. It's expected now that people will do what they're paid to do without any close supervision. But if there were no pressures from outside effort would fall off.

Trust was sometimes thought of in collective terms, as a question of the relations between departments, or of the degree of interest in a department shown by top management:

Communications is appalling! Other departments get to hear what's coming up in our department before we do. It's not always been like that. It's developed over the last five years. I wouldn't say *anyone* trusts anyone else.

The problem is, they set up too many systems that aren't working harmoniously. They need more co-ordination. And someone needs to cut down on inter-department conflict.

Communication is one of the worst aspects of this company. Rumours are always flying around, for example that more reorganization, and redundancy, is likely. People will tend to believe these stories when they have little trust in the company.

Managers concerned with employee relations strategy explained that severe departmental rivalry and obstructionism remained widespread, as a hangover from the mergers and restructuring some years previously. Overcoming this, one personnel planner complained, was 'a thankless task' that required the vigour and ruthlessness of the 'Neanderthal man' which he personally claimed to be. Departments fought one another by withholding information and by insistence on following procedures to the letter. Senior managers took action without warning or explanation. When the fieldworker asked him in what manner this was done— did it tend towards being autocratic, or more paternalist?—he commented:

Very senior people say: 'I don't see why people need to know what I'm up to; and I don't want to know what *they're* doing.' Paternalistic? It's your word, but I must say it's spot on [for the existing system]. But things are changing.

He illustrated the nature of the change by the behaviour of younger managers in handling grievances. They were, he maintained, far readier to analyse common problems—of discipline, tenure, or promotion—in a logical manner, while trying to weigh the outcome of differing solutions. They did not simply react, as older managers did, in order to protect their personal authority or some hallowed company rule.

Informants confirmed that replacement of the old paternalist culture by such pro-active management was a slow process. The move away from paternalism did not involve any outward change in the company's attitude towards trade unions. The position of the union was no less secure than it had been before the recession, but remained in some ways an ambiguous one. The head office recognized the union for pay-bargaining, but officially it neither encouraged nor discouraged membership. Whether the union had influenced the redundancy programme or the introduction of new technology in any significant way was not agreed, by managers or by union members, but it had made an effort to do so.

The earlier changes, and the continuing anxiety about future reorganization of the company, might have increased union membership sharply if the firm had handled them clumsily. But there was no serious evidence that change was being undertaken in order to undermine the influence of the union. Indeed, the situation was strongly reminiscent of that at the unionized subsidiary: the head office seemed to prefer to keep the union alive at a relatively low level of activity and influence, rather than to see it disappear altogether. No managers believed a policy of derecognition had ever been seriously considered, or was likely to be introduced in the near future. In one vital respect, though, the position of the union differed: the union was far more visible, vocal, and eager to promote itself than its counterpart at the unionized subsidiary. The head office had not welcomed unionization when it occurred a decade or so earlier. The Association of Scientific, Technical, and Managerial Staffs (ASTMS)[5] had won the right to represent the lower and middle grade staff by ballot in the 1970s only against determined management opposition. What is more, fieldworkers were assured, the company had chosen the wording of the ballot itself, with great care, to maximize the chance of rejection. It had also stipulated that more than half the employees of a given grade had already to be members for the grade to be included in the ballot. It had then been 'very surprised indeed' that over 80 per cent of returned ballots were in favour of recognition. Several informants could remember these days, and agreed they had voted for unionization mainly to combat arbitrary management:

I joined up with the union because I felt under very serious threat at the time. The company was very paternalist indeed in those days, in the traditional sense—if your face fitted, you'd never get fired; if it didn't, then it was OUT. There was a series of take-overs to make us feel still more vulnerable. So finally I signed up.

I joined ASTMS in 1977 and I'll tell you why I did. I worked for a right old moo, a real bitch—she used to hate me speaking my mind, which I always did, and she could make my life very awkward, a real misery, so I joined ASTMS, though in the event I never actually needed their support. If I'd been in another department I'd not have bothered.

Since then membership had declined somewhat. But around half of the head office's employees in eligible grades were current union members. A major reason for allowing membership to lapse was promotion:

I left because ASTMS only represents lower grades and I got promoted out of them.

Another reason was the atmosphere of the Swindon site, which in many ways differed from that of a traditional workplace:

I was in ASTMS when I worked in Manchester. It was a strange reason I joined in the first place. The fact is, at the Manchester site it was just the norm to join ASTMS, it was the thing you did. When I came down here I came to a different climate, where you join the union only if you feel like doing it a favour.

Motives for continuing to support the union were often explained rather hazily, though they usually touched on the issue of job security in one way or another:

I can't think for the life of me why I'm still in it. It's there for people 'in the works' in a manner of speaking, not people like us [white-collar employees]. For us, it's a very easy-going company, they never sack you. Union protection is superfluous.

I rejoined ASTMS because the company was going through a bad spell and I was disillusioned with the reorganization, what with the wages negotiations dragging on and getting nowhere. I thought I'd lend some weight to get them going.

The strongly instrumental tone of this latter statement was characteristic of this site. But it also shows that 'lending weight' was thought to be worth while, and implies that the union already had some ability to press claims effectively. In many ways it suggested why the union was able to hold on to its membership at head office, and even to increase its following a little, though union representatives considered that the great majority of staff were, in strict party political terms, opposed to the Labour Party, and in favour of most of the new employment legislation. What mattered above all was how highly employees rated the union's influence. In this respect, this case-study in particular bears out Gallie's remarks in Chapter 4 on the importance of unions being capable of 'delivering' benefits: almost by definition, union members were those people who believed the union had, or could develop, some real bargaining power at the site:

Yes, the union does have some influence here. They're always holding union meetings in the firm's time, and lots of people go to those meetings. They have an influence on pay, on holidays, and maybe behind the scenes too.

Ideological or moral reasons for joining the union were only very occasionally voiced, and then only in somewhat apologetic tones:

Greed always operates in the end, and this forces people to resist it when it makes their lives a misery. Employers demand more and more output and suddenly the wheel turns. It could turn here too.

The overall picture was one of overriding pragmatism and instrumentalism, of limited support for a style of trade unionism concerned with pursuing attainable benefits by using persuasion and 'reasonable' bargaining tactics.

It's quite a good union. I rate it highly. Before it came in there were no negotiations over the pay-rise, and it does have an impact there, and in the firm generally. Don't let anyone tell you the contrary.

As the defensive tone of the last remark suggests, a large minority of the head office staff seemed to remain doubtful about the true degree of the union's influence in the firm. For them, there was no point in paying subscriptions unless this investment brought a guaranteed minimum return. But strong ideological objections to unionism were rare. Management's handling of the union was governed by considerations that in many ways were similar to those affecting employee involvement in the union:

Because I worked in employee relations till two years ago, I know ASTMS here, and it's a very reasonable union. The local leaders take the view that some new technology will enhance the quality of working life of their members.

It's very moderate. It has *some* influence here, if not a great deal. That's the firm's choice, too. The firm could just disregard ASTMS if it wanted to. But I'm happy with things as they are. It makes life simpler in some ways. It's just easier to deal with one person representing all those others.

Local union representatives agreed that the firm had made no attempt when the time had been most opportune to withdraw recognition. It even allowed staff who were not union members to go to some authorized meetings in working hours, for which the company provided facilities. These representatives believed the firm treated the union 'seriously' as a pay-bargaining agent for the eligible grades. While union representatives thought ordinary members were never 'marked out' for joining the union or taking part in meetings, some of them alleged that they themselves suffered for their activism. One informant, who had held an important local civic office, commented sarcastically:

You tell me why I'm still in Grade X—because I've not got leadership or management ability?

A former union representative who had recently resigned his office stated candidly:

Now it's time for me to get some promotion. I have my family to think about nowadays. So that's why I've stopped being a union rep.

It was impossible to verify the claim that union representatives risked sacrificing all promotion. (Such assertions are as common as the claim that, in order to destroy their credibility, employers are more likely to promote 'difficult' activists.) The firm's explanation was simply that the demands of their union work made representatives less productive as employees, and 'less able to show exactly what they're worth'. Another view still, and an interesting one, was that some of the older union representatives had been relatively co-operative and easily managed by the personnel department, which had not wished to lose such pliable bargaining partners. Personnel managers acknowledged that the younger union representatives had a different style:

Our relations with ASTMS are pretty good. But you do find nowadays this new breed of slightly aggressive leaders—since the retirement of some older, highly responsible officials. But we're friendly enough to have lunch together occasionally.

As at both the unionized subsidiary and the public research centre (see next section), at the head office an established set of industrial relations procedures and understandings remained essentially intact. The research uncovered no evidence of pressure from a higher level to alter this aspect of the employment relationship. The personnel department had one or two reformist managers who were putting forward ideas for a more strategic approach to training and staff development, or for reducing the stiffness in the atmosphere of some departments, or for curbing the firm's 'appalling bureaucratic habits'. None of these proposals envisaged change to the existing employee representation system.

As they might have done in any long-established organization, the fieldworkers heard many complaints about personal mistreatment—unrewarded loyalty, favouritism, or blatant sexual harassment. However, the head office was notable for the rarity of complaints about its working conditions, its salary scales, or its promotion opportunities. Employees recognized, however reluctantly at times, that they enjoyed material advantages shared by relatively few other Swindon employees with comparable levels of training and skill.

Two objective findings suggest that job satisfaction was indeed relatively high at the head office site. First, the average length of service of currently employed staff (excluding temporary employees) was almost twenty years. In so far as the present job amounted in effect to a career, the head office had a very committed workforce. Second, the head office, purely as an employer, had the highest employee approval of the case-study employers: almost four out of five head office informants said they would highly recommend it as a firm to work for if asked by an outsider. (The non-union subsidiary received the next highest endorsement, but from fewer than half its informants.) The head office already had a workforce that in formal terms was loyal and committed. But this commitment was based squarely on self-interest, not moral involvement (Etzioni, 1975) with the employer; in a cynical view expressed by some people at the site, the firm simply bought loyalty and job satisfaction. Managers were, of course, well aware of the extent of this satisfaction, and its basis, which they regarded as a bulwark against the growth of any militancy in the trade union:

Just tell me: What is an 'active' union going to gripe about in an environment like this? People will want to get themselves noticed for stirring it up. But the scope for that is strictly limited.

However, managers had concluded that loyalty to the firm was entirely consistent with support for 'moderate' unionism (as they defined it). Fewer informants at head office were strongly anti-union or assertively apathetic about unions than at the other private sector sites. Like the informants of the public research centre (see Section 6), head office employees were more likely than not to say that unions were still important as local bargainers and representatives, though they could be very critical of unions for their policies or their leaders' behaviour at the national level. Their attitudes were not affected, so far as the case-study work could establish, either one way or the other by the firm's policy towards unions. This policy—perhaps surprisingly in an organization so often characterized as bureaucratic—in many respects itself lacked full definition, and clarifying it was not regarded as an urgent priority. (However, beside the unionized subsidiary, it was a model of precision and transparency.)

While there is little evidence that attitudes towards trade unionism in general were much affected either way by the firm's employee relations policies, the fact that the head office management continued to recognize the union as a bargaining agent, and as a valid representative in disciplinary cases, no doubt accounts for much of the support it received from employees. Without this recognition, its future would in all probability have been a short one. Continued support from management for local industrial relations arrangements once again largely accounts for union survival at the head office.

6. PUBLIC SERVICE UNDER STRESS: THE RESEARCH CENTRE

Research and development, especially scientific research, had been widely portrayed as a characteristic activity of the new Swindon economy by the time of the research. The public research centre (PRC), like the private sector head office, had relocated from London, but much more recently. It sponsored and co-ordinated several publicly funded specialist branches of scientific research. Together with other ministerially funded research centres, the PRC formed part of a wider public research domain. Of the almost 400 staff at its Swindon base, about half were shared with other centres. It directly employed several hundred others at a dozen or so sites spread around the United Kingdom.

The employee relations regime at the PRC was a product of three main factors: Civil Service employment rules; the PRC's work processes, which required highly trained professional and administrative staff; and the hitherto well-established representation and negotiation system 'Whitleyism', still in place in the 1980s in the national-level public service in Britain.

Four features of the Whitley system should be noted at the outset. First, Whitleyism awarded full recognition to designated unions in employee grades reserved for them. Second, bargaining covered a wide range of issues. Because of this wide scope, and the more or less equal representation of management and union representatives on committees, employee relations had become, in effect, subject to extensive joint regulation. Third, Whitleyism was systematic: in the PRC, Whitley committees or sub-committees existed at three levels, and in several functional areas. Finally, the Whitley system embodied an ideal—an ideology almost—of consensus: both sides were bound by existing rules, but there was an unspoken assumption that procedure would be oiled by the good faith and goodwill of each side. Hard bargaining could occur within this secure procedural framework, with the underlying understanding that agreement would always be reached.

The PRC employed an overwhelmingly white-collar workforce, with many professionally and technically qualified staff. But there were sharp status divisions between three main staff branches: (1) scientific and administrative professionals; (2) routine administrative employees; and (3) technicians, secretaries, and clerks. (In addition, there was a small group of manual workers at the site.) Most of the PRC's women employees (about 40 per cent of the site workforce) were in office or lower-graded data-processing posts. Very few worked in the scientific grades. Clerical employees had better terms of employment and working conditions than many local private sector employees, although their pay was often poorer. They mostly had low commitment to the PRC or to their work role, and very few thought of their employment as a career.

Though the scientific staff and the administrative specialists both thought of themselves as following a career within the public service, the first group tended to think of themselves as professionals with strong academic links, and the second as organizers and controllers. Members of both echelons, however, subscribed to the strong public service ethos which had hitherto shaped the PRC's work, vigorously defending the contribution of publicly funded scientific research to education and national life. However, the value of public provision of basic research, and *a fortiori* public service as a vocation, was now played down by the PRC's ministerial supervisors, and openly belittled by its ultimate political masters. So too were Civil Service employment and the Whitley system of employee representation. Not surprisingly, many informants at the PRC felt that institutions they considered valid and worthwhile had come under sustained attack.

The eventual privatization of the agency was considered likely by many of them, although the immediate prospect of it had been lifted at the time of the research. In reality, more strain in everyday workplace relations had resulted from a drive to cut staffing levels. The cuts already made, though much less severe than those suffered by some other public services, had created a keen sense of threat to personal security and promotion prospects, especially among higher-grade staff. For a minority, however, the perceived threat was also that to the value of publicly supported science itself.

But the PRC did not present a united face on these issues. Few clerical-graded employees shared the fears of the professional and scientific staff. With its clearly defined work roles, precise lines of authority, emphasis on written documents or their electronic equivalents, and rule-governed discipline, the PRC closely resembled the textbook definition of a bureaucratic organization. Yet it lacked the overall cohesion attributed to such organizations. Radically differing terms of employment and reward, overlapping those of training and values, created sharp cleavages between its three main employee echelons. The PRC, in fact, possessed a rigidly segmented internal labour market. Because interests were so divided, opposition to the tide of change was weaker among lower-grade employees, exactly where in many private organizations it would have been strongest. In the view of some lower-graded staff, the opposition to change of the 'boffins' and administrators reflected their self-interest and personal political values.

The split between grades was reflected in the complexity of the representative system. With five different unions on the site, this fragmentation was somewhat offset by the long-standing agreements, procedures, and ideology of the Whitley Committee system. Local management still applied the agreements in good faith, even scrupulously. The PRC also provided the union representatives with office facilities and paid time off work that the representatives acknowledged to be 'very fair'. This helped the unions to maintain a united resistance to ministry (in effect, government) policy. The strongest support from union members for a Civil Service defence campaign occurring at the time of the fieldwork was concentrated in the higher grades.

Union representatives considered daily workplace industrial relations in the PRC to be otherwise very harmonious, despite this being the only site where industrial action occurred during the course of fieldwork. The unions were almost apologetic about this dispute. Officially, the action was represented as being 'in favour of a better Civil Service'. Its logic was national and propagandist (or political), rather than local and instrumental. The local protest strikes and picketing had involved criticism of government policy towards the Civil Service; it had been hard work for union organizers to explain and justify the action taken to employees (union members or not) in clerical grades. A strong union supporter in this grade said that those who were wives of servicemen at a large local air-base were particularly hostile to trade unionism. (Many of these staff were also said to be strong government supporters.) For some union representatives, however, an equally serious problem was that most of these employees regarded the PRC no differently from any private sector employer offering half-casual employment. For them, almost inevitably, the action lacked relevance, let alone legitimacy.

Unions thus had only weak support in the lower grades. Their position was an odd one in many other respects. Membership among the upper grades remained around 70 per cent and the commitment of these members to unionism was often strong. The segmented structure of union representation made communication between unions more difficult, and they were under official attack at national level. Yet union influence at the site remained evident enough, and local management was making no attempt to subvert or to bypass the Whitley institutions. Furthermore, the professional-grade unions usually had access, informal as well as formal, to local and higher management. (Some union officers themselves held administrative posts.) Local managers considered the Whitley system a rational and effective way of managing employee relations, although some had begun to take an interest in changes taking place in the private sector.

In the 1980s, then, the PRC had experienced rapid and upsetting changes. First, it had been relocated from central London. Not all the scientific and administrative staff who followed it to Wiltshire had welcomed this change, which some at the time experienced as an indirect loss of status—a banishment from life in a lively capital city to 'a town nobody pretends is anything but a dump'. Since then, the advantages of closeness to a rural environment had become better appreciated, especially given the sharp deterioration in the quality of life in London in the 1980s. Nevertheless, the shock of enforced movement had been real enough at the time.

Second, it was rapidly followed by a redefinition of the unit's mission, or at least of the way the PRC should use its expertise. The PRC had been constrained (as many informants saw it) to undertake increasing amounts of research under realistically costed contract to the private sector, and at the time of the fieldwork in 1987–8, the agency had built up substantial earnings from these sources. The incitement to think commercially—to 'charge the corporate customer up'—had been greatly intensified a year or so earlier, and this renewed financial pressure had coincided with a wave of staff cuts. Local professional staff were as a result experiencing great uncertainty about the agency's future role.

Many of the agency's professional employees opposed more commercial-minded working methods, fearing they would bring a drop in the quality or reliability of their work. Some office staff said they could not understand 'the mentality of the boffins', and had little sympathy with them. Support staff claimed to know still less about 'the politics of what goes on here'. Like that of the office workers, their main attitude was one of indifference. One or two higher-grade informants who seemed prepared to accept change in a pragmatic spirit (or were at least ready to state a case for doing so), considered opposition to be founded in some degree on 'a panic stations attitude'. Others, even some who otherwise accepted much of the government's programme, regarded the 'growing commercialization' of the PRC as an inappropriate public approach to scientific research.

For the scientific professionals, the logic of the changes ran counter to non-commercial norms and values they drew from three spheres—traditional science, the universities, and the Civil Service—out of favour in the 1980s. These staff believed the new market-oriented culture and 'money-spinner' ideology must lead sooner or later, via a lowering of technical standards, to the weakening of all meaningful scientific values in their work. Even if this did not result in lower ethical standards too, as was widely feared, their sense of scientific identity would be compromised.

While opposing pressures on the PRC towards 'silly forms of commercialization' (including eventual privatization) some of the professionals said they none the less supported parts of government policy on public accountability and privatization. For others, recent treatment of the PRC resulted from unthinking application of political dogma. One or two argued forcefully that the official demand for commercial thinking was a sure sign of imminent privatization, while others believed a change of government would soon remove the possibility completely. (The Conservative victory in the June 1987 General Election, which occurred during fieldwork, revived their fears.) The underlying consensus seemed to be that present policies would continue, with the PRC slowly disappearing in the face of politically inspired fervour for private enterprise, and continuing government disfavour towards higher education, public employment, and basic or 'curiosity' science.

The strength of the belief that privatization was imminent is in some ways surprising. A feasibility study of privatization, commissioned by the ministry from a firm of international management consultants, had recently been undertaken. The report concluded that none of the agency's satellite research stations or laboratories could make enough money in the foreseeable future to turn them into an attractive investment for private buyers (including their present scientific employees). Without switching to new activities in which the PRC and its satellites were quite inexperienced, privatization could not be made financially viable—or not sufficiently so to attract private risk capital.

In addition, information had been supplied free or at cost to many government departments and nationalized industries, or was already sold to large private firms and a number of foreign governments at very attractive prices. Privatization would make it unprofitable to provide these services, or price the PRC out of this market. All such scenarios also overlooked the PRC's function of promoting strong basic research in universities and other branches of higher education. Was this role to be completely wound up? The report went on to suggest that the implications for the quality of British research needed to be considered. Where, it asked, were future specialists in this area to come from without the agency's sponsorship?

At the same time, union sources alleged, the report had pointed out that the PRC had already made great strides in tapping other funding sources by its competitive bidding for research contracts from public or private clients. Unless it did produce costings comparable to private agencies in these new markets, private competitors would lodge claims of unfair competition. In this sense, the PRC was already behaving in a commercial manner, and doing so successfully.

This positive bill of health did not remove the possibility of full privatization, some informants argued, because the government's motivation was essentially doctrinaire—any means of cutting public employment was valid for the Prime Minister herself.

However, so long as the PRC remained part of the public service, no radical alteration of the agency's control regime would be envisaged. This still left room for piecemeal adjustments to the system—fewer informal contacts between supervisors and staff, tighter monitoring of work performance, less generous provision of time off for union business, a stricter interpretation of the Whitley procedures, or a rejection of the accommodative spirit of Whitleyism. Changes like these would together add up to a significant modification of the existing regime.

Fieldwork found little evidence of such changes. The corporate plan put into operation a year or so earlier had brought in its wake (voluntary) early retirements and (compulsory) redundancies. But the unions had been fully involved in this scheme. Although the corporate plan had, it was said, sapped morale, and was continuing to create uncertainty, it seemed so far to have altered the actual tone of relations between employees and managers rather little, and then mostly at the intermediate to lower staff levels.

Most importantly, it was widely acknowledged that the staff cuts had not been used primarily to increase compliance with work discipline, or to boost output, or to cow union representatives into a compliant frame of mind through generating a sense of job insecurity. In any case, and unlike some of their opposite numbers in the private sector, local managers had been given no extra authority to operate such policies—nor tried to arrogate it. (The idea of their seeking such autonomy by stealth, as those at the non-union subsidiary may perhaps have done, does not bear much scrutiny.)

Another kind of change does require comment here. Part-time and contract work seemed to have been growing substantially in the agency as a whole. Could not this drive towards numerical flexibility be seen as part of a strategy for making employment precarious in the PRC? One-year, three-year, and five-year contracts for scientific and technical staff were being introduced at those of its satellite centres which had come to rely more on their limited-term research contracts. The headquarters' scientific staff in Swindon were not yet affected by them. The Swindon management also recognized that the agency's escape from long-term commitments to any contracted employees was only to be bought at the cost of lower motivation among staff who were supposed to exercise personal initiative. A short-term contract system would also increase recruitment costs thanks to the 'premature' departure of employees to take up permanent posts outside the PRC, while bringing pressure on research directors to provide non-money inducements to forestall early resignations.

According to personnel managers, the introduction of part-time work also primarily reflected growing labour-market scarcities in Swindon, and the preference of some employees themselves for part-time work, rather than a policy for tightening management control. The PRC claimed to re-employ former women employees after a period of child-bearing, and to meet any wishes they might have for part-time employment. It operated a job-sharing scheme in the administrative grades. (In the scientific grades, managers claimed, it was 'harder for technical reasons to flex the work around between—say—morning and afternoon work periods'.)

Many informants reported changed work organization. For higher grades this reflected a redrawn authority structure, and the reduction of control of the Swindon headquarters over the budgets of the agency as a whole, as well as over those of individual satellite centres, in line with the corporate plan. In the clerical grades the changes often resulted from a policy of job rotation. Frequent changes of task were seen as an aspect of good modern management; that is, either as ways of counteracting boredom with jobs that were for the most part easily mastered, or as a method of expanding the range of an individual's skills. The PRC's declared motive was, in fact, to cut recruiting costs by retaining staff who were 'ready to move for just 10p an hour more'. Any increase in productivity was treated as a windfall gain.

Such changes did not foreshadow a new pattern of control. They confirmed the existing division of staff grades. These divisions, personnel staff said, had been much sharper ten years previously, when it was commonplace (as at the time it still was in government departments such as the Ministry of Defence) for staff to insist on being addressed as 'Sir/Madam'—or by their formal job-titles. However, this did not reflect an internal policy of informality so much as broader social change, and the growing stress on flexible organizations in management education and writing.

A final, but noteworthy aspect of the control system at the PRC was the stress on staff training. At all levels, staff appeared to be very well trained indeed for their work. A great range of courses was available through the Civil Service, through the PRC itself, through other locally based government research agencies, or were sub-contracted to local further education colleges. While these courses focused on problems or techniques most relevant to public service organizations such as the agency, many were relevant to work in other public sector organizations. Most would also have been a good preparation for work in private sector firms. Any claim that the agency's training effort was directed at locking individuals into their work role at the research centre does not bear examination. On the contrary, it seemed that in the increasingly tight Swindon job market of the later 1980s its training effort must if anything have facilitated, or even encouraged, individual mobility. In truth, the PRC was a net supplier of human capital to a local economy where many private employers had an indifferent record as trainers.

There seems good reason, then, to accept the view of the personnel department that there existed no other policy for employee relations than to continue as long as circumstances permitted with a system combining the embedded formal employment structures and practices of the public service with those of the existing Whitley Committee system of staff representation. This system, it was agreed by those involved, was always modified locally in important ways by the personalities of people holding leading roles on the management and union sides, and in Swindon the 'extended-family sized scale' of the site aided this customization. But the formal properties of the system always prevailed.

Such industrial relations institutions were those most distrusted, and at times condemned most scathingly, at the highest government level during the 1980s, increasing the expectation of a general attack on Civil Service trade unionism in due course. Many informants pointed to the example of the government's nearby security information gathering and processing establishment (the GCHQ Cheltenham site),[6] where de-unionization had actually been pushed through. This was seen as a harbinger of a wider campaign to run down the Whitley system and promote de-unionization. At the time of the fieldwork, there were perhaps good grounds for such anxieties, though there were already other signs that union influence in the Civil Service was no longer a major government preoccupation since its former influence had visibly diminished.

The employee relations regime at the PRC differed from those of the three private sector employers in its high degree of coverage, its systematization, and the degree of positive support from local management it could continue to count on. It offered a well-defined and formally secure role for unions. There existed a high degree of consensus between managerial staff, most employees, and union representatives on the nature of the agency's mission and how it should be achieved. For many staff and managers, as well as active supporters of the unions, a sense of being beleaguered by hostile government policies may actually have brought about an increase in normative and procedural agreement. Some informants reported a growth of closer understanding between staff and local management comparable to that reported for some private firms in Swindon in the SCELI 'core' surveys. However, its main source was not the threat of tougher market competition but—as one particularly forthright informant put it—'the unpredictability of a paymaster playing conviction politics'.

However, there were limits to such solidarity. In its feel, the atmosphere of the PRC was far from easy-going or 'matey', especially in comparison with the non-union subsidiary. The PRC remained in many ways a very formal workplace indeed. (Only one in ten of PRC informants claimed to be on first-name terms with 'almost everyone' they met at work—this was the lowest proportion by far at any of the four sites.) Individuals also worked in relative isolation more often, and seemed to prefer doing so. Personal aspirations were likewise higher in general, with almost four out of five of PRC employees saying they regarded their job as a career, or that they felt pressure to work effectively because of the high professional standards demanded by colleagues. At the same time, management had imposed more stringent standards in annual appraisals of performance. But this new toughness was thought to be 'civilized':

Relations have got more difficult because things are firmer here. Once it was slack—I don't think it's disloyal to say that—but it's not slack now. It's objective. We were carrying passengers. But there is more scope here, compared to most organizations, public or private, to express the human element officially, for example in the treatment of staff under pressure from personal or family problems.

There are degrees of trust, it depends on grade. There's a greater degree of alienation at the lower levels. On the other hand, the degree of distrust that does exist is not as high as it could be. People are moderate in their degree of criticism of management—they don't want to make its job any harder.

Relations were always good, if you discount a hiccup over staffing two years ago. Lots of staff had to go and there was no real consultation with unions about it. But if you look at the recent strikes, picketing, and other action, this isn't against management.

Several informants pointed out that the PRC's Swindon site, as a unit, was regarded as 'the boss' by its satellite centres around the United Kingdom. As such it was in turn treated with suspicion. Several administrators noted that this gave rise to special stresses on them, which made it easier to appreciate the demands of their own ministerial superiors in London:

If you think of the research centre as a whole, the [ministry in London] has tremendous confidence in [local managers] like us. The [ministry] doesn't impose its will, except on the budget. We have great autonomy. As for building a closer relationship with staff, well no—the Civil Service isn't so much affected by that. That's happening in the private sector. We always had a close relationship of our own sort with the staff, through the unions, the Whitley system.

The endorsement of union membership undoubtedly had an effect on recruiting. As noted earlier, the PRC was by far the most heavily unionized of the four sites, with an overall rate estimated at 70 per cent and a virtually complete coverage in some grades. Over three out of five informants at this site—the highest proportion by far for all the sites covered in the Related Study— said it had become more important to be member of a union over the previous five years. But there was general agreement that the influence of Civil Service unions, especially over pay and manning levels, had greatly weakened. Continuing support for trade unionism among staff did not arise from hostile relations in the workplace, but in important part because local management continued to recognize and support membership of a union. In this sense, there was some resemblance between the PRC and the two unionized private sector employers discussed earlier.

Individual support for trade unionism had many bases, but was expressed more strongly by the staff of the most highly qualified grades. Most of these informants, it should be added, were knowledgeable and articulate in their views of unionism, and they gave cogent reasons for their own involvement. It is not easy to present their comments briefly—informants laced their replies with illustrations and qualifications. However, running through this complexity was a single, clear theme: despite some failings, their union did a good job for its members:

For a small union, the [name] is quite good. It tries hard to keep members informed, to get the broad mass involved in arriving at decisions; and it's got a realistic attitude.

Union influence has fallen quite a lot. But [name] still can have an important questioning role, and maybe in changing minds, though any union can only do that when the minds in question are willing to be changed.

Unionism in general remained important to many of the PRC's union members because, as informants saw it, of a continuing need for a collective guarantee of individual rights, or of terms and conditions of employment. One informant did point out that as a signed-up Labour Party member he had given an undertaking to join a union 'even if it was a pretty useless union or unaffiliated to the Party'. Otherwise, there was little ideological commitment—or ideological opposition—to trade unionism. For nearly all these high-graded staff, any political role for the union should be restricted to that of a strictly non-aligned lobbyist or pressure group:

[Unions] are sounding-boards for a collective membership, increasing a democratic debate. That [democratic debate] is affected by what democratic structures they have. Personally, I believe they should avoid getting enmeshed in the government process or state structures. That's the royal road to losing their *raison d'être*.

The proper place for any union action was in the workplace:

Middle-level union leaders, even in white-collar unions, adopt an old-fashioned 'industrial' style—that's so out-of-date, it's mass hysteria, showmanship. That style, the extreme stance, perpetuates itself. They can attack mass-unemployment, but they should also be making efforts at the local level because workplace things affect individuals more.

At this level, union organization and support should be strong:

[Because] the only communication that is paid any attention these days must have size and power to back it up, and for employees that means a union. There's no future in individuals representing themselves—but the union is there to *represent* individuals and mustn't forget that.

Yet, in the PRC, just as in the private firms, much of the new employment legislation was welcomed—or, at the worst, not perceived as wholly unwelcome for unions. A strong Labour supporter even commented:

They [the new laws] are producing some short-term effects through reducing morale, getting unions involved in the law and courts, through sequestration of their funds, and forbidding secondary action. But I think some parts of the legislation should have been carried through by unions themselves long ago, and for them to have done so would have strengthened them immensely . . . making sure national and other leaders have to be voted in, and can't be voted in for life. Likewise for strike-ballots—mostly these have been going in favour of action as it so happens—and new legislation affecting unions' rule-books, which were often very vague or contradictory. Changes affecting these things will—yes, I mean it—*strengthen* unions by giving members a democratic reason for supporting a call for action.

As Duncan Gallie points out in Chapter 4, the Work Histories/Attitudes sample fully confirmed a trend reported in all other studies of British trade unionism in the later 1980s: employee involvement in unionism had clearly fallen much less in the non-industrial public sector than in the private sector. Membership held up well in national and local administration. The large industrial disputes of these years were nearly all in public sector industries, local government, or the Civil Service. There are several reasons for this resilience. This case-study brings out two factors which help explain this relative strength.

First, in the public sector, a very sharp distinction between the *employer*, which ultimately is the government in some form or another, and *management*, especially local managers in person, can be drawn by the actors. Government policies towards public sector employment in the 1980s involved retrenchment based on cash limits to expenditure and the 'capping' of other services. The inevitable reduction in job security and relative rewards often brought functional management and employees into closer sympathy because the cuts hit overlapping economic interests. Perhaps less often, but still often enough to matter, they conflicted with shared values about public service and about the way industrial relations should be organized and conducted.

Second, workplace industrial relations in the public sector are for the most part long-established and heavily institutionalized. They form a part of the employment relationship that is not merely accepted *de facto* but is internalized and carries normative force with both management and employees. They certainly were continuing to do so at the time of the Related Study: at the PRC, there was far stronger, more positive support for a trade union role in employee relations than in any of the private sector firms. On the surface there was rather little about this support that seemed ideological or radical in a political sense. With one exception, the agency's local union representatives themselves seemed to have had a somewhat reserved, apolitical view of their role, and a decidedly proceduralist view of how it should be played.

For their part, union members could, unprompted, embark on very cogent discussions of the reasons for and against belonging to their own union (or to any union) at a time of falling bargaining strength, open political hostility, and a wider, more diffuse social disfavour. Most of such commentaries were also phrased in terms of material costs and benefits, not abstract ideals such as employee solidarity. If these pragmatic and instrumental explanations are to be accepted at face value, they point to a paradox: support for the Civil Service unions had remained strong, and might even be hardening in the professional grades, as these unions were growing less able to deliver material benefits. It seems possible to conclude, therefore, that there was a stronger normative aspect to the support for the agency's unions than the members themselves were aware of, or were prepared to acknowledge.

It was to be expected that many of the PRC staff, with their professional or scientific training, and public service ethos, would phrase arguments in analytical terms rather than in those of shared attitudes and values. It may be, none the less, that the strict objectivity of their 'case for unionism' sometimes disguised a strong normative component in their involvement, which should not be overlooked here (or, perhaps, be discounted by policy-makers). For a large minority of the PRC's unionists, the right to union representation, and the readiness of management to accept unions as partners, apparently formed part of an unwritten contract of employment. Such expectations set them apart from most other employees in the Related Study.

7. CONCLUSION

The Related Study in Swindon was undertaken to gain a better understanding of how management policies, organizational context, and employee attitudes affected trade unionism in selected workplaces in Swindon. The main working hypothesis was that smaller and more recently established employers in the faster-growing industries would strongly prefer non-union employee relations regimes, and would be more likely, where unions were recognized, to operate personnel strategies bypassing an existing union, with the ultimate goal of achieving a non-union workplace. The case-study workplaces were therefore chosen because the employer in each case appeared to have a good opportunity to alter union influence if it wished to do so. If such change was occurring in the three unionized workplaces, how far would it be aimed at reducing, or even completely removing, union influence? In the non-union firm, how strongly had the employer resisted union recognition, and did its policies seem likely to be effective in preventing growth in support for unionization among its staff?

The Work Histories/Attitudes survey, analysed by Duncan Gallie in Chapter 4, confirms that employer attitudes to union membership were a major determinant of individual membership in the SCELI employee sample. These results lead to the question of how far employer policies may account for employee attitudes towards trade unionism in general. The Work Histories/Attitudes data on the policies towards unionism of the interviewee's current employer are, however, limited to assessments by the interviewee of how far the employer encouraged or discouraged union membership. Valuable as these data are for documenting the link between employer policies towards trade unionism and individual attitudes towards it in the later 1980s, the material available provided little further detail about the employer's approach to industrial relations in the workplace, personnel management practices, human resources policies, or sponsorship of non-union forms of representation in the workplace. The latter may form part of carefully devised employee relations strategies that are designed to result in a well-defined regime of control. The possible effects of the employer's regime of control on the employee's involvement in trade unionism cannot be assessed on the basis of this survey.

Similarly, Gallie and Rose in their examination of the Employers 30 case-studies in Chapter 2 report many SCELI employers describing significant changes in their relations with trade unions over the five years (the mid-1980s) preceding the study. Yet the results for these 191 establishments showed, in fact, that unionized employers were more likely to report an improvement in their relations with trade unions than otherwise in these years, while determined attempts to prevent unionization in non-union workplaces seem to have been relatively uncommon, and plans to achieve de-unionization where unions were present were reported in only one case out of almost 200. Once again, however, although the link between policies towards union recognition and other aspects of management control strategy could be explored in this survey, the possible impact of employee relations policies on employee involvement in trade unionism could not be followed up. The four intensive case-studies in the Related Study in Swindon allowed such links between employer policies and worker attitudes to trade unionism to be examined more carefully.

The three main findings seem clear. First, the four cases presented in this chapter show how complex—at times unclear, and apparently inconsistent—employer policies towards trade unionism and the development of employee relations could be in practice: in all but one case it seemed inappropriate to term them 'strategies'. Second, the findings fail to show any serious attempt to remove a union presence from the unionized workplaces, or to alter employee attitudes in the expected direction. Third, only in the case of the non-union subsidiary were policies definite enough to be considered a true non-union strategy, but they apparently had little effect on employee attitudes towards and involvement in trade unionism.

In terms of the categories used in the Work Histories/Attitudes survey, the PRC encouraged individual union membership, the non-union subsidiary discouraged it, while the unionized subsidiary and the head office were largely neutral towards it. Three of the employers 'encouraged' membership to the extent of recognizing unions as bargaining partners—albeit of a very indefinite kind in the case of the unionized subsidiary. In these three very different workplaces, a majority of those informants eligible for membership of the unions present in them said that, even though they might not wish to take it up, it mattered to them personally that the possibility of membership at least was open to them, and that they could participate in union meetings at the workplace if they wished to do so. They thought the union had at least some (more rarely, a great deal) of influence in their own workplace. A majority of the Related Study informants as a whole even considered the national contribution of unions to have been 'positive overall' over the years. These results amplify (and corroborate) the findings of the Work Histories/Attitudes survey that while relatively few employees may have remained enthusiastic, committed trade union supporters in the later 1980s, only a small minority held views strongly antagonistic to trade unionism.

However, it was only in the two white-collar workplaces, the public research centre and the head office, that majorities of eligible employees said they actually *did* participate in union meetings or elections. Even more strikingly, the overall employee verdict in the two white-collar workplaces was that whatever the trade unions' (political) faults and mistakes at the national level, or however inadequately they might be performing as bargainers in the workplace concerned, they still had an important role in industrial relations, which should continue. In both the unionized and non-union manufacturing firms, however, majorities said it was not important to them that a union was (or was not) recognized. It was in these manufacturing firms also that informants were far more likely to say that unions had lost much of their influence as plant-level bargainers in recent years, and had behaved irresponsibly at the national level.

These findings no doubt reflect in part the decline of manufacturing industry, and especially the decline of the mass-production factory as an industrial relations context. The newer manufacturing plants, employing a greater proportion of women, offering more individualized payment systems, and demanding a high degree of functional flexibility, contrast sharply in this respect with the 'Fordized' factories of the earlier post-war period, with their armies of semi-skilled male workers, complex piece-rate systems, and strong inter-group rivalries. It is tempting to conclude that lack of involvement in the more active form of trade unionism for which such plants were noted, or even experience of any union involvement whatsoever, may account for the lower support for unionism in the two manufacturing plants. However, such an explanation seems inadequate. Nearly all informants at the unionized subsidiary had in fact been union members at some time, and so had many of the manual worker informants at the non-union subsidiary. Nearly all respondents in both workplaces had fathers who were, or had been, union members. Most female employees in them had current partners who were union members. Thus most of them had some personal experience of unionism, usually of a direct kind. It is thus worth considering how far their reluctance to take up or resume membership in fact stemmed from this experience itself.

As noted earlier, some manual workers at the non-union subsidiary said that in previous jobs they had found strict closed shop rules offensive, or had resented the power of shop-floor leaders and higher-level union officials. Yet these employees usually held somewhat inconsistent views on the question of union membership. For unions, an optimistic interpretation of their attitude would seem to be that such lapsed members might sometimes have been recovered if unions had been offering a style of unionism closer to the employee's requirements—in particular, his or her immediate workplace difficulties. On the other hand, it seemed quite possible that this firm's non-union policy might become harder to maintain if the employer lost touch with its employees through the firm's growth and a consequent formalization of control systems.

Yet the sheer lack of interest by younger employees in unionism, in both the manufacturing firms, may amount to a more formidable obstacle to be faced in future in union recruitment. It may have pointed to a permanent social change, with a new generation adopting a radically individualist view of work and employment that could only be altered by (for example) a reversion of employers in general to primitive methods of control and motivation. It should be emphasized once more how firmly some younger informants in the manufacturing firms asserted their apathetic attitudes towards union membership. Not merely was it considered by them irrelevant to their immediate needs, wants, and opportunities in the workplace: it formed part of a class of subjects they considered intrinsically inconsequential and exasperating ('boring'). Even so, this attitude might still be one that later work experience would modify, if Peter Elias's analysis in Chapter 5 is correct. It may even be worth pointing out that the study was undertaken at a time when 'conspicuous self-reliance' had reached a high-point of fashionability, which has since waned. None the less, the depth of such 'assertive indifference' towards trade unionism could be impressive.

What evidence is there that employer policies helped to shape or reinforce such attitudes in any significant way? The fieldwork began with the assumption that employers might well attempt to harness any potentially anti-union sentiment for their own ends, as well as building control systems that sought to redirect (even to appropriate) the group solidarity which formerly employees might have expressed through union membership. However, refusal of union involvement on the part of an employee of course does not logically imply readiness for positive identification with an employer, or with any ideological aims and values implied in management policies. This was also found to be the case in practice at the two manufacturing firms.

In the unionized subsidiary, management in any event showed little inclination (or perhaps ability) to operate such a programme for building identification. Even in the non-union subsidiary, such evidence as was found for any successful normative engineering seemed less than conclusive. The assertively apathetic young employees at the non-union subsidiary could also possess a keen awareness that their own interests or needs might clash with the demands of production or with the authority of supervisors. They maintained that they were confident of being able to handle these tensions successfully as individuals, without fully trusting in the goodwill of the firm. They obviously preferred working for a 'matey' firm but gave no signs of wishing to become members of any plant social community. The scope for any programme of social integration, along Japanese or neo-Mayoite lines, would seem to have been rather limited if such young people were typical recruits to Swindon's new factories.

When these young employees explained that they were 'in it strictly for Number One' most of them probably meant exactly

what they said. Their radical individualism seemed far more
closely in tune with a 1980s 'go-for-it' ethos than with the spirit
of plant collectivism pursued by the Human Relations in
Industry movement in the early post-1945 years (Kerr and
Fisher, 1956), or for that matter with the notion of a 'community
of fate' (Cole, 1979) espoused by large Japanese companies. The
firm's populist rhetoric had so far harnessed this individualism
with considerable success, and some managers asserted that it
was set aside if an appeal for self-sacrifice ('putting the target
first') was skilfully phrased. For example, these managers cited
the readiness of their young, go-getting employees to 'all muck in
together' during crises, seeing in it a proof of a deeper, longer-
term commitment to the firm as a working community. A more
sceptical view is that 'putting the target first' had made sense in
terms of personal advancement at a time when rapid growth had
been bringing two promotions a year for some staff who had
joined the firm when it started up. Rather than reflecting moral
involvement, it may merely have constituted another mode of
calculative involvement (Etzioni, 1975).

The managers at the non-union subsidiary also believed that
their success in building team spirit accounted largely for the
rejection of union representation when they consulted employees
(by ballot) on the question. The timing, and wording, of the ballot may indeed have helped to produce this result, though perhaps no more than marginally so. In itself this result provided
rather weak evidence of employee *commitment* to the employer
and to a team spirit in the firm. (As such evidence, it was largely
circumstantial.) No clear conclusions about the strength, consistency, and stability of any sense of positive involvement in the
firm on the part of employees could really be drawn on the basis
of this result. On the other hand, the employer's known preference for a non-union workplace may have had an important
influence on the votes of undecided employees, or even on potential union supporters, at the time the ballot was taken. It
undoubtedly provided the non-union policy with powerful legitimacy, and was continuing to do so at the time of the fieldwork.
It was less evident that it would always continue to do so in
future. The non-union subsidiary could perhaps consolidate the
attitudes to trade unionism which most employees had brought
with them to the firm—in some cases hostile, but for the most

part ones of indifference. There seemed no strong reason to believe that the personnel practices, methods of supervision, or more diffuse management philosophy of this employer had thereby created a degree of positive employee identification which would render it union-proof once and for all.

This employer had by far the most pro-active policy towards employee relations as a whole, and gave it a higher priority than any of the other three employers. In this respect it differed from them to a marked degree. The unionized subsidiary provided an instance of outdated supervisory styles, a fusty management philosophy, and widespread resentment of them among employees—the bases, perhaps, for a revival of support for the union in due course. The union gave no sign of either wishing, or being able, to harness underlying employee dissatisfaction. Senior managers believed that a pseudo-parental personnel 'philosophy'—their conviction, in effect, that the firm 'always knew best'—created a close personal bond between the 'girls' and the firm. They were for the most part deluding themselves. The firm, as represented by these managers, was regarded as distant and uncaring by most of the 'girls', whose daily experience of work was soured by their aversion to the supervisory style of the 'whitecoats'. When senior managers extolled the architectural distinction of the factory, they implied that the basis of the loathing of the 'girls' for this award-winning building ('No windows, are there?!') should be treated as another typical piece of silliness on their part. Even non-smokers among the staff thought the firm should not have imposed a creeping ban on smoking without first putting the issue to a vote. The management response ('Yes—we know they're saying that. But the fact is, most of them are in favour of a ban anyway. So why do we need a vote?') seems characteristic. Yet the dissatisfaction of the 'girls' with the casual and patronizing high-handedness of management seemed most unlikely to result in a revival of support for the union.

The head office presents a further contrast. Managers themselves (at least in the personnel department) and several employee informants expressed considerable impatience with the firm's still-paternalist atmosphere, its red tape, and its indifference to innovations in employee relations practice. Its tradition of corporate formalism, they complained, was too highly resistant to change for its own good. (Its more open forms of paternalism were said to be in slow decline.) None the less, employee informants strongly approved of it as an employer. Despite its own half-hearted experiments with a populist approach, and its relative sophistication as a paternalist, for most informants the head office remained 'what it's always been—traditional, hidebound, conservative'. If few approved of this immobility, none were alienated by it.

Fortunately for all its employees, the head office also remained relatively prosperous, with few pressing financial incentives to change. Its ability to offer outstanding rewards and other benefits had recently been affected, but not drastically, by market changes; and it increasingly insisted on results. It was widely agreed that there were reasonable grounds for seeking such improvements. (It was suggested that some results could be 'toned up' by creative accountants or gifted statistical masseurs in management: true or false, it is noteworthy that the allegation was made so readily.) Personnel staff, who talked at length of their frustrated efforts to establish 'a clear manpower strategy and pro-active human resource policies', reported similar resistance to change on the part of senior management. They had been given verbal backing at this level for (cautiously incremental) change, but neither the staff nor budgets necessary to implement it.

This failure to engage the support of senior management for a more carefully planned—and in that sense more strategic—approach to the development of employee relations perhaps precluded, in any case, any plans for bypassing the union or reducing its influence. But there was no suggestion at any point that this was the underlying motive, or even a major reason, for seeking a change in the main features of the regime of control at the head office. When a fieldworker asked why the relative weakness of the union had not led to a drive for a non-union workplace, the suggestion was treated with open incredulity: 'You can see how busy I am already! What do you expect me to do, bargain with five hundred people separately on top of that?'

In several respects, the management regime at the public research centre was undergoing the most radical change at the time of the fieldwork. Hitherto, the agency had possessed a largely consensual public service corporate philosophy. Imposition of market-based performance standards and the threat of privatization had brought this system and its ideology under severe strain. In the face of it, staff in the administrative and the scientist professional grades were drawing together. The recent industrial action had required some severe tests of their own union involvement. Key management staff had been bound by their contracts to oppose the strike and its aims, yet managers had sympathized closely with the strikers. ('I crossed a picket-line, I felt *this high*', one commented, stretching his palm towards the floor.) The local managers had no wish to alter the system. Relations were changing because of external, ministerial pressure.

In the PRC, too, ever larger uncertainties were arising over the future of the existing employee representation bodies: the Whitley system had thus become, for many employees, the main emblem of organizational consensus and unity. Ironically, as the real bargaining position and informal influence of all Civil Service unions had weakened, support or sympathy for the professional-grade unions had been growing strongly among their actual and potential members.

The main activities of the case-study workplaces—electronics, scientific research, administration—were typical of those figuring in the 1980s in many portrayals of Swindon as the Sunrise City of the M4 growth corridor. None of the employers had originated in Swindon, and three had moved to the town or started up there recently. They are in both these senses typical of many new employers in the area. Yet those which recognized unions continued to follow patterns of management action and employee relations that would have been found in the great majority of British workplaces of their size and type throughout much of the post-war period. (The familiarity of the atmosphere in each one struck the senior fieldworker—the present writer—strongly.) Certainly, the tone of social relations in all of them was very much less formal in terms of dress and status etiquette than it would have been even ten years earlier. Many routine workers had higher job discretion too, and, except in the unionized subsidiary, supervisors had adopted what appeared to be genuinely more participative styles in the everyday management of subordinates. Yet even the employee relations arrangements of the non-union subsidiary hardly lived up to the Sunrise City image of Swindon that was frequently being conjured up in the later 1980s.

Some further remarks on the typicality of the case-study employers are perhaps due at this point. As noted in the opening section, the Related Study tried to find firms that were typical in terms of actual growth points in Swindon employment, without assuming these firms would all fit what might be called the Sunrise City profile. It was, however, hoped that the employers chosen would be more likely to provide a context which facilitated employee relations experiments. A few employers more closely matching the Sunrise City stereotype—small firms with single employee status, paying good wages, investing highly in firm-specific training, employing demanding but participative managers, and hostile to unions—were probably present in Swindon at the time of the survey. It is not, however, clear that there is any good reason to regard the approach to employee relations of such firms as in some sense prototypical for this labour market as a whole, rather than as just a new baby in an already varied family of employee relations regimes. Some firms of this kind could indeed have been found at the time, as they would be now, in most large employment centres anywhere in Britain. Perhaps, in the case of Swindon, observers have always had in mind the best-known 1980s newcomer firm, the Honda Motor Company. A green-field employer, Japanese owned, and designated a non-union workplace, Honda fitted the Sunrise City profile to perfection. (It became an instant favourite with makers of documentary programmes on Swindon.) Yet in the late 1980s, Honda had barely begun operating. Rather than setting the tone for Swindon's industrial relations, this company had made no impact on them that the case-study research could point to, though understandably Honda's employee relations philosophy was a point of reference when union officials speculated on future trends. (By early 1994, it should be added, it had become uncertain whether Honda would continue to operate its Swindon plant at all.)[7]

By the same token, no single one of the case-study workplaces exemplifies a 'Swindon model' of employee relations. Rather, each is perhaps representative, to greater or lesser extent, of some of the more common new variants of workplace regime that had been emerging in the Swindon area. Yet it will be evident from the case reports that not one of them was pioneering particularly novel regimes of control or approaches to industrial relations.

These newer employers are notable for their continuity in both these respects. This conclusion, if it is correct, discredits speculations that very different models of the employment relationship, whether Japanese or neo-liberal, would spread rapidly in the area. Significant change had undoubtedly been occurring in Swindon workplaces during the 1980s, above all in the contract of employment, in work organization, and in management style, but to a much lesser extent in employee representation and the position of trade unions.

Yet nothing in the SCELI data on trade unionism as a whole suggests that the degree of continuity to be found in Swindon differs very greatly from that present in the other SCELI localities. On the contrary, the data that are available all point to the *typicality* of Swindon as an industrial relations context, and suggest that the SCELI findings may in turn provide a good guide to trends in British workplace trade unionism as a whole in the later 1980s. If this is correct, the conclusion must be that if a new system of industrial relations was appearing, it was doing so very gradually indeed, while older patterns, although much modified compared with ten years earlier, remained the first point of reference.

This gradual change has no doubt been continuing in the 1990s, as the most recent Workplace Industrial Relations Survey (Millward *et al.*, 1992) suggests, and may in time modify employee relations patterns in as yet unforeseen ways. The main patterns actually observed in the Related Study, however, appear to be variants of long-established, distinctively British models. This observation applies no less to the non-union subsidiary than to the other employers examined here: its non-unionism and drive to build a novel form of workplace participation—like some of its production system itself—in some important respects took on an extemporized, under-capitalized appearance, especially compared to those of well-known American employers. Taking the four case-study employers as a whole, continuity rather than change remains the most striking feature in these findings, whether the focus is upon the attitudes of management, the capacity to plan and implement change in a truly strategic manner, or even the involvement in trade unionism of employees themselves.

An obvious question remains to be answered: why should employers themselves have preferred such continuity? Neither of the unionized private employers in the Swindon Related Study would have risked determined opposition if they had set out to reduce the role of unions, or had even withdrawn recognition altogether. Yet neither had taken such a step or seriously contemplated it, despite the unusually favourable conditions for such action. In their Related Study of trade unionism in Rochdale (see Chapter 7), which also undertook intensive interviewing and observation, Penn and Scattergood were concerned mainly with inter-union relations in the 1980s. However, their incidental findings on the continuity of workplace representation and bargaining arrangements, and the reasons their Rochdale employers gave for their survival, are not merely consistent with those of the present chapter but strikingly similar to them. Among this larger selection of employers, Penn and Scattergood also found very little readiness to embark on a process of derecognition of unions or to build alternative systems of employee involvement and representation.

An underlying assumption in much debate in the 1980s on the future of British trade unionism, as in government policy itself, was that many British employers actually did wish to embark on some kind of anti-union offensive. This assumption, surprisingly, was only rarely (Longstreth, 1988) challenged at the time. One reason for this was the preoccupation with the political influence of trade unions at the national level discussed in Chapter 1. As Marsh (1992) rightly points out, much of the debate thus took place on grounds largely chosen by political scientists unfamiliar with the realities of workplace industrial relations. The continuing utility to management of ongoing workplace institutions was therefore overlooked. At the same time, the costs of establishing alternative, non-union regimes of employee relations, and the uncertainties surrounding their viability, were not given proper consideration—indeed they were given hardly any consideration at all.

It was never explained exactly what motivation most employers might have for discarding an established system in favour of alternatives that were unclearly specified, probably costly to establish, and possibly troublesome to operate. A more valid question would in fact have been: why should employers *not* prefer continuity? Both the Swindon and the Rochdale Related Studies suggest, however, that the great majority of employers that recognized unions did not wish—or did not wish strongly enough—to remodel their systems of involvement and representation. To state things more simply, most unionized employers did not wish to do without trade unions—whatever the government might have expected of them. This preference for continuity was, in turn, based upon essentially simple and cogent grounds: some employers saw no clear advantage in making the effort to do without unions, though they may have considered doing so; but most unionized employers appear to have been essentially satisfied with the arrangements they had. In both Swindon and Rochdale, the fieldworkers asked employers why they had not taken the favourable opportunity to further reduce, or remove, union influence. The answer was always that the existing, union-based system performed functions that were either necessary or useful.

A further matter should be dealt with at this point. The concept of employer strategy has been treated with some caution in this chapter. The term 'strategy' was one of the more overworked words of industrial relations and industrial sociology in the 1980s, and a relatively hard test for its existence was applied in the case-study establishments. It was not felt that the approach to trade unionism of three of the four case-study employers actually did amount to a coherent strategy. It might be objected, therefore, that the results of the Related Study in Swindon were affected by choosing employers that were less likely to envisage change to their workplace employee relations systems because they were less capable of taking a strategic view of their businesses in general. Moreover, the most strategic (in terms of employee relations strategy) of the four employers *was* making an effort to do without a union. Might the more strategic of British employers at least have been more likely to have similar aims?

This is a reasonable objection, but in the light of some strong evidence from SCELI, turns out to be ill founded. Firms in the Employers 30 survey provided detailed estimates for how far ahead they planned a variety of business activities. These estimates can be regarded as providing a reasonably objective measure of the overall capacity of the employer to adopt a strategic approach as a whole. According to this measure, those employers that planned their business furthest ahead, and in this sense could be considered the most 'strategic' employers, were no more likely than the others to express dissatisfaction with their own industrial relations—yet their workplaces tended to be rather more heavily unionized, and their everyday involvement with unions was far heavier. This analysis also shows very clearly indeed that the great majority of employers—but particularly the more strategic employers—were far more concerned with carrying out technical change and setting up more flexible work systems in the 1980s than with attacking union influence in the workplace (Rose, 1994). It appears that once union influence at the national level had been removed, British employers were able to undertake changes in working practices and manning which union power had previously blocked. Indeed, the evidence from SCELI is that they henceforward received considerable support for technical change and work reorganization from unions at the workplace level. Very specific documentation of such union-supported reorganization was provided during the case-studies described in this chapter. Evidently, this co-operation reduced still further any incentive to undertake de-unionization. Finally, it should be noted that although it had by far the most developed employee relations policies, the non-union employer was not necessarily more strategic in other respects: the public research centre tried to establish integrated programmes of scientific work lasting up to ten or more years; the head office was acknowledged to be a shrewd long-term player in its own product markets.

The case-study evidence examined in this chapter suggests that one of the most important reasons for the survival of workplace-level trade unionism in Swindon in the 1980s was, in essence, the wish of managers in unionized workplaces for it to do so. The claim of one of the case-study employers (the unionized subsidiary) to have 'put the union on a life-support machine' may have been an overstatement, but it is significant none the less. It seems probable that a union presence would not have survived in this and in some other Swindon workplaces without some such assistance. But there is no reason to believe that Swindon was in any way atypical in this respect. It is tempting to conclude that British trade unionism might have declined further in the 1980s but for positive support from British management.

Such support might be less forthcoming in the future. Longer-term survival depends also on the support trade unions can attract from their members and potential members. The present chapter suggests that in the 1980s trade unions were failing to take full account of changes in employee needs and attitudes, especially among manual workers. In Chapter 7, Penn and Scattergood argue that unions were also slow to redefine their aims and to seek out new member constituencies. The involvement of employees in trade unionism as shown in the Work Histories/Attitudes survey is examined in detail by Duncan Gallie in the next chapter.

NOTES

1. For a description of the core surveys of the SCELI programme, see the Methodological Appendix to this volume. Related Studies examined special questions, for which the core surveys could provide background data. Fieldwork for the related study in Swindon began in late 1986 and ended in mid-1988. Approximately 135 people were interviewed. For interviews with the 96 employee informants an interview guide was used; although it contained many open-ended questions, and the order of putting enquiries could be varied, a number of standardized questions were also asked. Most of these questions were taken from the Work Histories/Attitudes questionnaire, partly for convenience, partly to provide some comparability. However, because the initial question could be followed by probing questions, it was also possible to examine certain aspects of the validity of the findings from these questions in the core survey itself. (For example, it was possible to obtain further detail on the real extent of changes in skill reported by informants.) The interviews with employee informants covered their own work, relations with managers, view of their employer, and their involvement in and view of trade unionism. Selection of employee informants used *systematic* sampling from lists supplied by personnel departments, aiming to produce a varied set of informants, rather than a random sample of the workforce. The guided interviews with the employee informants took place at each site, between spring and late summer 1987, in offices provided by the employer. They lasted up to two hours. Replies to some questions were field-coded to provide simple quantified data. Interviews with management and trade union informants occurred throughout the whole period of the research. Most were arranged formally, but some occurred informally as the fieldworkers were given a 'free run' at all four sites after initial clearance, and a few were conducted by phone.

All interviewing was undertaken by the author (Team Co-ordinator) and by the team's Research Officer (Dr Sarah Fielder), the load being split approximately 2 : 3 for employee informant interviewing, and 3 : 2 for other interviewing. The quantified results of the employee interviews are available through the University of Bath as part of its SCELI data-set.

2. The six localities were in fact the six travel-to-work areas (TTWA) surrounding the main town. TTWAs are defined by the Department of Employment, usually centre on a large central town, but extend considerably beyond it, to include small towns that are in effect satellites of its labour market. The SCELI travel-to-work areas varied considerably in geographical and spatial terms. Aberdeen, for example, included a large hinterland of very sparsely populated Scottish countryside stretching into the Highlands. The Swindon TTWA embraced small but substantial towns such as Wootton Bassett, Hungerford, Marlborough, and Shrivenham. As explained in the Methodological Appendix, the TTWA localities were not selected for reasons of demography or urban geography, but for their historic and contemporary differences in industrial structure and employment levels; any important 'locality effects' would presumably reflect such variations. In the event, surprisingly few significant variations between locality samples were found, even before controlling for occupational and industrial structures.

3. The railway engineering works (BREL) that once made the town famous remained a large employer until shortly before their closure in the mid-1980s. The railway workshops were noted for their traditional craft union traditions and paternalist management. The motor industry became the largest single employer at one point in the 1960s, declined sharply from the mid-1970s, then revived somewhat in the later 1980s, following the establishment of an engine plant by the Honda Motor Company and the improved performance of the Rover Cars group.

4. The firm's product had very high profit margins, thanks at first in part to its novelty value. But there was already growing public suspicion at the time of the survey that margins remained high thanks to co-operation between producers. The firm's growth and relatively high manual wages could not have been maintained without these high margins.

5. The Association of Scientific, Technical, and Managerial Staffs (ASTMS) was later renamed the Manufacturing, Scientific, and Finance Union (MSF).

6. The GCHQ installation monitors radio communications between foreign intelligence services, from military space satellites, etc. In 1984

the government decided that union membership was incompatible with this security role, withdrew recognition from unions, and required all union members at the base to resign their membership. This led to a prolonged dispute.

7. Honda's Swindon engine plant had been built following a technical co-operation agreement with Rover Cars in the early 1980s, while Rover was still a nationalized company. Rover was sold by the government to the British Aerospace Corporation (BAe) in 1988, and then sold by BAe to the German BMW company in early 1994. Honda were not consulted during the negotiations for the disposal or given the opportunity to make a counter-bid. It announced that it was unable to continue its co-operation with the new owners of Rover, and the logic of the take-over seemed that Rover would cease using the Honda engines from Swindon.

4

Trade Union Allegiance and Decline in British Urban Labour Markets

DUNCAN GALLIE

The 1980s have witnessed a dramatic decline in British trade union strength—with membership falling by 26 per cent between 1979 and 1990 (Department of Employment, 1993). This raises fundamental questions about the nature of British trade union allegiance and its implications for the longer-term strength or fragility of the unions' power. Does membership decline indicate a crisis of legitimacy for the unions or can it be seen primarily as the result of structural changes that have made the recruitment and retention of membership more difficult?

One interpretation of the membership crisis would be that British trade unionism has become increasingly vulnerable to a major erosion of membership due to a decline in the level of commitment of its membership. As its strength grew and it became progressively institutionalized, the basis of its membership, it could be argued, altered fundamentally. Membership was no longer an act of choice, rather the unions were able to use their institutional position to make it a condition of having the job. The relatively high level of trade union membership in Britain, then, could be seen as largely the product of constraint rather than choice. As such, with the changing political, legal, and economic context of the 1980s, the unions were very vulnerable to membership loss from a weakly committed membership. Support for the unions may have been further undercut both by a heightened sense of economic crisis accompanying the sharp rise in unemployment and by the sustained critique of the power of the unions by the Conservative Government. A second type of argument emphasizes the way in which changes in the labour market have been creating structural conditions that are much less favourable to union recruitment. Technical change and the expansion of new sectors have led to a shift in the occupational composition of the workforce, marked by the decline of manual occupations, which constituted the traditional bastion of trade union strength, and an expansion of non-manual employees with historically lower levels of commitment to trade unionism (Bell, 1974). Moreover, whereas previously the trend towards larger-sized establishments favoured trade unionism, this has been reversed to the benefit of small establishments (Millward and Stevens, 1986). There may have been a decline in the earlier supportive attitude of employers to trade unions and the growth instead of strategies that seek to develop direct lines of communication with employees and to dissuade them from trade union membership (Beaumont, 1987). Finally, the changing geography of employment has meant that employment decline has been in the areas with the strongest historical traditions of trade union support, while expansion has been in areas where trade union traditions have been much weaker. The combination of these different factors implies a growing polarization of conditions, with the unions retaining high levels of allegiance in the areas of employment decline, but facing heavy loss of membership in the more dynamic labour markets.

In this chapter the issue of the relative importance of commitment and structural favourability will be addressed drawing on data from the Work Attitudes/Histories survey carried out in each locality. This covered all individuals aged between 20 and 60 (for details see the Methodological Appendix). First, we look at the reasons why people originally became and currently remain trade union members, to explore the extent to which membership was experienced as constrained. Second, we look at the relative importance of individual and structural factors in accounting for membership levels. Finally, we shall examine the motives of those that have left trade unions.

Overall 45 per cent of people in employment in our six localities and 40 per cent of the labour force were trade union members. However, as can be seen in Table 4.1, there was a marked variation between localities. The industrial centres that had suffered most in the recession were also the areas in which trade union membership strength was greatest. The most highly unionized labour market was that of Coventry—renowned for its strong tradition of workplace bargaining in the car industry.

TABLE 4.1. *Trade union membership and commitment*

Area	Trade union membership (%)	
	Overall workforce (employees and unemployed)	Employees
Aberdeen	36 (821)	40 (724)
Coventry	49 (713)	57 (602)
Kirkcaldy	44 (749)	53 (593)
Northampton	34 (749)	38 (654)
Rochdale	44 (752)	52 (628)
Swindon	32 (737)	35 (641)
All	40 (4,521)	45 (3,842)

Area	Favourability to trade unions (%)		
	Overall, very or quite favourable	Employees very or quite favourable	Trade union members very or quite favourable
Aberdeen	35	35	53
Coventry	41	46	55
Kirkcaldy	47	47	58
Northampton	29	31	50
Rochdale	39	41	55
Swindon	31	31	53
All	36	38	54

Note: The figures in brackets refer to the sample number upon which the analysis was based.

Source: SCELI Work Histories/Attitudes Survey

Here some 57 per cent of employees were currently union members. This was followed fairly closely by Kirkcaldy with 53 per cent and by Rochdale with 52 per cent. However, if we turn to the labour markets that had been more dynamic over the preceding decade we find a very different picture. In all cases membership failed to exceed the 40 per cent level. Union density in Aberdeen was 40 per cent, while in Northampton and Swindon it was even lower (38 per cent and 35 per cent respectively). In short, the pattern fitted closely the more general picture of

greater union weakness in the expanding areas of the economy
and therefore provides a good basis for examining theories of
union allegiance and decline.

1. REASONS FOR MEMBERSHIP AND
ATTITUDES TO TRADE UNIONISM

The argument relating membership decline to a low level of legitimacy of the unions would be plausible if it could be shown that
membership was largely a matter of constraint. Arguments about
coerced membership have tended to emphasize the role of the
closed shop. However, this in itself is inconclusive: it is possible
for people to be union members in a closed shop establishment,
but to feel that they would wish to be members irrespective of
this. Conversely, those that are not in a closed shop may still be
subject to strong informal pressures to join. It is necessary then
to consider directly how people perceived their own membership
decisions. The first step is to explore the reasons why people initially joined trade unions, focusing in particular on the extent to
which they were experienced as constrained or as an act of
choice. Such initial reasons can then be compared with current
reasons for union membership, giving some indication of whether
the individual's commitment has become more or less positive
over time.

To begin with, people were asked why they had *first* joined a
union. It is clear from Table 4.2 that by far the most frequent
reason was simply that union membership had been a condition
of the job. This was cited as the sole reason by 31 per cent of
current union members. A further 10 per cent mentioned that it
was a condition of the job, but gave positive reasons as well,
indicating that they had regarded membership as a personal
choice. There could be other pressures, however, of a less formal
kind—for instance employer recommendation, union 'advice', or
the threat of workgroup sanctions. Where these factors were
mentioned, interviewers were specifically instructed to check
whether the respondent had regarded membership as voluntary
or not. In practice, another 10 per cent of respondents cited pressures of this type as the main reason why they had joined—most
particularly informal pressures coming from the workgroup.

Duncan Gallie

TABLE 4.2. *Reasons for initial membership of current members, by social class (%)*

Reasons for initial membership	Service	Lower non-manual	Technical/ supervisory	Skilled manual	Non-skilled manual	All
Condition of job	21	20	37	42	40	31
Other constrained	9	17	9	8	9	10
Condition of job but voluntary	6	5	17	14	12	10
Solidarity/social justice	8	5	5	7	6	7
Pay/conditions benefits	14	10	5	5	7	9
Protection	28	24	16	15	15	21
Influence	7	11	8	6	7	7
Other	7	8	4	4	5	6
N	571	259	114	287	504	1,735

Note: N = sample number.

Source: SCELI Work Histories/Attitudes Survey.

Overall, then, 41 per cent of current trade union members had originally joined primarily because membership was a condition of the job or because of strong informal pressures. At first sight this would appear to give some support to the view that, despite its apparent membership strength, British trade unionism was highly vulnerable due to the low commitment of much of its membership. Yet before drawing such a conclusion, it is necessary to consider how people's attitudes to trade unionism may have evolved over time, as a result of the experience of membership or of employment itself.

What was the relationship between people's initial reasons for joining trade unions and their current attitudes to unionism? The evidence suggests that allegiances to trade unionism have grown stronger rather than weaker over time. Taking *current* reasons for membership the striking point that emerges in Table 4.3 is the substantially reduced importance of involuntary membership. This was now mentioned by only 17 per cent as their principal reason for membership and only 21 per cent mentioned it at all. Although those who had originally felt coerced into membership were far and away the most likely to cite it as a factor in their present situ-

TABLE 4.3. *Most important current reason for being a trade union member at present (%)*

Reason	Service	Lower non-manual	Technical/ supervisory	Skilled manual	Non-skilled manual	All
Condition of job	11	15	21	23	22	17
Way of creating a more just society/ solidarity	19	17	11	15	14	16
Higher pay and better conditions	17	20	27	25	23	21
Everyone else is a member	1	4	5	2	6	3
Protection if problems come up in the future	51	44	35	33	34	41
Other	1	1	1	1	1	1
N	569	258	113	289	504	1,733

Note: N = sample number.

Source: SCELI Work Histories/Attitudes Survey.

ation, none the less only about half (47 per cent) of these reluctant joiners still mentioned it as a major factor influencing the fact that they were still trade unionists. Attitudes to trade unionism would, then, appear to have become more favourable over time. Our evidence suggests a trajectory in which the experiences of those who are currently trade union members had led them to an increasing awareness of the advantages of membership.

For the 1980s there is more direct evidence about the way in which attitudes had been changing. Trade union members were asked: 'Thinking back over the last five years, has it become more important or less important to you to be a trade union member or has there been little or no change in its importance?' As can be seen in Table 4.4, the main shift in attitudes over this period has been towards an increased emphasis on the importance of the unions. Overall 39 per cent said that the unions were more important to them then than five years previously, while only 15 per cent regarded them as less important.

TABLE 4.4. *Change in importance of trade union membership in last five years (%)*

Area	More important	Less important	No change
Aberdeen	39	15	46
Coventry	37	17	46
Kirkcaldy	37	12	51
Northampton	41	12	47
Rochdale	39	10	51
Swindon	42	23	34
All	39	15	47

Source: SCELI Work Histories/Attitudes Survey.

Our evidence, then, indicates that the great majority of trade unionists regarded their present membership as voluntary rather than as a result of constraint. This does not offer much support for the view that the crisis of membership of the 1980s was primarily a crisis of legitimacy. The unions were seen to be serving a positive role in the workplace, in particular through the protection they provided their members. In so far as there was a change in attitudes over time, the allegiance of members to their unions would appear to have been strengthening rather than weakening.

2. STRUCTURAL AND PERSONAL DETERMINANTS OF MEMBERSHIP

A second approach is to look at the factors that distinguished those employees who were trade union members from those who were not. The view that the trade unions have lost membership as a result of a decline in commitment assumes that individual preferences are the major determinants of membership. However, a number of authors have pointed to the importance of structural constraints on membership (Bain *et al.*, 1973; Booth, 1986; Payne, 1989). Is membership, then, best explained in terms of the characteristics of people's employment situation or in terms of their personal views about trade unionism? If the employment situation is important, which particular features contribute most to increasing or decreasing opportunities for membership? We will begin by examining the various structural explanations of membership and then turn to the significance of individual values.

2.1. Class and Trade Union Membership

There has been a sustained debate in the literature on the relationship between class and trade union membership. Trade union membership has been shown in a number of studies to be weaker among non-manual employees than among manual. This has been attributed variously to the greater stake of non-manual employees in the *status quo*, their closer involvement with the exercise of authority, the more individualized nature of their work situation, and their greater security of employment (Bain, 1970; Bain *et al.*, 1973; Bell 1974; Prandy *et al.*, 1983). Even where white-collar workers have become unionized, it is sometimes argued that the nature of this membership is quite different from that of manual workers—more instrumental, less militant, and lacking the durability that comes from a deeper commitment to collectivism. Given the long-term shift in the occupational structure with the expansion of non-manual and the contraction of the manual categories, it is arguable that one of the most important structural supports of trade unionism has been steadily eroded.

Much of the discussion of the relationship between class and trade union membership has deployed a conception of class boundaries that is based on a rather crude division between manual and non-manual employees. This can conceal important variations within these categories and it treats the categories themselves as unproblematic. If instead trade union membership is analysed in terms of the more robust class categorization provided by the Goldthorpe class schema (Table 4.5), it can be seen that the very assumption that there is a major class differential in membership levels becomes doubtful. While skilled manual workers are the most highly unionized (53 per cent), and lower non-manual employees the least (39 per cent), the level of membership in the service class (which brings together professionals, administrators, and managers) is fully comparable with that among technicians and supervisors and among non-skilled manual workers. Given that it is the service class that contains the most rapidly

TABLE 4.5. *Trade union membership and commitment, by social class (%)*

Commitment	Service	Lower non-manual	Technical/ supervisory	Skilled manual	Non-skilled manual
Members	48	39	49	53	42
Voluntary members	43	34	39	41	33
Very or quite favourable to unions	56	46	49	60	54
Never attend union meetings	39	56	47	52	54
Consider that membership has become more important	49	38	36	32	32

Note: Voluntary membership is calculated by excluding members who gave 'condition of the job' as the first reason for currently being a member.

Source: SCELI Work Histories/Attitudes Survey.

expanding occupational strata, it is difficult to conclude that trends in class composition have *necessarily* been undercutting trade union support.

Further, it should be noted that whether or not there is a significant difference in membership between the broader categories of manual and non-manual employees depends crucially upon the location of workers in retailing and personal services. These are difficult to place unambiguously in terms of the manual/non-manual divide. If they are included among non-manual employees, 43 per cent of non-manual employees are unionized, compared with 50 per cent of manual. If, however, they are classified with non-skilled manual workers, as Goldthorpe now advocates (Goldthorpe, 1987), the differential in unionization between the broad categories of manual and non-manual disappears. The class differential then is largely an artefact of the particular system of occupational classification deployed.

Is there a difference in the quality of trade unionism between manual and non-manual employees? In the first place, it is worth noting that trade union membership would appear to be much more clearly an act of choice for non-manual employees than for manual. Whereas 42 per cent of skilled manual workers and 40 per cent of non-skilled said that the main reason for first joining a union was that it had been a condition of the job, this was the case for only 20 per cent of lower non-manual employees and 21 per cent of those in the service class (Table 4.2). The same picture emerges for the principal reason for currently being a trade union member: manual employees were twice as likely as those in the service class to say that it is a condition of the job (Table 4.3). Indeed, if an estimate is made of the current 'voluntary' membership by class, it was the non-manual classes rather than the manual that emerged as the most committed to trade unionism (Table 4.5). Whereas 39 per cent of all non-manual employees are voluntary members, this was the case for only 34 per cent of manual. The highest level of voluntary membership was in the expanding occupations of the service class (43 per cent).

Second, the positive reasons given by non-manual and manual employees for union membership do not suggest that there are fundamental differences between classes in the nature of union commitment. Certainly non-manual employees show no very high level of solidaristic collectivism: only 19 per cent of service class and 17 per cent of lower non-manual members gave the concern either to create a fairer society or to show solidarity with fellow workers as their main current reason for membership. However, there is no evidence that this was a particularly strong motive for membership among manual workers either. Rather, collectivist reasons were given marginally less frequently by both skilled (15 per cent) and non-skilled (14 per cent) manual workers. Among all types of employee, by far the most frequent reason for membership was the need for protection against future problems at work.

A number of other indicators reinforce the view that service class membership is no less committed than that of manual workers and in some respects may be more so. Service class members are more likely to be favourable to trade unionism than those that are non-skilled manual workers or that come from the manual supervisor–lower technician category (Table 4.5). They are more likely to attend union meetings frequently than any category other than skilled manual workers (to whom they are very close) and they are the least likely of all never to attend meetings. Only 39 per cent of service class members never attend union meetings, compared with 52 per cent of skilled manual, 54 per cent of non-skilled manual, and 56 per cent of lower non-manual employees. Finally, service class members were by far the most likely to consider that it had become more important for them to be a trade union member over the last five years. In short, in terms of the voluntary character of membership, union attendance, and the perceived change in the importance of membership, the service class emerges as an even more solid bastion of trade unionism than the manual working class.

The argument that trade unionism is necessarily weakened by changes in the class structure, in particular the expansion of non-manual work, would appear unsubstantiated. The most dynamic sector of the expanding non-manual occupations, the service class, has a level of unionization that is significantly higher than that of the declining non-skilled manual class. Moreover it is clear that trade unionism in the service class is in some ways more robust than in the manual working classes: it is more frequently chosen rather than being the result of constraint and it is more likely to be accompanied by a belief in the increasing importance of membership.

2.2. Size of Establishment and Membership

The structural factor affecting trade union membership that is perhaps most commonly cited in the literature is the size of the establishment in which people are employed (Bain and Price, 1983; Bain and Elsheikh, 1979; Elsheikh and Bain, 1980). Larger establishments are held to be conducive to higher levels of union membership for a variety of reasons. First, employees in large establishments are likely to have a more distant and impersonal relationship with their employers, leading to more strained authority relations. Second, larger establishments are likely to be more attractive to union organizers, because of the lower per capita costs of recruitment. Third, employers in larger establishments may be more favourable to the unions, as a way of ensuring more effective communication with the workforce and of enhancing the legitimacy of work arrangements. Whereas in the past there appeared to be an inexorable trend towards larger establishments, thereby favouring union membership, this was being reversed in the 1980s and the relative proportion of smaller establishments was growing.

As can be seen in Table 4.6a, the likelihood of someone being a union member did indeed rise markedly as establishment size increased. In small establishments (with 24 or less employees), only 29 per cent were members of trade unions. In contrast, in large establishments (500+) this was the case for 65 per cent. The proportion of employees that were members rises regularly across the size categories. But if the general association between size and membership is confirmed, what factors account for this?

The argument that links the effect of establishment size to the level of worker grievance is not supported by our data. An indicator of worker dissatisfaction was constructed from a list of items relating to promotion opportunities, pay, relations with supervisors, job security, the ability to use initiative on the job, the ability of management, the nature of the work task, and the hours of work. Worker dissatisfaction was not significantly related to size of establishment and it was not a significant predictor of trade union membership itself.

It seems more likely that the size effect works through its implications for employer policies. People were asked whether their current employer encouraged trade union membership, accepted it, discouraged it, or was unaffected due to lack of interest among employees themselves. Employees in larger establishments were considerably more likely to report that they had pro-union employers: in small establishments (24 employees or less), only 13 per cent of employers were seen as actively encouraging unions, compared with 30 per cent in the large workplaces (500+). Further, it is notable that size made very little difference to membership levels where employers were pro-union (Table 4.6b). Where employers were favourable to unions, 87 per cent of employees in large establishments were members; however, this was also the case for 79 per cent of employees in the smallest size of establishment. It is mainly where the employers are unfavourable to unions that size of establishment had a clear independent effect, raising the proportion of members from 6 per cent in the small establishments to 35 per cent in the largest.

TABLE 4.6. *The effect of establishment size and trade union membership*

(a) Trade union membership (%)	Size of establishment			
	1–24	25–99	100–499	500+
Employees in unions	29	42	55	65
Employers encouraging unions	13	19	25	30
Employers discouraging union	16	19	14	11
N	1,273	824	845	823

(b) Employer attitudes	% employees unionized by employer attitudes and establishment size				
	Size of establishment				
	1–24	25–99	100–499	500+	All
Employer encourages	79	82	85	87	84
Employer accepts	59	68	67	68	66
Employer discourages	6	16	20	35	17
Employer unaffected	4	6	13	19	7

Note: N = sample number.
Source: SCELI Work Histories/Attitudes Survey.

2.3. *Industry and Ownership Sector*

Historically, the heartland of trade union strength has been in manufacturing industry. Yet the major trend of change in the economic structure of Britain, as with other advanced industrial societies, has been a decline in the relative share of the employed population in manufacturing and a major expansion of the service sector. For authors such as Daniel Bell (1974), progress towards a 'post-industrial' society necessarily leads to the erosion of trade union membership and a decline of the role of trade unions in society. The service sector, he argued, provided much less fertile terrain for trade unionism because of the dispersion of employees into much smaller work units, the greater use made of

TABLE 4.7. *Percentage of employees unionized, by industrial sector*

Unionized employees (%)	Manufacturing	Services
Trade union members	46	46
Men	49	56
Women	39	38
Employees in establishments sized		
1–24	20	31
25–99	35	47
100–499	50	62
500+	68	66
Full-time employees	48	54
Part-time employees	25	27

Source: SCELI Work Histories/Attitudes Survey.

part-time workers, and the more satisfying employment conditions deriving from a person-centred task.

As can be seen from Table 4.7, however, there was no significant difference, in these six urban labour markets, between the overall levels of trade union membership in manufacturing and services. Men in the service sector were more likely to be unionized, while women's membership rates were virtually the same in the two sectors. There is certainly evidence of the presence in the service sector of the factors that were thought to work heavily against trade unionism. A considerably higher proportion of the workforce is employed in small establishments: 43 per cent compared with only 20 per cent in manufacturing. But, this is counteracted by the fact that, in every size category except the largest, service sector employees were more likely to be unionized than their counterparts in manufacturing industry. It is also the case that a larger proportion of the service workforce consists of part-time workers and that the level of unionization of such workers is exceptionally low. However, this is partly offset by the fact that the smaller proportion of full-time workers in service employment are more highly unionized than their equivalents in manufacturing.

The major reason, however, for the negligible significance of the manufacturing–service division for trade unionism is that it is crosscut by the much more fundamental divide between the public

TABLE 4.8. *Percentage of employees unionized by class and industry/ownership sector*

	Service	Lower non-manual	Technical supervisory	Skilled manual	Non-skilled manual	All employees	N
Public manufacturing	68	46	*	88	65	73	153
Private manufacturing	25	32	38	50	52	42	1,068
Public services	74	62	65	74	58	67	1,175
Private services	23	26	28	28	20	23	1,092
All public	74	62	72	83	60	69	1,417
All private	22	26	34	44	34	31	743

Note: * = N lower than 15.
Source: SCELI Work Histories/Attitudes Survey.

sector on the one hand and the private sector on the other. Overall, 69 per cent of employees in the public sector were in unions compared with 31 per cent in the private sector (Table 4.8). If manufacturing and the service industries are divided into their public and private components, the dominant influence of ownership is immediately apparent. Overall levels of membership in public manufacturing are very similar to those in the public services, while both differ sharply from those prevailing in the private sector. Whereas 73 per cent of employees in public sector manufacturing were in unions and 67 per cent in public services, the proportion falls steeply to 42 per cent in private manufacturing and to 23 per cent in private services. The key divide, then, is not one of industry but of ownership. This pattern emerged clearly for all social classes, although it is most pronounced for service class employees and least for non-skilled manual workers.

One possibility is that this difference between the public and private sectors is a result of differences in establishment size. For instance, it might be that people in the public sector services are typically employed in much larger establishments than in private services. Given the powerful association between size and union membership discussed earlier, this might largely account for the different levels of union strength. Thus Bain and Price (1983: 27) suggest that: 'although adequate data on employment concentration do not exist for the public and the private sectors of the economy, this factor is clearly important in explaining the very different degrees of unionisation'.

While employees in the public sector were likely to be in larger establishments (Table 4.9), the difference was rather modest: 30 per cent of public sector employees were working in small establishments (24 people or less), whereas this was the case for 36 per cent of private sector employees. At the other end of the scale, 27 per cent of public sector, compared with 19 per cent of private sector, employees were in workplaces with at least 500 people. Not only is this difference relatively small, but it cannot account for the different levels of unionization in the public and private sectors. Within each of the size categories, sector made an important difference to the likelihood that a person would be unionized. Indeed, the effect of sector was strongest for people working in small and medium-small establishments. Where there were 24 or fewer employees, 58 per cent of those in the public

TABLE 4.9. *The effect of ownership sector*

	Public	Private
% employees by size of establishment		
1–24	30	36
25–99	22	22
100–499	21	23
500+	27	19
% of trade union members by size of establishment		
1–24	58	15
25–99	74	24
100–499	72	46
500+	78	55
% employers		
encouraging membership	32	15
discouraging membership	5	21
% members where employers encourage membership	85	81
% members where employers discourage membership	40	13

Source: SCELI Work Histories/Attitudes Survey.

sector were members of unions compared with 15 per cent of those in the private sector. The percentage difference between public and private sectors narrows to 26 per cent in establishments of between 100 and 499 employees and to 23 per cent in establishments of 500+ employees. Further, apart from the transition from very small to medium-small establishments (25–99 employees), size made very little difference to union levels in the public sector. It is mainly in the private sector that the size effect was pronounced. In short, it seems unlikely that differences between the levels of trade unionism in the public and private sectors can be explained in terms of differences in the size composition of establishments.

What would appear to be more decisive is the difference in employer attitudes to the unions in the two sectors. Government action, which has been historically one of the major factors encouraging the institutionalization of industrial relations, has been most directly effective in influencing employment relations in the public sector. Employees in the public sector were twice as likely as those in the private to report that their employers encouraged trade union membership (32 per cent compared with 15 per cent). Further, anti-union employers were heavily concentrated in the private sector. Indeed, 87 per cent of those reporting hostile employer policies were private sector employees. It has been seen already that employer policies were powerfully related to the probability of membership. If employer policies were controlled for, a good deal of the difference between membership levels in the two sectors disappeared. For instance, where employers are pro-union, 85 per cent of public sector, but also 81 per cent of private sector, employees are in unions. Where employers discouraged unionism, the proportion of members in the public sector declined to 40 per cent and in the private sector to 13 per cent.

2.4. Gender and Trade Unionism

The explanations that have been considered so far focus on the characteristics of the immediate employment situation in which people find themselves. However, it is also possible that major sources of variation in unionization may lie in attitudes to employment and collective organization that are either individual in character or derive from cultural influences outside employment. For instance a consistent finding in the literature is that women have lower levels of trade union membership than men (Bain and Price, 1983: 8; Bain and Elias, 1985), and one explanation that has been advanced for this is that women have a lower commitment to employment.

In each of the localities, the general pattern of lower levels of union membership among women emerged very clearly. Overall, 38 per cent of women employees were members, compared with 52 per cent of men. Further, in terms of indicators of union commitment, those women that were in trade unions appeared to be less attached to them than their male equivalents. For instance, whereas 59 per cent of male trade unionists were favourable to unions, this was the case for only 46 per cent of women. Yet, despite their generally lower level of enthusiasm, women trade unionists became more rather than less attached to the unions over the 1980s. Indeed, this occurred more frequently among women than among men: 42 per cent of women thought that the importance of union membership to them had increased over the previous five years, compared with 37 per cent of men. Further, if the union membership of men and women is examined by class (Table 4.10a), while women were substantially less likely to be in unions than men in four out of five classes, in the most rapidly expanding class—the service class—the relationship was reversed. In fact the relatively high level of unionization in the service class was mainly attributable to the high levels of unionization of women in this class. Men in the service class were notably less likely than those in any other class to be in unions, while women in the service class were more likely to be unionized.

None the less, despite these signs of change, the most striking feature of the data remained the generally lower level of member-

TABLE 4.10. *Trade union membership, by social class, sex, and employment status*

(a) Social class	Percentage of employees unionized	
	Men	Women
Service	46	53
Lower non-manual	52	35
Technical	55	31
Skilled manual	55	38
Non-skilled manual	55	30
N	2,172	1,673

(b) Membership status	Employees (%)			
	Men full-time	Women full-time	Women part-time	All
Member	52	47	26	38
Former member	25	20	38	28
Never member	23	33	36	34
N	2,124	929	729	1,670

Note: N = sample number.

Source: SCELI Work Histories/Attitudes Survey.

ship among women. Can this be accounted for in terms of women's lower level of commitment to employment? One factor that might appear to support such a view is the sharp difference in membership levels between full-time and part-time employees (Table 4.10b). Full-time women workers are relatively close in their level of membership to men: 47 per cent are members, compared with 52 per cent of full-time men. In contrast, membership among part-time women workers falls as low as 26 per cent. The major break in patterns of membership would appear to be less between men and women as such, than between people in full-time work and people in part-time work.

Yet the assumptions that part-time work implies lower levels of commitment to employment, and that commitment to employment itself is a major influence on the decision to join a trade union, cannot be taken for granted. Bain and Elias (1985) and Booth (1986), for instance, have shown from regression analysis that the personal characteristics of women—such as marital status and family responsibilities—which might be thought to be major factors behind the level of commitment become insignificant when job, establishment, regional, and industry characteristics are controlled for. Here a more direct approach is taken by using a measure of employment commitment developed by the Social and Applied Psychology Unit (Warr, 1982) that compares people in terms of whether or not they would wish to continue working if there were no financial necessity. It is notable (Table 4.11) that the differences between men and women, and between full-time and part-time women workers, are not very substantial. Men in full-time employment are the most likely to say that they would continue working even if there were no financial need (67 per cent), but this was also the case for 64 per cent of full-time and 60 per cent of part-time women workers. If the assumption that part-time work involves a low commitment to employment is incorrect, it is also the case that a low commitment to employment would *not* appear to be a disincentive to trade union membership. While the differences are not large, whether one takes women in full-time work or in part-time work, those that would stop work if there were no financial need are more likely to be in unions than those that would continue to work. While part-time work then is powerfully related to women's low level of unionization, this is not because it implies a low level of interest in

TABLE 4.11. *Trade union membership employment status, and work commitment*

Work commitment (%)	Employees		
	Men full-time	Women full-time	Women part-time
Would continue to work if no financial necessity	67	64	60
Would stop working if no financial necessity	33	36	41
N	2,096	911	731

Work commitment (%)	Percentage of employees unionized		
	Men full-time	Women full-time	Women part-time
Would continue to work if no financial necessity	49	45	24
Would stop working if no financial necessity	57	51	28
N	2,096	911	731

Note: N = sample number.
Source: SCELI Work Histories/Attitudes Survey.

employment, but, more plausibly, because it reflects distinctive employment conditions or the concern of trade unions to recruit such workers.

2.5. Commitment to Trade Unionism

The most plausible individual influence on membership is people's personal commitment to trade unionism. This may have little to do with direct experience of the employment relationship, but may rather be related to people's wider values, to political influences, and to early socialization.

As a general measure of commitment, people were asked how favourable or unfavourable they were to trade unions. A first point to note is that there was little sign that trade unionism generated a great deal of enthusiasm. Only 12 per cent of employees declared themselves very favourable to trade unions and a further 26 per cent were quite favourable. On the other hand, there was also relatively little sign of marked antagonism: 7 per cent said that they were not at all favourable to the unions and 19 per cent were not very favourable. The most commonly found response was one of neutrality (36 per cent).

The likelihood of being a member varied clearly with the level of favourability, and personal commitment had an effect even when factors such as size of establishment and ownership sector were controlled for (Table 4.12). What is equally striking is how powerfully the implication of individual preference for actual membership is constrained by the employment situation in which people find themselves. For instance, while 85 per cent of those that were favourable to the unions in the public sector were trade union members, in the private sector this was the case for only 48 per cent. While 81 per cent of employees favourable to unionism in large establishments were members, in the small establishments the figure fell to 43 per cent. The effect of employer policy

TABLE 4.12. *Membership and favourability to trade unions*

Percentage of members	Favourability to unions		
	Favourable	Neutral	Unfavourable
In public sector	85	65	41
In private sector	48	26	18
In establishment with			
<25 employees	43	28	16
25–99	62	34	19
100–499	72	47	33
500+	81	56	48
Where employer encourages			
membership	88	84	67
Where employer discourages			
membership	28	8	11

was even more drastic. Where employers encouraged membership, 88 per cent of those who were in principle supportive of
trade unionism were members; where employers were hostile the
proportion fell to 28 per cent. In short, the employment situation
imposed very heavy constraints on the extent to which individual
preferences could be actualized.

While heavily constrained, the individual's personal commitment or favourability to trade unionism must still be included in
an adequate explanatory account. What types of factors, then,
make people more or less favourable to trade unions? It seems
plausible that people's judgement might be affected by their
wider social values, as reflected in their party allegiances. Taking
a measure of political allegiance based on people's reported vote
in 1983 and their voting intentions in 1986, it is possible to distinguish consistent supporters of a particular party from those
with less secure party attachments. Political allegiances are, in
fact, strongly associated with commitment to trade unionism.
Among Labour supporters, 63 per cent were favourable to the
unions, while among Conservative supporters the proportion fell
to 19 per cent. Similarly, 50 per cent of Conservative supporters
were unfavourable to the unions, but this was the case for only
10 per cent of Labour supporters. The influence of party remains
virtually the same if one controls for trade union membership.

Party allegiances and their associated values are themselves
likely to be related to longer-term factors. For a sub-sample of
our respondents, information was collected on the political preferences of people's parents when the respondent was between 12
and 14 years old. Where the father was a Conservative supporter,
only 15 per cent of our respondents were currently Labour.
However, where the father was a Labour supporter the proportion rose to 52 per cent. This suggests that Labour support may
have been heavily affected by early socialization.

It is also possible that attitudes to trade unionism are formed
directly through socialization in the parental family. Research
into the formation of political attitudes has pointed to the importance of family socialization for early political identities and for
moulding patterns of belief that subsequently influence political
allegiances (Greenstein, 1965; Easton and Dennis, 1969). To
explore whether similar influences were at work in establishing
trade union loyalties, people were asked about their father's atti-

tudes to trade unions at about the time they got their first job. The assumption was that this was the time at which parental influence over attitudes to trade unions would be greatest, since ties with the family were still likely to be close and advice would have relevance as people confronted an unfamiliar situation. There was, indeed, a strong relationship between father's and child's attitudes. Where the father was favourable to unionism, 60 per cent of respondents were favourable and only 17 per cent unfavourable. In contrast, where the father was unfavourable, only 25 per cent of respondents were favourable to the unions and fully 49 per cent unfavourable.

While such political and early family influences suggest that there are important sources of commitment to trade unionism that are not easily traceable to people's employment experiences, the experience over time of membership itself would also appear to be a significant factor. Some evidence for this has already been seen in the changes that occur over time in the reasons that people give for membership. Further, current trade unionists were much more likely to report that the importance to them of trade union membership had increased over the previous five years than that it had become less important. If a measure is constructed from people's work histories of the amount of time that they have spent in trade unions during their work lives, there is a strong association between the length of such experience and their current favourability.

It is possible to get some indication of the relative importance of the factors that affect people's personal favourability to trade unionism from the regression reported in Table 4.13. The single most important influence leading to a higher level of favourability to the unions was allegiance to the Labour Party. It is also notable that father's favourability to the unions when the person was young continued to have a very significant influence even when current party allegiance was controlled for. Experience of trade union membership over the work history emerged as the second most important influence after party allegiance. In contrast factors such as establishment size and employer policies had only a weak impact on levels of commitment.

Overall, then, the SCELI evidence suggests that personal attitudes to trade unionism—whether positive or negative—were not usually of an intensity that might be expected to structure in a

TABLE 4.13. *The determinants of favourability to trade unions*

Variables	Beta coefficient	*t*-value	Significance
Labour supporter	0.22	13.70	0.000
Time in trade union	0.20	11.69	0.000
Father's favourability	0.17	10.79	0.000
Conservative supporter	−0.13	−7.95	0.000
Redistribution	0.10	6.15	0.000
Employer policy	0.06	3.73	0.000
Sex male	0.07	4.58	0.000
Public sector employee	0.05	3.38	0.000
Size of establishment	0.04	2.78	0.006

Note: Constant: 1.72; Adjusted R^2: 0.28; N: 3143.

Source: SCELI Work Histories/Attitudes Survey.

decisive way patterns of trade union membership. While personal commitment to trade unionism retained an independent influence, its implications were very heavily constrained by the structural conditions in which employees were located. The variations in commitment could be traced in part to people's wider values and to their early socialization. However, the evidence also points strongly to a process of internal socialization within unions whereby people become increasingly aware over time of the benefits of membership. Commitment itself was then partly determined by structural factors associated with the employment situation rather than purely by the characteristics of the individual.

2.6. Area

It was noted earlier that there were significant differences in levels of trade union membership between the higher unemployment and lower unemployment labour markets. To what extent can these be accounted for in terms of the factors that are significant in explaining levels of trade union membership in general?

As can be seen in Table 4.14 (*a*), once establishment size was controlled for, the differences between the labour markets in membership levels emerged clearly within each size category. When, however, the localities were compared by industrial and ownership sector, it was notable that the pattern was based heav-

TABLE 4.14. *Trade union membership, labour market area, establishment size, and ownership sector*

| (a) | Percentage of employees unionized | | | |
| | Size of establishment | | | |
Labour market area	1–24	25–99	100–499	500+
Aberdeen	29	33	47	59
Coventry	31	51	66	78
Kirkcaldy	30	58	63	73
Northampton	27	37	44	54
Rochdale	37	46	65	74
Swindon	18	29	47	51

| | Percentage of employees unionized | | | |
| | Labour market | | | |
Ownership sector	Public manufacturing	Private manufacturing	Public services	Private services
Aberdeen	57	31	67	26
Coventry	72	59	69	27
Kirkcaldy	72	51	73	23
Northampton	51	29	63	19
Rochdale	71	46	77	28
Swindon	90	32	53	17

Source: SCELI Work Histories/Attitudes Survey.

ily on particular areas of employment (Table 4.14(*b*)). The more recessionary labour markets showed their higher levels of membership most clearly in private manufacturing and to a lesser degree in the public services. In private services, the level of unionism was low in all of the labour markets and there was no consistent difference in terms of labour market type. Further, when the level of personal commitment to trade unionism was controlled for, there was a marked decline in the distinctiveness of the different types of labour market. As can be seen in Table 4.15, the introduction of successive controls, particularly those of

TABLE 4.15. *Area and trade union membership: beta coefficient with successive controls*

Area beta	0.17	0.17	0.15	0.16	0.13	0.11	0.11	0.08
Variable in regression	Area	Area Class	Area Class Size	Area Class Size Industry	Area Class Size Industry Owner-ship	Area Class Size Industry Owner-ship Emp. policy	Area Class Size Industry Owner-ship Emp. policy Sex	Area Class Size Industry Owner-ship Emp. policy Sex Fav. to TUs

Source: SCELI Work Histories/Attitudes Survey.

ownership and favourability to trade unionism, reduced substantially the influence of 'area' on trade union membership, although there was a clear residual effect that remains unaccounted for.

2.7. Determinants of Membership: Overview

The relative importance of the various influences on trade union membership that have been considered can be summarized in the logistic regression reported in Table 4.16. For each variable, the odds of being a trade union member associated with any given category are expressed in relation to the first level of that variable. It is clear that the most important predictors of membership are whether or not people are employed in the public sector and the attitude of their employer to trade union organization. Those in the public sector are six times more likely than those in the private to be in trade unions, even when other factors are controlled for, and the odds of membership increase by a similar amount where a person has a pro-union employer.

The effects of other variables are notably weaker and, in several instances, are very unstable when one compares male and female employees. There is a striking difference for instance between men and women in the odds of membership associated with different class categories. The pattern for neither sex offers

TABLE 4.16. *Parameter estimates for the odds of union membership of employees (logistic regression)*

Variable and level	Multiplicative estimates	
	Men	Women
Constant	0.01	0.03
Class		
Service	1.00	1.00
Lower non-manual	2.51	0.77
Technical/supervisory	1.98	0.61
Skilled manual	3.03	1.00
Non-skilled manual	2.29	0.91
Size		
1–24	1.00	1.00
25–99	1.59	1.38
100–499	2.85	2.64
500+	3.95	2.42
Industry		
Primary	1.00	1.00
Manufacturing	1.71	2.13
Service	2.18	1.48
Ownership		
Private	1.00	1.00
Public	6.43	6.33
Employer attitude		
Not encouraging membership	1.00	1.00
Encouraging membership	6.48	5.55
Employment status		
Full-time	1.00	1.00
Part-time	0.89	0.42
Age		
<25	1.00	1.00
25–34	2.60	1.57
35–44	2.23	1.80
45–54	2.29	2.51
55+	2.58	2.01
Favourability to unions		
Unfavourable	1.00	1.00
Neutral	1.89	2.03
Favourable	4.45	4.16
Area		
Low unemployment	1.00	1.00
High unemployment	1.63	1.84
	N = 1,572	N = 1,439
	Pseudo R^2 = 0.32	Pseudo R^2 = 0.31

Note: All variables are significant at the 0.01 level or better.

Source: SCELI Work Histories/Attitudes Survey.

much support for the view that there is a fundamental divide
between manual and non-manual employees. However, the
insignificance of this distinction is particularly striking for
women, for whom the odds of membership in the service class
are the same as those for skilled manual workers. Similarly, the
effect of size of establishment on membership appears to be very
much weaker for women.

Overall, the data support the view that it is structural factors
rather than individual preferences that are most important in
determining whether or not people are trade union members.
There is little reason to think that membership is necessarily
undercut by changes in the class structure, the movement to a
service economy, or the shift in the gender composition of the
workforce. What does strongly affect the feasibility of union
organization is the ownership sector in which people are
employed, and the policies of their employers. The importance of
structural factors in determining membership suggests that
changes in personal views about trade unionism are unlikely to
have been a major factor in explaining membership decline.

3. SOURCES OF LOSS OF MEMBERSHIP

The evidence examined so far has suggested that there had
occurred no major collapse of commitment to the unions among
trade union members in the 1980s and that structural factors
were the most decisive influences on the level of membership. It
would seem implausible, then, that the loss of membership in the
1980s was due principally to an erosion of individual support for
trade unionism. However, the crucial test for this must clearly lie
in the circumstances and motives of the leavers themselves. What
types of people were these and how did they account for the fact
that they were no longer union members?

As can be seen in Table 4.17(*b*), the largest single category of
former members was of people still in employment (47 per cent);
only a minority were out of paid work. Within this overall picture, however, the composition of the ex-membership differed
substantially between labour markets. In the more dynamic
labour markets, former members still in employment constituted
an absolute majority of the ex-membership. In the recessionary

TABLE 4.17(*a*). *Percentage of former trade unionists, by labour market*

Aberdeen	Coventry	Kirkcaldy	Northampton	Rochdale	Swindon
33	35	41	36	36	32

TABLE 4.17(*b*). *Percentage of former trade unionists, by activity status*

Labour market	Self-employed	Employed	Unemployed	Non-active
Aberdeen	6	56	13	26
Coventry	7	40	20	33
Kirkcaldy	5	39	25	31
Northampton	9	54	15	22
Rochdale	9	41	25	25
Swindon	10	55	15	21
All	8	47	19	27

Source: SCELI Work Histories/Attitudes Survey.

labour markets, however, those without paid work constituted a larger proportion of former members than those in jobs. Any analysis of the loss of membership sustained by the unions in recent years needs then to take into account that it may have very diverse sources. Given that these are likely to be linked to very different motives for leaving, the case of former members currently out of paid work will be examined separately from those still in employment.

3.1. Loss of Membership Among Those Without Work

It cannot simply be assumed that all former members who were currently unemployed or non-employed had left membership as a result of leaving paid employment. It is possible that they had decided to leave membership at an earlier period in their lives. However, the overwhelming majority did in practice give reasons that are consistent with a break of membership on leaving their job. Taking first the unemployed, 75 per cent said that they had ceased being members because they were no longer employed (Table 4.18). Only 15 per cent of the unemployed gave reasons

TABLE 4.18. *Most important reason for no longer being a trade union member*

Reason	Percentage		
	Unemployed	Non-active	Current employees
No longer employed	75	85	—
Moved to a job without a union	6	4	45
No benefit in joining	7	4	27
Disagree with unions in principle	8	4	14
Management against/ job prospects	1	1	4
Other	3	2	10
N	392	547	950

Note: N = sample number.
Source: SCELI Work Histories/Attitudes Survey.

that appear to relate to a stage of their employment history prior to unemployment. For instance, 6 per cent said that they had left because they had moved to a job in which there were no unions and a further 8 per cent had left because they had come to disagree with the unions in principle.

The non-actives were even more likely to give reasons that indicated that they had left membership only on leaving work. Eighty-five per cent attributed their decision to stop being a member to the fact that they were no longer in employment, while only 9 per cent gave a reason relating to a previous job or to a change in their own attitudes to the unions.

These two sources of outflow are, of course, heavily differentiated by gender. The loss of members into unemployment is to a greater degree a loss of male membership: 54 per cent of former members who were unemployed were men; in contrast, the overwhelming majority of former members who had become non-active were women (85 per cent).

3.2. Loss of Membership Among Those in Work

Did the fact that those in employment in the more dynamic labour markets formed a larger share of the ex-membership indicate that employee loyalties to trade unions were being more rapidly eroded in this type of setting? The evidence would suggest that this was not in fact the case. The proportion of current employees who had left trade union membership was remarkably similar across the different labour markets. Just over a quarter of employees were ex-members and there appears to be no systematic difference in this respect between types of labour market. The more prosperous labour markets were certainly distinctive in that they had a lower proportion of people who were currently in trade unions, but this reflects the fact that they had a higher proportion of consistent non-members and not that they had suffered a disproportionate loss of membership among people in employment.

What were the reasons for leaving membership among those that were still in employment? Again, only a fairly small proportion (14 per cent) appear to have left because they had come to have objections to the unions in principle. Northampton was the labour market in which such reasons were most frequently given, but even here they accounted for only 20 per cent of all reasons for leaving. Instead, the most frequent reason given by people for no longer being members was that they had moved to jobs where there were no unions present in the workplace. Overall, this reason was given by 45 per cent of former members and, although the proportions differed substantially between labour markets, there was no consistent pattern by labour market type. This was followed by those who said that their main reason for leaving was that they could see no benefit in being a member (27 per cent). The reasons underlying this response, of course, could be diverse. It might be that there were unions in the establishment, but these were felt to be ineffective in defending employee interests; alternatively, unions may have been absent at workplace level, making it seem that there was little to be gained from retaining membership. In practice, fully 70 per cent of the former members still in employment that gave this response were working in establishments where there were no unions to represent them. The findings here are very similar to that of research

TABLE 4.19. *Comparison of employment situation of current and former trade union members*

	Members	Former members
Percentage		
in establishments 1–24	21	41
in establishments 500+	31	14
in private manufacturing	27	35
in private services	15	37
in private sector	43	79
with employers encouraging unions	37	9
with employers discouraging unions	5	27
service class	33	28
non-skilled manual	29	35
women	36	46
part-time workers	12	28

Source: SCELI Work Histories/Attitudes Survey.

(Spilsbury *et al.*, 1987) which has shown the importance of the presence of a union for the membership of young adults as they move between jobs. A comparison of the structural location of the former members with those of current trade union members in Table 4.19 reveals sharply the way in which the former members were constrained by their current employment situation. They were twice as likely as current members to be people who were now working in small establishments, to be working in the private service sector, and to be engaged in part-time work—all conditions that have been shown to be heavily inimical to trade union membership. The evidence, then, for those that have left trade unions clearly confirms the conclusions reached earlier: the most significant factors affecting whether people were union members or not were structural.

4. CONCLUSION

Our evidence points clearly to the importance of structural factors, rather than to any decline in commitment to trade unionism, in accounting for the high level of membership loss during the 1980s. In the first place, there was little evidence of widespread alienation from the unions among trade union members. While it was the case that a significant proportion of the membership had been recruited originally through institutional pressures, rather than through some clear act of choice, this did not imply that members experienced their current membership as the result of constraint. Rather, the experience of trade unionism over time made people increasingly aware of the advantages that trade unions offered. Second, the analysis of the sources of membership and non-membership among those currently in employment suggested that the most powerful influence over whether or not people were members lay in the structural contexts in which they were employed rather than in their individual preferences. The most important factors here were the extent to which employers accepted and were prepared to facilitate trade union organization, and whether or not people were in the public sector. Finally, the explanations given by former members for why they had left trade unions confirmed the overwhelming importance of structural factors. For a large proportion, their membership had ceased because they had become unemployed or because they had withdrawn from the labour market. Among those that had remained in employment, the principal reason for dropping membership was that people had moved to an establishment in which there was no union to join. Overall, only a very small proportion of former members would appear to have left because they were disenchanted with trade unionism as such.

It should be noted, however, that the type of structural explanations for patterns of union membership that are pointed to by the data are not highly deterministic in type and cannot be seen as implying any *necessary* long-term trend for the future of union strength. (Elias's analysis in Chapter 5 provides further grounds for such caution about long-term trends). Certainly, it is probable that the long-term shifts in the class structure and in the sectoral composition of the economy will continue, but these were not found to be major influences on union membership. Rather, the aspects of the employment situation that did emerge as of key significance—in particular the policies of employers—are in principle open to influence, whether through the activities of the trade unions themselves or through government intervention. The future pattern of trade union membership is not, then, predetermined, but will depend upon the organizational skills of trade unions and the longer-term development of government policies.

5

Growth and Decline in Trade Union Membership in Great Britain: Evidence from Work Histories

PETER ELIAS

1. INTRODUCTION

From the end of the Second World War until the late 1960s, the proportion of the employed population in the United Kingdom who were union members remained around the 40 per cent mark. Between 1969 and 1979, this proportion rose to an all-time peak of 53 per cent. Subsequently, union membership has declined to the rates which prevailed in the 1945–69 period.

A variety of explanations has been proposed to account for this growth and decline in trade union membership. These range from changes in the legislative environment, facilitating or impeding the ability of unions to recruit and retain members; changes in the industrial and occupational composition of the labour force, more recently away from sectors which have traditionally been heavily unionized and towards sectors and jobs which have only ever been weakly organized; to 'business cycle' explanations which rely upon arguments about the perceived benefits of membership in times of high inflation or the ability of employers to oppose collectively organized labour in times of high unemployment. At present there is an emerging view that the business-cycle explanation of changes in membership provides a reasonably satisfactory account of these changes. Carruth and Disney (1988: 13) use such a hypothesis to argue:

The present economic environment—a combination of persistent unemployment, steady real-wage growth and a Conservative government—looks particularly unfavourable to trade unions in the foreseeable future.

The purpose of the present chapter is to present an alternative view of the dynamics of trade union membership, using a unique source of information on membership changes, the life and work history information collected from over 6,000 people in six localities in England and Scotland, in the SCELI Work Histories/ Attitudes Survey. The intention of this study is to examine the role of secular influences on trends in membership, particularly those which are associated with underlying changes in the composition of the labour force or the propensity of younger workers to join and leave unions compared with their older counterparts. These will be contrasted with the business-cycle 'explanations', particularly the role of inflation or unemployment as possible causes of membership growth and decline.

The plan of this chapter is as follows: Section 2 discusses the formulation of earlier empirical models of union growth or decline. Section 3 illustrates the membership information available from the Work Attitudes/Histories data-set and portrays the dynamics of union membership from this new data source. Section 4 present a pooled time-series–cross-sectional model of membership. Section 5 examines in detail the dynamics of union membership, the processes of joining and leaving trade union membership. Finally, Section 6 pulls together these results with a summary of the impact of secular versus business-cycle influences on membership.

2. PREVIOUS WORK ON THE DYNAMICS OF UNION MEMBERSHIP

There have been four major empirical studies of union growth and decline in the United Kingdom. Table 5.1 lists these studies, together with a brief account of the variables which were included in these analyses and the time period through which union growth and decline was investigated.

There are some common elements to these studies. First, they are all versions of the 'business-cycle' specification of union growth. This stems from the fact that structural variables in such aggregate analyses are virtually indistinguishable from long-term trend effects. For more recent periods, say from 1961 onwards, the occupational and industrial changes in employment structure

TABLE 5.1. *Four models of union growth and decline in the UK*

Author and date of publication	Time-period covered by study	Dependent variable	Independent variables
Hines (1964)	1893–1961	ΔD_t	D^*_{t-1}, $\Delta P_{t-1/2}$, $\pi_{t-1/2}$ (−) (+)
Bain and Elsheikh (1976)	1893–1970	ΔT_t	ΔP^*_t, ΔW^*_t, U_{t-1}, U_{t-2}, D^*_{t-1} (+) (+) (−)
Booth (1983)	1895–1980	Z_t	Z^*_{t-1}, Z^*_{t-2}, ΔP_t, ΔW^*_t, U^*_t, U^*_{t-1} (+) (−) (+) (−) (+)
Carruth and Disney (1988)	1896–1984	$\Delta \log T_t$	$\Delta \log E^*_t$, $\Delta \log P^*_{t-1}$, $\Delta \log W^*_{t-1}$, (+) (+) (−) $\Delta \log U^*_t$, $\Delta \log T^*_{t-1}$, $\Delta \log T_{t-2}$, (−) (+) $\Delta \log T^*_{t-3}$, $(\log T - \log E)_{t-1}$, (−) $D.Pol^*$ (+)

Key
Δ = 1st difference operator, periods t and t–1
D = T/M where T = total union membership, M = labour force
P = retail price index
π = level of real profits
W = index of money wages
U = unemployment rate
E = level of employment
Z = $\log [D/(1-D)]$
$D.Pol$ = Dummy variable taking a value of 1 in years in which there is a Labour, Liberal, or coalition government.
  * The variable is statistically significant at the 5% level.

Note: A plus or minus sign in brackets indicates the sign on the estimated coefficient for each variable.

which took place do not account well for the 'plateau' in membership trends which lasted until 1969, followed by the growth of the 1970s and decline of the 1980s. Second, with the exception of Booth's (1983) study, there is strong evidence of a positive relationship between inflation and trade union membership; as the rate of inflation increases, the overall level of membership of trade unions rises. Bain and Elsheikh (1976) and Carruth and Disney (1988) find separate effects for wage inflation and Booth finds a positive correlation only between the rate of increase of money wages and trade union membership.

Bain and Elsheikh (1976) trace the origin of this postulated link between inflation and labour organization to the work of Commons and Sumner (1911) and Perlman (1923), elaborated in later US studies by Davis (1941), Dunlop (1944b), and Bernstein (1954). Bain and Elsheikh summarize these theoretical arguments:

. . . in as much as workers perceive an increase in the rate of change of retail prices as a threat to their standard of living . . . they are more likely to become and remain union members in an attempt to maintain this standard. In addition . . . employers may be more prepared to concede worker demands . . . partly because . . . increases in labour costs can be passed on more easily to customers. (Bain and Elsheikh 1976: 62–3)

The link between unemployment and trade union membership is less clear from these studies. This may, at first sight, appear surprising, given that these models have been estimated over time periods which span the Great Depression of the early 1930s. Union membership declined rapidly in the 1920s, falling from a peak of 43 per cent to a trough of 25 per cent by 1935. Nevertheless, it is only in two of these studies that there is statistical evidence of any link between unemployment and membership. Both Booth's study and the work of Carruth and Disney indicate that union membership and the change in the unemployment rate are negatively correlated; in times of rising unemployment, membership levels fall.

The theoretical reasoning underlying a direct relationship between unemployment and trade union membership presents a weaker case than for inflation. Bain and Elsheikh suggest that:

When unemployment is high or increasing, employers may be better able and more willing to oppose unionism. For in as far as unemployment reduces the level of aggregate demand, production lost as a result of strikes and other forms of industrial action will be less costly to employers. (Bain and Elsheikh 1976: 65–6)

However, they recognize that the relationship is likely to be weak, given that union members are unlikely to discontinue their membership immediately upon becoming unemployed.

Other studies of trade union membership have been undertaken, but these are all cross-sectional in nature, indicating the variations that exist between patterns of membership in different industries, different establishments and between individuals. Bain and Elsheikh (1979) and Elsheikh and Bain (1980) illustrated clearly the importance of industry sector and establishment size as variables which account for a considerable proportion of inter-industry or inter-establishment variations in union membership. Bain and Elias (1985) pursued these cross-sectional variations further, showing that certain individual factors (gender, qualifications, and work experience) also contribute to variations in membership between individuals, whilst confirming the overwhelming importance of structural factors (industry, occupation, establishment size) as key factors in understanding such variations. The importance of the working environment as the principal factor influencing trade union membership was evidenced in a study of membership conducted at the intra-firm level. From a detailed analysis of union membership among the employees of a multi-plant employer in the UK electronics industry, Guest and Dewe (1988) conclude that instrumental reasons (union best represents specific interests—wages, job security, working conditions) were the most significant reason for membership of trade unions and that such attitudes and perceptions are more important than background and biographical factors as influences affecting trade union membership in the particular workforce they studied.

The two strands of empirical investigation present an apparent paradox. On the one hand, time-series models of trade union membership (or density—membership as a proportion of the population 'at risk' of membership) appear to track the growth and decline in membership quite well over long periods of time. With just a few variables, notably price or wage inflation, these models can account for the growth and decline of membership in certain key periods. On the other hand, cross-sectional models illustrate the importance of structural factors in account-ing for inter-industry, inter-establishment, and, given their influ-ence through work experience, individual level differences in membership. In the face of the major structural changes that have occurred over the last three decades, why then do structural factors appear to be so unimportant in the time-series models?

The answer could rest with the nature of the data which have been available for the study of trends in membership. Time-series models cannot incorporate structural factors at the aggregate level, because such factors are virtually indistinguishable from time trends. For example, the construction of a variable representing the proportion of manual workers in the national workforce would rely heavily upon interpolation of point observations from the Censuses of Population for 1961, 1971, and 1981. An annual time-series constructed for such a variable would approximate a linear trend.

The integration of these two approaches requires longitudinal information on trade union membership, providing information at the level of the individual and/or establishment, and containing information on the evolution of trade union membership through time for the unit of observation. The next section describes such a body of data for which the unit of observation is the individual.

3. A LONGITUDINAL ANALYSIS OF MEMBERSHIP CHANGES

The aggregate time-series studies of union membership, which purport to show a simple and elegant link between membership, inflation, and, to some extent, unemployment, contrast markedly with the cross-sectional analyses that indicate the strength of structural factors affecting membership. In this situation, it is of interest to combine these approaches to study the time profile of union membership changes at the individual level. At issue is the relative influence of structural patterns of economic change (the decline of particular occupations and industries that were traditionally heavily unionized), and the role of business-cycle variables, particularly unemployment and inflation as factors that affect the decision to join or remain in a trade union.

These issues are addressed using life and work history data collected within the Social Change and Economic Life Initiative. The historical trade union membership information which is available for this study is derived from the work histories of approximately 6,000 respondents to the Work Attitudes/Work Histories surveys conducted in six localities in England and Scotland in 1986 as part of the Social Change and Economic Life Initiative (SCELI). Respondents to these surveys were a randomly selected group of 20–60 year olds, predominantly living in urban locations outside the South East of England. Sampling procedures yielded a deliberate over-representation of unemployed persons; non-co-operation yielded a slight over-representation of females. These factors, predominantly the urban dimension, must be borne in mind in the subsequent investigation of these data.

An obvious question to ask of these survey data is whether or not the trade union membership histories of respondents reflect the decade of growth (1969–79) and decade of decline (1980–9) in membership. This is a complex question to answer from work history information, because it has been shown in cross-sectional studies that trade union membership is strongly associated with work experience, which is, in turn, correlated highly with the age of an individual (Bain and Elias, 1985). In investigating work history information to detect change associated with calendar time, one is of necessity studying information which confounds the effect of age or work experience with time-varying changes. This is demonstrated in Figure 5.1, which plots the rate of union density (trade union members as a percentage of the employed) for two age groups or cohorts of survey respondents: those aged 30–4 years old at the time of the survey and those aged 55–60 years. Obviously, the younger age group has a shorter employment history than the older group, a fact that is represented by the shorter historical plot of union density for this age group.

For males, there is some indication that union membership builds up during the first ten years of the working life of the age group. For men aged 55–60 years in 1986, this took place between 1947 and 1956. For 30–4 year olds, a corresponding rise took place from 1969 to 1978. For women the evidence of this age or work-experience effect on membership is less clear, presumably because many women experienced a significant interruption to their employment associated with family formation. Nevertheless, there is some indication of an upward trend in the membership rate in the early part of the working life of both age groups of women respondents.

Apart from work experience or age-related influences on membership, Figure 5.1 also gives some indication of a significant time-related effect. For both males and females and for both age groups, trade union membership commenced to dip at or around 1979. This reflects the time-series work of Carruth and Disney (1988), who find that a dummy variable that takes a value of

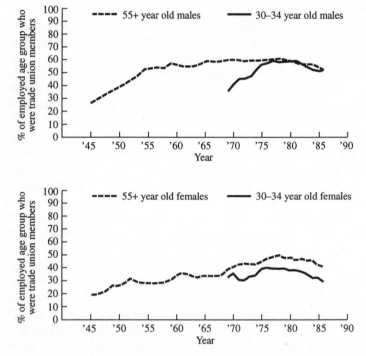

FIG. 5.1. Percentage of employed members of two age groups who were
trade union members: 30–4 year olds, and 50–60 year olds, all SCELI
localities
Source: SCELI Work Histories/Attitudes Survey.

unity for years in which there is a Labour, Liberal, or coalition
government has a significant and positive relationship with tem-
poral variations in union membership.

Another way of looking at these longitudinal data is to examine particular years within the work histories, portraying as a
cross-section the trade union membership rates prevailing within
the work histories of respondents within the years selected for
study. This allows one to examine whether or not these individual work histories reflect the national trends in trade union
membership, particularly the trends in the 1970s and early 1980s.
As the preceding analysis has shown, this must be performed in
such a manner as to control for the influences of age or work
experience. Table 5.2 attempts this by comparing the trade union

membership of 20–39 year olds in 1986 with the membership in 1976 of 30–49 year olds at the time of the survey and the membership in 1966 of 40–59 year olds at the time of the survey. Thus, in each year selected, membership data refer to 20–39 year olds. Interestingly, the growth in membership in the period 1966–76 is not strongly in evidence, reflecting the major differences that exist between localities. Coventry and Northampton both show a significant increase in trade union membership from 1966 to 1976. Aberdeen shows signs of only modest growth in membership. Kirkcaldy and Swindon show little change in union density among 20–39 year olds between 1966 and 1976. Rochdale exhibits a declining rate of union membership among this age group over the same period. For the period 1976–86, there is clear evidence of a decline in membership among this age group. With the exception of Northampton and Rochdale, for which only a slight decline is noted, these locality-based estimates of membership of young workers reflect the national downward trend which took place in the same period.

Table 5.3 expands the information shown in Table 5.2 to include details of the changing nature of the labour force within which these 20–39 year olds were working at each point in the three decades. First, it can be seen that the proportion who were

TABLE 5.2. *Membership of trade unions of employed persons in 1966, 1976, and 1986, for respondents aged 20–39 years in each period (%)*

Locality	1966[a]	1976[b]	1986[c]
Aberdeen	45.8	47.6	31.9
Coventry	58.6	64.0	47.5
Kirkcaldy	58.7	58.9	48.2
Northampton	27.7	38.7	35.2
Rochdale	53.9	48.0	46.8
Swindon	39.0	39.0	27.6
All areas	47.6	48.9	39.1
BASE = 100%	2,514	3,047	3,455

[a] 40–59 years old at time of survey.
[b] 30–49 years old at time of survey.
[c] 20–39 years old at time of survey.

Source: SCELI Work Histories/Attitudes Survey.

Peter Elias

TABLE 5.3. *Changes in the status of survey respondents: 1966, 1976, and 1986, for respondents aged 20–39 years in each year*

All localities	1966[a]	1976[b]	1986[c]
% of respondents in labour force	69.8	75.7	78.5
unemployed	1.4	3.6	16.6
% of employed			
Trade union member	47.6	48.9	39.1
Manufacturing	36.8	30.9	24.6
Public sector	29.1	32.7	31.0
Large workplaces	48.4	44.8	39.5
Manual work	57.5	50.1	44.1
Self-employment	4.1	5.4	7.8
Part-time work	9.6	15.2	17.9
BASE = 100%	2,514	3,047	3,455

[a] 40–59 years old at time of survey.
[b] 30–49 years old at time of survey.
[c] 20–39 years old at time of survey.

Source: SCELI Work Histories/Attitudes Survey.

working, or looking for a job, is significantly higher in 1976 and 1986 than in 1966. This is because of the higher rate of labour force participation among married women in the later periods. The growing experience of unemployment among 20–39 year olds is clearly in evidence, though in part this is an artefact of a strategy devised to over-sample the unemployed in 1986.

Among survey respondents who were in employment in each year, the decline in manufacturing sector employment is clearly apparent, as is the decline in employment in large workplaces and in manual occupations. Countering such trends is the growth of self-employment and part-time work. The proportion of employed 20–39 year olds in public sector employment in each year rose slightly then declined.

Separate analysis of these trends for the six localities revealed some interesting differences. In Aberdeen, the proportion of employed 20–39 year olds working in the public sector declined from 37 per cent in 1966 to 27 per cent in 1986. In Coventry this same proportion grew from 24 to 29 per cent and in Northampton from 27 to 32 per cent. The growth in public sector employment in Rochdale is remarkable, from 20 to 31 per cent between 1966 and 1986. In other areas, this proportion remained relatively constant.

The need to restrict these cross-sections of work history information to survey respondents who are in the first half of an average working life (20–39 years) obscures the overall dynamics of the changing pattern of trade union membership. While trade union density may change because new entrants to the labour market do not take up membership, or may leave membership at some stage in the first half of their working life, it may also be the case that changes may arise due to patterns of early retirement or high levels of unemployment among older workers. Table 5.4 indicates the scale of these wider dynamic influences by focusing upon the latter period, 1976–86, and changing the age group studied to include all respondents aged 30–60 years at the time of the surveys. Comparing the membership history for 1976 with that for 1986, respondents have been characterized into six groups: 'continuous membership', consisting of respondents who were trade union members throughout the decade; 'joiners', who were not members in 1976 but joined a union at some time between 1976 and 1986 and were still in a union in 1986; 'leavers', the obverse of the 'joiners' category; 'continuous non-members', who never belonged to a trade union throughout the decade; 'intermittent members', who joined *and* left a union at least once between 1976 and 1986. A small residual category consists of those whose membership histories could not be categorized. The results of this classification of membership changes is shown for each locality and by gender in Table 5.4.

Before examining this table, it is important to consider the nature of the sample of work histories used in its construction. The sample of respondents will be ten years younger in 1976, therefore any significant influence of age upon trade union membership must be taken into account. Counteracting such a trend, the decade from 1976 to 1986 saw membership levels decline nationally by approximately 10 percentage points (Disney and Mudambi, 1987). Among the sample of 30–60 year olds, membership declined from 36 per cent of the full sample to 30 per cent. Previous work (Bain and Elias, 1985) indicates that the accumulated work experience from one decade would have increased membership by approximately 4 per cent. Taken together, this implies that the national downward trend in membership is well reflected in the sample of work histories portrayed in Table 5.4.

TABLE 5.4. *Percentage of trade union members among 30–60 year olds, by localities and gender, 1976–1986*

Pattern of membership 1976–86	Aberdeen	Coventry	Kirkcaldy	Northampton	Rochdale	Swindon	All areas
Males							
Continuous member	33	41	33	18	32	23	30
Joiner	5	5	5	8	7	5	6
Leaver	12	22	20	14	16	17	17
Continuous non-member	38	21	25	47	32	42	34
Intermittent member	8	10	14	10	11	11	12
Not known	4	2	3	4	2	2	2
BASE = 100%	297	321	316	315	294	316	1,859
Females							
Continuous member	13	14	13	7	11	11	11
Joiner	8	8	10	8	11	5	8
Leaver	11	12	9	10	14	8	11
Continuous non-member	59	54	53	61	52	70	58
Intermittent member	6	10	12	9	11	5	9
Not known	3	3	4	4	2	1	3
BASE = 100%	415	388	409	403	408	411	2,434

Source: SCELI Work Histories/Attitudes Survey.

The main component of change in the membership histories of men aged 30–60 years is the major difference between joiners and leavers. This difference of 11 per cent varies significantly by locality, from 17 per cent in Coventry to 6 per cent in Northampton. For women, the difference between joining and leaving is not so marked, nor are there significant variations by locality in terms of the dynamics of membership. Swindon, however, stands out as an area in which a high proportion of women aged 30–60 years have never been members of a trade union. It is interesting to note, for both men and women, that about one respondent in ten is classified as an intermittent member, joining and leaving a union at least once during the decade. A more detailed analysis of this group indicated that the net effect of intermittent membership had little influence on the overall level of membership among 30–60 year olds between 1976 and 1986.

The differences in the dynamics of membership across localities and by gender are quite striking. Male survey respondents in Northampton exhibit a low absolute level of membership, but had the highest inflow over the ten-year period and the lowest outflow, yielding a relatively low decline in membership when compared across the six localities. For females, the proportion of continuous members is much lower than for males. The main reason for this is the fact that many women in this age group will have experienced a break in their employment for family formation during this decade. For this reason, one would expect the proportions shown as joiners and leavers to be considerably higher than for males. This is certainly the case for joiners, but the outflow from membership (leavers) is considerably lower than for males. In other words, although union membership levels are significantly lower among women than men, the decline in membership is predominantly a male phenomenon.

In summary, the growth in membership shown for the decade 1966–76, as evidenced in the work histories of certain respondents to these surveys, persons aged 40–59 years in 1986, appears to be somewhat lower than expected. It has been argued earlier that work experience effects alone would be expected to have increased membership by about 4 percentage points, the approximate magnitude of the increase in membership observed among this group. Nationally, trade union membership increased by about 12 percentage points between 1966 and 1976. The lower than expected increase in membership among the employed most probably reflects the varying experiences of the different urban locations in which these surveys were conducted, together with the differential effect of migration, which, over a long period of time, results in a sample from each locality who are predominantly 'stayers', particularly among the older age groups. It could well be the case that a high proportion of persons who have left each locality since 1966 are predominantly ex-trade union members who joined a union during this decade.

Despite this weakness shown by the data from the period 1966–76, the preceding analysis has revealed three interesting features. First, there is evidence of the decade of growth and decade of decline in these membership histories, particularly for Coventry and Northampton. Second, membership changes seem to be more apparent for men than women and, during 1976–86, arose due to an excess of leavers over joiners. Third, the changes in membership are associated with some significant changes in the structure of employment, notably the proportion of respondents working in the public sector, in manufacturing, in large workplaces, in manual occupations, self-employment, and part-time work. The next section of this paper investigates these influences on membership, in particular, the role of business-cycle influences as opposed to structural effects.

4. MODELLING TRADE UNION MEMBERSHIP

This section of the paper attempts to unravel the complex relationships that give rise to the observed trends and variations in trade union membership. This is performed by estimating the parameters of a series of statistical models, thereby characterizing systematic relationships from variables that may influence the probability that an individual is a member.

A 'probabilistic' approach to the study of members may, at first sight, appear confusing, because the trade union membership information categorizes each individual as either 'in a union' (category '1') or 'not in a union' (category '0'). If we postulate that various factors can contribute to whether or not any individual is a union member, the effect of these factors (X) can be represented as:

Probability that individual i is a union member $= f(X) + \varepsilon_i$ (1)

where ε_i is a random disturbance term for individual i. In this formulation, the factors in X can be viewed as contributing to a threshold probability, some unobserved or latent variable which, once a particular value has been crossed for each individual, will result in that individual either joining or leaving a trade union.

Opinion is varied about the functional form of (1) and the associated techniques that are available for the estimation of structural parameters. At its simplest though, for for initial exploratory analysis, there are strong arguments to adopt a linear functional form, a restrictive set of assumptions on the nature of the ε_i terms, and to estimate (1) using ordinary least squares (Amemiya, 1981).

The potential explanatory factors that may contribute to these threshold probabilities can be viewed as belonging to one of three groups. The first section of this paper presented the theoretical reasoning behind the inclusion of certain macro-economic influences as factors affecting the propensity or ability of individuals to join and retain their membership of a trade union. Time-varying, macro-economic factors are postulated as a set of influences that may be experienced by all individuals simultaneously. Such factors are those which are typically used in aggregate time-series models of trade union membership to investigate the correlates of secular changes in membership, for example, inflation, economic growth, unemployment. These factors are deemed to be common to all individuals but vary through time. Second is a set of influences that can be described as specific to the individual, not the job in which he or she works. The theoretical rationale for individual-specific influences may appear intuitive; certain individuals may have a greater or lesser propensity to join a union than others for reasons associated with their early socialization. However, the ability to identify such factors and discriminate between them and what might be termed job-specific factors is extremely difficult. For example, one could argue that the holders of higher educational qualifications are less likely to unionize. Empirical work has shown (Bain and Elias, 1985) that, *ceteris paribus*, male degree holders are less likely to be union members at any point in their working lives than males without degrees. But possession of a university degree may be more a characteristic of the job in which such males work than a characteristic of the individual. There are, however, certain influences that can be deemed individual-specific. Kochan (1980) suggests that an important part of the individual's decision-making process is their degree of commitment to the job. His argument rests upon the length of the time horizon facing a prospective union member. Those who expect to move on to other jobs shortly 'are unlikely to be willing to invest the energy and resources necessary to unionize' (Kochan, 1980: 145). Another individual-specific influence is a proximity effect. Shister (1953) argues that the propensity to unionize is dependent upon an individual's awareness that comparably situated workers are in a better position. This awareness he terms a proximity influence, given that it is likely to be related to the proximity of unionized workplaces. The individual-specific factors used in this analysis include age, gender, previous work history, previous trade union history, and place of residence as a proxy for proximity influences. For the reasons outlined above, some of these may not strictly be interpreted as individual-specific. They obviously vary between individuals and may also vary through time. Finally, a set of influences or explanatory factors are included which can be termed job characteristics. These are factors which relate to the type of work a person does at a particular point in his or her working life. Examples are the industry sector in which they work, size of workplace, and occupation.

Table 5.5 shows the relationships that exist between trade union membership of individual i in time period t, for each year of employment in the individual's work history. These data have been developed from SCELI Work Attitudes/Work Histories survey data using the IDEAS software package (Elias and Jones, 1990). The 'dominant event' method has been used to characterize each year of a respondent's working life. Each survey gives rise to approximately 17,000 'employment years' of work history information. An employment year forms the basic unit of observation in this analysis. Student t-statistics are not shown, given that the estimation procedure is likely to yield inefficient estimates. Instead, an exacting 1 per cent confidence interval is used to determine the statistical significance of parameter estimates.

Studying the business-cycle specification first, Table 5.5 indicates that, at the level of the individual, there exists a weak but systematic relationship between trade union membership and the national unemployment rate in each year (U_t). With the exception

TABLE 5.5. *Pooled time-series–cross-section model of trade union membership: simple business cycle specification*

	Aberdeen	Coventry	Kirkcaldy	Northampton	Rochdale	Swindon
Trend	0.008*	0.014*	0.007*	0.003*	0.003*	0.007*
ΔP_t	0.001	—	-0.001	0.003*	—	0.001
U_t	-0.011*	-0.020*	-0.013*	—	-0.003	-0.013*
Post-1979 dummy	-0.044*	-0.055*	0.009	0.002	—	-0.012
F	51.6	154.6	31.6	39.2	27.2	35.6
n	17,362	16,879	16,915	16,999	16,717	16,884
Mean dependent variable	0.417	0.542	0.554	0.324	0.486	0.357

Note: An asterisk denotes that the coefficient is statistically significant at the 1% level.
ΔP_t is the annual rate of change in the retail price index;
U_t is the national unemployment rate;
F measures the overall significance of the regression equation;
n is the number of observations (person-years of employment).

Source: SCELI Work Histories/Attitudes Survey.

of Northampton and Rochdale, there is some evidence of a decline in trade union membership associated with an increase in unemployment nationally. This is countered by the positive trend in trade union membership through time. There is no evidence of a relationship in these data between union membership and inflation, where inflation is defined as the annual rate of change of the retail price index. This is a surprising finding, given the importance of inflation in the time-series work on trade union membership. The specification of this model was varied, to examine for a link between changes in the national unemployment rate and trade union membership, but no such relationship was detected.

A dummy variable is also included in this model, to account for the changed political environment in which trade unions found themselves in the post-1979 period. This variable takes a value of unity for each year after and including 1979 in the work history information. The coefficients shown in Table 5.5 demonstrate that a 'post-1979' effect can only be detected in two localities, Aberdeen and Coventry, but that it is quite a substantial influence.

Table 5.6 shows the individual-characteristics specification of the model of trade union membership. This formulation shows a positive relationship between age and trade union membership, with the propensity to belong to a trade union increasing with age but at a decreasing rate. These results also indicate that, in any particular year, men are about 5 per cent more likely to belong to a union than women. This formulation does not, however, take any account of the characteristics of the jobs in which women work as opposed to those in which men work. The results also indicate a strong relationship between each individual's work history and his or her membership of a trade union in a particular year. Considerable care must be exercised though, in interpreting this result, because this formulation does not account for observed or unobserved heterogeneity, apart from distinguishing the gender of the respondent. Thus, factors that could influence the probability of a respondent becoming a trade union member will be reflected in terms of his or her prior history of trade union membership, which will, in turn, yield a correlation with their membership in a particular year. Hence, the observation that each year that a respondent has spent as a trade union member increases the probability of their membership in each successive year by 5 per cent does not necessarily imply that state dependence exists in trade union membership histories.

There is an inverse association between union membership and unemployment at some time during the same year, which relates to the observation of employment in each respondent's work history. If a respondent has recently experienced, or is about to experience, a spell of unemployment, the probability that they will belong to a trade union during the dominant employment event in that year is correspondingly reduced by between 6 and 9 per cent.

A negative relationship was found between the cumulative number of years each individual has been employed and their propensity to belong to a union. This effect is additional to the influence of age, which has a curvilinear effect on membership. In other words, the effect of ageing increases the probability of membership, but at a decreasing rate. In contrast, each year of employment reduces the average probability of membership by about 2 percentage points in each successive year. This is not particularly surprising, given that this model also includes the cumulative years as a trade union member. In the absence of other identifying characteristics, the variable measuring cumulative years of employment may simply be acting to discriminate between those persons who would never join a trade union and those who are 'prone' to membership.

Proximity influences are apparent from the analyses presented in Table 5.6. These influences are strong and relate to the locality in which the individual was observed in 1986. For each year in which the respondent was living in the locality, the probability that they belonged to a trade union is between 3 and 13 per cent higher.

The individual-characteristics specification of membership is a more powerful model of membership than the business-cycle specification represented in Table 5.5, yet it ignores information about the characteristics of jobs in which respondents work. By way of contrast, Table 5.7 shows the job-characteristics specification. Particularly strong influences on membership are attributable to industry sector, occupation, part-time working, self-employment, workplace size, and public sector employment. Further, these influences are in line with previous research findings in the UK and the USA (Bain and Elias, 1985; Scoville, 1971; Elsheikh and Bain, 1980; Antos *et al.*, 1980; Spilsbury *et al.*, 1987).

Three additional variables are included in this specification that have not hitherto been available in UK studies. These are 'promotion prospects', a respondent's evaluation of whether or

TABLE 5.6. *Pooled time-series–cross-section model of trade union membership: individual-characteristics specification*

	Aberdeen	Coventry	Kirkcaldy	Northampton	Rochdale	Swindon
Male	0.070*	0.060*	0.050*	0.032*	0.055*	0.050*
Age	0.017*	0.026*	0.017*	0.004*	0.026*	0.016*
$(\text{Age})^2 \times 10^{-2}$	-0.016*	-0.035*	-0.019*	—	-0.031*	-0.022*
Unemployed in previous year	-0.049	-0.024	-0.029	-0.055*	-0.031	-0.072
Unemployed at some time in current year	-0.094*	-0.084*	-0.080*	-0.087*	-0.062*	-0.074*
Cumulative years employed	-0.024*	-0.022*	-0.028*	-0.019*	-0.027*	-0.016*
Cumulative years as trade union member	0.049*	0.047*	0.047*	0.050*	0.049*	0.050*
Living in locality	0.079	0.136*	0.106	0.030*	0.046*	0.081*
F	1,442.2	1,296.7	1,222.7	1,118.1	1,300.4	1,411.8

Note: An asterisk denotes that the coefficient is statistically significant at the 1% level. For sample size and mean of dependent variable, see Table 5.5. *F* measures the overall significance of the regression equation.

Source: SCELI Work Histories/Attitudes Survey.

TABLE 5.7. *Pooled time-series–cross-section model of trade union membership: job-characteristics specification*

	Aberdeen	Coventry	Kirkcaldy	Northampton	Rochdale	Swindon
Mining, energy	0.075	0.241*	0.284*	0.056*	0.085*	0.057*
Manufacturing	0.308*	0.218*	0.329*	0.055*	0.074*	0.177*
Construction	0.178*	-0.194*	0.178*	-0.047*	-0.075*	-0.169*
Transport, communication	0.437*	0.237*	0.412*	0.316*	0.125*	0.253*
Services	0.146*	-0.022	0.112*	0.002	-0.041	-0.089*
Manual occupation	0.175*	0.198*	0.206*	0.110*	0.200*	0.129*
Nurse	0.142*	0.168*	0.202*	0.157*	0.120*	0.114*
Teacher	0.281*	0.326*	0.393*	0.387*	0.410*	0.394*
Part-time	-0.097*	-0.033*	-0.081*	-0.121*	-0.178*	-0.050*
Self-employed	0.008	-0.070*	-0.138*	-0.057*	-0.138*	-0.071*
2–24 employees	0.062*	0.018	0.049*	0.025*	0.085*	0.018
25–99 employees	0.166*	0.175*	0.195*	0.129*	0.168*	0.010*
100+ employees	0.226*	0.272*	0.223*	0.209*	0.270*	0.144*
Public sector	0.262*	0.218*	0.244*	0.235*	0.270*	0.257*
Promotion prospects	0.095*	0.064*	0.059*	0.079*	0.028*	0.051*
Closely supervised	0.013	-0.060*	0.006	0.062*	0.008	-0.043*
Inside mobility	0.041*	0.059*	0.059*	0.016*	0.001	0.052*
F	323.8	443.5	390.6	282.7	254.9	345.4

Note: An asterisk denotes that the coefficient is statistically significant at the 1% level. For sample size and mean of dependent variable, see Table 5.5. F measures the overall significance of the regression equation.

Source: SCELI Work Histories/Attitudes Survey.

not there were promotion prospects for people doing the same kind of work when they worked in a particular occupation for a particular employer. 'Closely supervised' indicates those jobs in the respondent's work history for which people doing the same kind of work were closely supervised. 'Inside mobility' indicates employment spells in which the respondent moved between jobs without changing his or her employer.

For the first variable in this group, the relationship between being in a job in which people doing the same kind of work were closely supervised, and trade union membership, is not particularly clear. Not all parameter estimates are statistically significant and the direction of influence appears unstable. This is not the case for promotion prospects and insider mobility, where the results indicate that respondents who were employed in jobs with promotion prospects, and/or actually demonstrated occupational change without changing their employer, were more likely to be union members. These findings are suggestive of the work of Carruth and Oswald (1987), who argue that trade union behaviour may represent a form of 'insider' power, restricting entry to union jobs in times of slack labour demand, thereby promoting internal mobility among union jobs within the employing organization. Given that, in 1989, 30 per cent of union members were engaged in some form of closed shop arrangement (Stevens *et al.*, 1989) the potential impact of the union on internal mobility is a distinct possibility. Alternatively, this revealed internal mobility and the availability of promotion can be viewed as an expression of labour market segmentation, with employees in the 'primary' segment of the workforce having access to internal labour mobility as well as the benefits of union membership.

Table 5.8 shows the effect of combining the business-cycle specification with the individual-characteristics model. As expected, the size of the trend effect identified in the pure business-cycle specification is reduced, as the influence of age picks up what was identified in Table 5.5 as a time-trend effect. The influence of national trends in unemployment is, however, unchanged even after including the personal experience of unemployment in each employment year of the individual's work history.

Finally, the combined influences of business-cycle variables, individual characteristics, and job characteristics are shown in Table 5.9. The business-cycle variables are little affected by the

TABLE 5.8. *Pooled time-series–cross-section model of trade union membership: simple business-cycle specification, with individual characteristics*

	Aberdeen	Coventry	Kirkcaldy	Northampton	Rochdale	Swindon
Trend	0.003*	0.006*	0.002*	0.003*	-0.001	0.002*
ΔP_t	—	—	—	0.003*	—	—
U_t	-0.012*	-0.020*	-0.013*	—	—	-0.012*
Post-1979 dummy	-0.041*	-0.043*	0.013	-0.007	0.004	-0.011
Male	0.072*	0.059*	0.049*	0.030*	0.056*	0.050*
Age	0.014*	0.019*	0.016*	-0.001	0.027*	0.014*
$(\text{Age})^2 \times 10^{-2}$	-0.009*	-0.022*	-0.016*	—	0.032*	0.016*
Unemployed in previous year	-0.032	-0.012	-0.018	-0.072*	-0.025	-0.054*
Unemployed at some time in current year	-0.072*	-0.066*	-0.068*	-0.107*	-0.056*	-0.056*
Cumulative years employed	-0.024*	-0.023*	0.029*	-0.018*	-0.027*	-0.017*
Cumulative years as trade union member	0.048*	0.047*	0.047*	0.049*	0.049*	0.050*
Living locality	0.095*	0.138*	0.117*	0.022*	0.051*	0.095*
F	987.1	907.0	826.1	759.4	867.9	962.7

Note: An asterisk denotes that the coefficient is statistically significant at the 1% level. For sample size and mean of dependent variable, see Table 5.5. F measures the overall significance of the regression equation.

Source: SCELI Work Histories/Attitudes Survey.

addition of information on job characteristics except for the scale of the 'post-1979' effects in Aberdeen and Coventry which, although remaining statistically significant, are reduced in size. The parameter estimates that do change significantly with the inclusion of job characteristics are those that display the effects of gender on membership and 'living in the locality'. The coefficient on the former variable reduces in size to a marginal 1–3 per cent effect in the combined model. In other words, the inclusion of variables that categorize the jobs in which men or women work serves to reduce gender *per se* as a significant factor influencing the probability that a respondent was a trade union member in each employment year of their work histories. The scale of this reduction, from a range of 3.2–7.0 per cent in Table 5.6 to 0–3.6 per cent in Table 5.9, raises the question of whether or not additional information about job characteristics would eliminate gender as a separate variable entirely. For the variable 'living in the locality', its positive effect on membership is narrowed from the range 3.0–13.6 per cent shown in Table 5.6 to the 4.6–12.0 per cent shown in Table 5.9. Thus, knowledge of the type of work undertaken by each respondent does not serve to eliminate the locality effects. The interpretation of these locality effects is not straightforward. They may indicate a true urban locality influence on trade union membership—a proximity effect of the type suggested by Shister (1953). Alternatively, it could simply serve to identify migrants into the locality as a particular group with a higher propensity to unionize when working in an urban locality. The latter hypothesis was explored further by adding a variable to the regressions describing ethnic origin. This variable was not significant.

Examination of the relative size of the parameter estimates shown in Table 5.9 gives some indication of the magnitude of the effects of particular variables on the changing pattern of membership. The most significant variables in this respect are public sector employment, working in workplaces with 100+ employees, part-time working and self-employment, working in a manual occupation, and the sectoral distribution of employment. Without exception, these are all job characteristics, indicating that the business-cycle model does not measure well against a model based upon the changing characteristics of jobs held by survey respondents throughout their working lives.

5. MODELLING THE DYNAMICS OF TRADE UNION MEMBERSHIP

The type of analyses presented in the previous section are termed 'pooled time-series–cross-section'. They are useful as a means of exploring the combined effect of time-series as opposed to cross-sectional influences, but limited in that they do not control for 'unobserved heterogeneity', differences between individuals in terms of their propensity to unionize, which are not captured via any of the variables used in the pooled time-series–cross-sectional analysis. Further, the estimation technique used, ordinary least squares, gives imprecise estimates of the coefficients. This section remedies these weaknesses by modelling the dynamics of trade union membership at the level of the individual. This is performed by reconstructing the individual histories of trade union membership so that they portray persons joining or leaving trade unions in each year of their work history rather than observing whether or not they belonged to a trade union in each employment year. The variables that are used to study variations in the probability of joining or leaving are also reconstructed to represent changes between states rather than the representation of being in a particular state used in the preceding section. This results in what is termed a 'fixed-effects' model, in which each survey respondent is deemed to have a unique individual-specific propensity to join or leave a trade union. Maximum likelihood estimation procedures are used to estimate the parameters of a series of logit models (log of the odds) of the probability of joining or leaving a trade union. Tables 5.10 and 5.11 show the estimated parameters of these models, together with the associated asymptotic t-statistics.

Examination of these parameter estimates reveals some interesting insights into the dynamics of union membership. First, relatively few variables are required to model the systematic variations in the probability of joining or leaving a union. In terms of joining a union, and in the absence of any other information about an individual, one would estimate the probability of an individual joining a trade union in any particular year of his or her work history equal to the mean of the dependent variable, i.e. 4–5 per cent. It will be demonstrated later that with additional information about whether or not this individual joined a particular industry sector in that year, joined a workplace of a particular size, or

TABLE 5.9. *Pooled time-series–cross-section model of trade union membership: the combined effects*

	Aberdeen	Coventry	Kirkcaldy	Northampton	Rochdale	Swindon
Trend	0.003*	0.007*	0.002*	0.003*	—	0.003*
ΔP_t	—	—	—	0.003*	—	—
U_t	-0.011*	-0.016*	-0.009*	-0.002	0.002	-0.010*
Post-1979 dummy	-0.033*	-0.032*	0.014	-0.022	0.006	—
Male	0.036*	-0.008	-0.030*	0.015*	0.031*	—
Age	0.010*	0.021*	0.019*	-0.003	0.028*	0.013*
$(\text{Age})^2 \times 10^{-2}$	-0.006*	-0.020*	-0.017*	—	-0.031*	-0.013*
Unemployed in previous year	-0.019	-0.008	-0.015	-0.056*	-0.038	-0.057*
Unemployed in current year	-0.047*	-0.049*	-0.052*	-0.072*	-0.063*	-0.043*
Cumulative years employed	-0.019*	-0.022*	-0.026*	-0.013*	-0.024*	-0.016*
Cumulative years as TU member	0.040*	0.036*	0.037*	0.041*	0.041*	0.041*
Living in the locality	0.119*	0.120*	0.089*	0.049*	0.046*	0.093*
Mining, energy	0.092	0.113*	0.162*	-0.043*	0.027	0.046*
Manufacturing	0.194*	0.093*	0.202*	0.019	0.059*	0.064*
Construction	0.079	-0.141*	0.112*	-0.066*	-0.049*	-0.144*
Transport, communication	0.249*	0.151*	0.293*	0.222*	0.060*	0.115*

Services	0.096	-0.048*	0.057*	-0.026	-0.020	-0.078*
Manual occupation	0.091*	0.127*	0.124*	0.056*	0.118*	0.092
Nurse	0.114*	0.146*	0.185*	0.126*	0.087*	0.142*
Teacher	0.151*	0.177*	0.203*	0.235*	0.183*	0.173*
Part-time	-0.072*	-0.083*	-0.116*	-0.085*	-0.112*	-0.065*
Self-employed	0.040*	-0.073*	-0.097*	-0.059*	-0.132*	-0.052*
2–24 employees	0.036*	-0.010	0.072*	-0.002	0.041*	0.034*
25–99 employees	0.075*	0.087*	0.183*	0.065*	0.087*	0.083*
100+ employees	0.124*	0.182*	0.199*	0.128*	0.157*	0.114*
Public sector	0.187*	0.158*	0.151*	0.180*	0.177*	0.150*
Promotion prospects	0.066*	0.035*	0.047*	0.041*	0.024*	0.053*
Closely supervised	0.011	-0.004	0.016	0.052*	-0.010	-0.022*
Inside mobility	—	0.013*	0.032*	—	-0.004	0.020*
F	553.9	598.8	472.8	473.4	479.4	557.1

Note: An asterisk denotes that the coefficient is statistically significant at the 1% level. For sample size and mean of dependent variable, see Table 5.5. *F* measures the overall significance of the regression equation.

Source: SCELI Work Histories/Attitudes Survey.

TABLE 5.10. Probability of joining a trade union: OLS equivalents of maximum likelihood estimates of logit model

	Aberdeen		Coventry		Kirkcaldy	
	coefficient	(t-stat)	coefficient	(t-stat)	coefficient	(t-stat)
Cumulative years of employment	−0.0007	(−2.5)	−0.0011	(−3.8)	−0.0012	(−3.6)
Unemployed at some time during year	0.0168	(1.9)	0.0139	(1.5)	−0.0053	(−0.5)
Entered locality	0.0110	(2.2)	0.0012	(0.2)	0.0192	(3.2)
Joined public sector	0.0589	(11.1)	0.0701	(11.2)	0.0831	(12.6)
Joined part-time job	0.0237	(2.8)	0.0032	(0.3)	0.0029	(0.2)
Joined self-employment	0.0214	(1.0)	0.0173	(0.8)	0.0237	(0.8)
Joined job with promotion prospects	0.0311	(6.8)	0.0210	(3.8)	0.0326	(5.9)
Joined closely supervised job	0.0088	(1.6)	0.0056	(0.9)	−0.0033	(−0.5)
Began spell of employment with 'inside' mobility	0.0125	(2.2)	0.0179	(2.7)	0.0276	(3.9)
Joined workplace with 2–24 employees	0.0332	(5.1)	0.0294	(3.6)	0.0391	(4.7)
Joined workplace with 25–99 employees	0.0557	(8.7)	0.0686	(8.9)	0.0754	(9.9)
Joined workplace with 100+ employees	0.0674	(11.3)	0.0985	(15.0)	0.0744	(10.5)
Began manual job	0.0298	(5.7)	0.0421	(7.2)	0.0395	(6.4)
Began teaching job	0.0773	(6.9)	0.0648	(3.4)	0.1369	(6.5)

	Northampton		Rochdale		Swindon	
	coefficient	(t-stat)	coefficient	(t-stat)	coefficient	(t-stat)
Began nursing job	0.0319	(2.6)	-0.0037	(-0.2)	0.0787	(5.1)
Began job in mining and energy	0.0228	(2.7)	0.0856	(6.7)	0.0765	(7.6)
Began job in manufacturing	0.0580	(8.2)	0.0663	(9.6)	0.0936	(12.6)
Began job in construction	0.0544	(6.0)	-0.0052	(-0.3)	0.0587	(4.5)
Began job in transport and communication	0.0783	(9.4)	0.0632	(4.2)	0.0920	(7.4)
Began job in services sector	0.0158	(2.5)	0.0088	(1.1)	0.0074	(0.9)
Constant*	-4.387	(-38.0)	-4.011	(-38.3)	-4.138	(-38.3)
Log likelihood ratio	2,173.8		2,495.1		2,925.2	
Mean of dependent variable	0.042		0.050		0.054	
Cumulative years of employment	-0.0002	(-0.6)	-0.0006	(-2.2)	0.0001	(0.2)
Unemployed at some time during year	-0.0088	(-0.9)	0.0083	(0.9)	0.0165	(1.9)
Entered locality	0.0122	(2.4)	0.0141	(2.5)	0.0196	(4.1)
Joined public sector	0.0577	(10.4)	0.0635	(9.2)	0.0578	(11.3)
Joined part-time job	0.0025	(0.3)	0.0032	(0.3)	0.0037	(0.4)
Joined self-employment	-0.0100	(-0.4)	0.0010	(0.0)	-0.0126	(-0.6)
Joined job with promotion prospects	0.0227	(4.9)	0.0301	(5.7)	0.0267	(5.9)
Joined closely supervised job	0.0085	(1.6)	0.0088	(1.5)	-0.0085	(-1.5)

(cont./)

TABLE 5.10 (cont.):

	Northampton		Rochdale		Swindon	
	coefficient	(t-stat)	coefficient	(t-stat)	coefficient	(t-stat)
Began spell of employment with 'inside' mobility	0.0314	(5.8)	0.0171	(2.7)	0.0189	(3.6)
Joined workplace with 2–24 employees	0.0330	(4.7)	0.0516	(6.8)	−0.0029	(−0.4)
Joined workplace with 25–99 employees	0.0658	(10.3)	0.0864	(21.4)	0.0292	(4.6)
Joined workplace with 100+ employees	0.0820	(14.3)	0.1023	(15.9)	0.0356	(6.3)
Began manual job	0.0219	(4.1)	0.0460	(8.0)	0.0281	(5.7)
Began teaching job	0.1162	(8.8)	0.0831	(4.5)	0.0767	(5.5)
Began nursing job	0.0258	(2.1)	0.0017	(0.1)	0.0241	(1.9)
Began job in mining and energy	0.0514	(4.9)	0.0603	(4.2)	0.0701	(6.7)
Began job in manufacturing	0.0513	(8.2)	0.0465	(6.7)	0.0810	(14.3)
Began job in construction	0.0232	(2.1)	0.0369	(2.8)	0.0180	(1.4)
Began job in transport and communication	0.0794	(7.9)	0.0500	(3.2)	0.0832	(9.1)
Began job in services sector	0.0051	(0.8)	0.0109	(1.5)	0.0212	(3.4)
Constant*	−4.519	(−38.4)	−4.228	(−38.5)	−4.563	(−38.1)
Log likelihood ratio	2,149.6		2,380.2		1,893.5	
Mean of dependent variable	0.042		0.050		0.038	

* Logit estimate of constant term.

Note: 'OLS equivalent' parameter estimates have been computed at the mean of the dependent variable.

Source: SCELI Work Histories/Attitudes Survey.

joined a workplace in a public sector job, this probability can be set at its limits, 0 or 1, with a 70 per cent chance or more of being correct. In terms of leaving a union, the fit is even higher, with a 90 per cent or greater chance of correctly predicting when a survey respondent relinquishes membership.

In general, factors that influence the probability of joining a trade union also affect the probability of leaving, but not in a symmetrical fashion. The asymmetry could arise through a variety of processes: 'inertia'—once an individual has joined a union there is a tendency to remain a member even if the original incentive for joining is removed, or some other form of 'state dependence', for example, if individuals experience benefits from membership which are only perceived through membership itself. Examples of this asymmetry can be seen by examining the estimated coefficients on the variables that indicate the size of the workforce at the establishment the individual joined or left. From Table 5.10 it can be seen that joining a workplace with 2–24 employees, 25–99 employees, and 100+ employees increases the probability of joining a union by approximately 3, 7, or 9 per cent respectively. If a person stopped working at establishments with these sizes of workforce, the probability of leaving a union would increase by 2, 3, or 4 per cent. In other words, leaving different sizes of establishments has only about half of the effect on the probability of leaving trade union membership as joining different sizes of establishment has on the probability of joining a trade union. The same is true of public sector jobs. These act in much the same way and with an effect similar in magnitude to joining or leaving a workplace with 100 or more employees.

It is of interest to note that knowledge of whether a person joined or left part-time employment, or a spell of self-employment, does not generally have any significant impact upon the probability of that person joining or leaving a trade union. At first sight, this appears to be somewhat surprising, especially given that spells of part-time employment and self-employment are generally associated with reduced levels of union membership, as was shown in Table 5.9. This finding demonstrates the advantage of recasting the analysis into a dynamic framework. The negative association between part-time employment, self-employment, and trade union membership evidenced in Tables 5.7 and 5.9 probably results from sample heterogeneity. In other words,

TABLE 5.11. *Probability of leaving a trade union: OLS equivalents of maximum likelihood estimates of logit model*

	Aberdeen		Coventry		Kirkcaldy	
	coefficient	(t-stat)	coefficient	(t-stat)	coefficient	(t-stat)
Cumulative years as a trade union member	0.0009	(6.5)	0.0010	(6.2)	0.0008	(4.3)
Unemployed at some time during year	-0.0010	(-0.2)	0.0110	(2.1)	0.0256	(5.2)
Left locality	0.0238	(4.0)	0.0172	(2.1)	0.0323	(4.5)
Left public sector	0.0313	(7.9)	0.0270	(6.3)	0.0295	(6.3)
Left part-time job	-0.0008	(-0.1)	0.0014	(0.1)	0.0052	(0.5)
Left self-employment	0.0159	(1.0)	0.0052	(0.3)	-0.3813	(0.0)
Left job with promotion prospects	0.0185	(5.7)	0.0211	(5.9)	0.0285	(7.8)
Left closely supervised job	0.0148	(3.9)	0.0086	(2.0)	0.0047	(1.0)
Left spell of employment with 'inside' mobility	0.0081	(1.6)	0.0155	(3.0)	0.0215	(4.2)
Left workplace with 2–24 employees	0.0180	(4.0)	0.0258	(4.9)	0.0284	(5.2)
Left workplace with 25–99 employees	0.0350	(9.0)	0.0421	(9.1)	0.0434	(9.4)
Left workplace with 100+ employees	0.0425	(11.9)	0.0527	(14.3)	0.0473	(11.7)
Left manual occupation	0.0253	(6.5)	0.0249	(6.2)	0.0303	(7.0)
Left teaching job	0.0302	(2.7)	0.0633	(3.2)	0.0645	(3.4)

	Northampton		Rochdale		Swindon	
	coefficient	(t-stat)	coefficient	(t-stat)	coefficient	(t-stat)
Left nursing job	0.0161	(1.5)	-0.0064	(-0.3)	0.0563	(5.2)
Left job in mining and energy	0.0163	(2.7)	0.0493	(5.9)	0.0271	(4.5)
Left job in manufacturing	0.0237	(5.4)	0.0415	(11.4)	0.0434	(10.4)
Left job in construction	0.0283	(4.8)	-0.0051	(-0.3)	0.0179	(1.9)
Left job in transport and communication	0.0373	(6.4)	0.0211	(2.2)	0.0428	(5.8)
Left job in services sector	0.0050	(1.0)	0.0046	(0.8)	-0.0086	(-1.3)
Constant*	-5.235	(-47.9)	-5.377	(-44.3)	-5.172	(-45.6)
Log likelihood ratio	968.3		1,280.0		1,331.7	
Mean of dependent variable	0.020		0.022		0.025	

	Northampton		Rochdale		Swindon	
	coefficient	(t-stat)	coefficient	(t-stat)	coefficient	(t-stat)
Cumulative years as a trade union member	0.0018	(11.1)	0.0008	(5.6)	-0.0013	(8.8)
Unemployed at some time during year	0.0224	(4.4)	0.0157	(2.9)	0.0247	(5.4)
Left locality	0.0381	(4.8)	0.0156	(1.7)	0.0121	(1.2)
Left public sector employment	0.0333	(8.0)	0.0334	(6.9)	0.0318	(8.3)
Left part-time job	-0.0099	(-0.9)	0.0092	(1.2)	-0.0005	(0.0)
Left self-employment	-0.3365	(0.0)	-0.3809	(0.0)	-0.0073	(-0.3)
Left job with promotion prospects	0.0243	(7.2)	0.0203	(5.6)	0.0199	(6.0)
Left closely supervised job	0.0161	(4.1)	0.0135	(3.2)	0.0106	(2.5)

(cont.)

TABLE 5.11 (*cont.*):

	Northampton		Rochdale		Swindon	
	coefficient	(*t*-stat)	coefficient	(*t*-stat)	coefficient	(*t*-stat)
Left spell of employment with 'inside' mobility	0.0142	(2.6)	0.0086	(1.5)	0.0113	(2.3)
Left workplace with 2–24 employees	0.0142	(2.6)	0.0300	(6.6)	0.0207	(4.5)
Left workplace with 25–99 employees	0.0388	(9.1)	0.0336	(7.6)	0.0237	(5.5)
Left workplace with 100+ employees	0.0449	(12.0)	0.0366	(9.5)	0.0330	(9.3)
Left manual occupation	0.0242	(5.5)	0.0289	(7.6)	0.0216	(5.5)
Left teaching job	0.0440	(3.1)	-0.3927	(0.0)	0.0297	(2.3)
Left nursing job	0.0084	(0.8)	-0.0275	(-1.5)	-0.0067	(-0.5)
Left job in mining and energy	0.0443	(6.6)	0.0392	(4.2)	0.0447	(6.8)
Left job in manufacturing	0.0357	(8.8)	0.0387	(10.3)	0.0433	(12.0)
Left job in construction	0.0270	(3.0)	0.0174	(1.8)	0.0168	(1.9)
Left job in transport and communication	0.0469	(6.8)	0.0319	(3.4)	0.0393	(6.4)
Left job in services sector	0.0103	(2.0)	0.0132	(2.5)	0.0013	(0.2)
Constant*	-5.404	(-48.2)	-5.050	(-48.0)	-5.397	(-46.7)
Log likelihood ratio	1,244.8		2,954.3		1,037.8	
Mean of dependent variable	0.023		0.023		0.020	

* Logit estimate of constant term.

Note: 'OLS equivalent' parameter estimates have been computed at the mean of the dependent variable.

Source: SCELI Work Histories/Attitudes Survey.

people who are likely to become part-time workers or self-employed are much less likely to be union members, rather than it being the state of part-time working or self-employment in itself that gives rise to a reduction in membership.

The influence of joining or leaving jobs which were closely supervised is not particularly significant in terms of the dynamics of union membership. However, the influence of promotion prospects and internal mobility is again demonstrated in Tables 5.10 and 5.11. Once again, the issue of causality is problematical. Do unions create better job prospects for their members or do jobs with promotion prospects go hand in hand with union recognition in certain segments of the labour market? The results do not distinguish these possibilities but demonstrate an interesting link.

The influence of sectoral mobility on membership also remains strong in this model of the dynamics of membership. Particularly important in this respect are the manufacturing, and transport and communication sectors. Given the prevalence of closed shop agreements in many parts of the latter sector, these effects are hardly surprising.

Proximity influences remain in this dynamic formulation, suggesting that this effect is in fact due to geographical closeness rather than to heterogeneity associated with migration. The effect is relatively small, however, and in the case of Coventry, almost entirely disappears. The personal experience of unemployment (being unemployed at some time in the same year as the respondent had a spell of employment as his or her 'dominant' event) has a significant effect upon the probability of leaving a trade union. With the exception of Aberdeen, the effect is positive and well defined.

Each additional year as a trade union member increases the probability of leaving. This effect, though small, may relate to the observed curvilinear influence of age evidenced in Table 5.9.

A range of different variables were added to the basic formulation shown in Tables 5.10 and 5.11, but none was found to be significant in any locality. These included the rate of inflation, the rate of change of inflation, the rate of change of unemployment, and a set of variables indicating changes in the respondent's family situation (becoming married, separated, divorced, having children). The absence of any influence of these variables on the probability of joining or leaving a trade union reinforces the earlier findings, from the pooled time-series–cross-sectional analysis, that gender and marital status differences in union membership serve only to discriminate between the jobs held by men and women, single or married people, and women with and women without children, and are not related directly to the process of joining or leaving a trade union.

It is not easy to gain a clear indication of the relative influences of these changes on the dynamics of membership. Tables 5.10 and 5.11 display the estimated coefficients from a logit model as 'OLS-equivalent' parameters. This is achieved by evaluating the likelihood function at the mean value of the dependent variable. As Amemiya (1981) indicates, with a mean value for the dependent variable in the range of 0.3–0.7, logit parameters are equivalent to, but approximately four times greater than, the parameters of a linear model. In this case, however, the mean values of the dependent variables lie between 0.02 and 0.05. The averaging of individual coefficients shown in Tables 5.10 and 5.11 is less appropriate in such a situation.

An alternative approach is to specify some fairly typical transitions that an individual may make and, using the original logit parameters upon which Tables 5.10 and 5.11 are based, to estimate the effect these transitions have on the probability of such an individual joining or leaving a trade union. This has been performed for a typical individual with ten years of employment experience as a non-union member for the estimates of the probability of joining, and for ten years of employment experience as a union member for the probability of leaving.

Table 5.12 examines the impact of certain changes on the probability of this typical individual joining a union. These changes have been computed for two localities: Coventry, with its higher than average rate of union membership, and Swindon, which displayed the lowest rate of union membership of all the localities studied. To interpret this table, it is useful to consider the binary process that is being modelled and the rather abstract statistical process that has been postulated for estimation purposes. The logit model of joining (or leaving) a trade union gives rise to an estimated probability that, given certain transitions taking place in each year of the employment history of the individual, the individual will join (leave) a trade union. If a person crosses some threshold probability, say 50 per cent, it can be predicted that this person will join (leave) a union. The closer this predicted probability is to zero or unity, the greater is the chance that the prediction will be observed as an actual outcome.

The transitions that any individual makes tend to be combined in various ways. Table 5.12 shows three possible combinations of changes. In the first example, shown in the top row, the typical individual moves from a non-manual job in a medium-sized service sector establishment to a manual job in a large manufac-

TABLE 5.12. *Predicted probabilities of joining a trade union, given certain transitions in any particular year*

Combination of changes taking place in a particular year	Expected probability of joining a trade union	
	Coventry	Swindon
Non-member with 10 years' experience of employment in non-manual occupation in service sector workplace with 25–99 employees		
Changed from non-manual to manual work / Joined manufacturing from non-manufacturing / Started job with promotion prospects, previous job had no promotion prospects / Started job in which will demonstrate internal mobility / Joined workplace with 100+ employees, previous workplace was smaller	0.66	0.72
Changed from non-manual to manual work / Joined manufacturing from non-manufacturing / Joined workplace with 100+ employees, previous workplace was smaller	0.36	0.53
Changed from non-manual to manual work / Joined manufacturing from non-manufacturing	0.17	0.12

turing sector establishment. People who are working in similar jobs to this new job have got promotion prospects and the individual will demonstrate internal mobility in this new job. For this change, it is predicted that the individual will join a union. Approximately seven times out of ten this prediction will be correct. However, if the change only involved a move to a non-manual job in the manufacturing sector, with no accompanying move to a larger workplace and no change in promotion prospects (perceived or demonstrated), it is predicted that the individual would not join a union. In eight or nine times out of ten this would be a correct prediction.

From Table 5.13 it can be seen that, for the probability of leaving, the predictions are made with an even greater degree of certainty for these hypothetical changes. If the typical individual has been an employed trade union member for ten years, working in a manual job in a large establishment in the manufacturing sector, then experiences a change to a non-manual job in a smaller workplace in the non-manufacturing sector, and if this change is accompanied by a loss of promotional prospects (perceived and demonstrated), the model would predict a termination of membership. In nine times out of ten this prediction would be correct. Note, however, that a change of occupation and sector without accompanying changes in establishment size and promotional prospects do not lead to a predicted termination of membership.

Further simulations have shown that any combination of three or more of the significant influences shown in Tables 5.10 and 5.11 will produce a prediction of joining or leaving with a high probability of success. For example, movement into and out of large employment establishments in the public sector, coupled with a major occupational change, will almost certainly be associated with a change in membership.

In summary, the information that is most important in yielding this high degree of fit is as follows. Workplace size, expressed in terms of the number of employees at the workplace an individual joins or leaves in a particular year, is clearly a dominant factor. Following close on this variable is the public sector categorization of employment, the industry sector information, and the crude categorization of occupational change. Additionally, access to an internal labour market is clearly associated with trade union membership.

TABLE 5.13. *Predicted probabilities of leaving a trade union, given certain transitions in any particular year*

Combination of changes taking place in a particular year	Expected probability of leaving a trade union	
	Coventry	Swindon
Trade union member for previous 10 years employed in manual occupation in manufacturing sector workplace with over 100 employees:		
Changed from manual to non-manual work Left manufacturing for non-manufacturing Left job with promotion prospects, new job has no promotion prospects Left job in which demonstrated internal mobility Left workplace with 100+ employees, new workplace is smaller	0.86	0.9[1]
Changed from manual to non-manual work Left manufacturing for non-manufacturing Left workplace with 100+ employees, new workplace is smaller	0.56	0.65
Changed from manual to non-manual work Left manufacturing for non-manufacturing	0.19	0.14

6. SECULAR VERSUS STRUCTURAL INFLUENCES ON TRADE UNION MEMBERSHIP

Time-series analysis of trends in union membership has an intrinsic elegance. With one or two macro-economic factors it is

possible to track the course of periods of growth and decline in
union membership over the last 100 years, in much the same way
that Phillips (1958) produced a simple model of the relationships
between the rate of change of money wages and unemployment.
Time-series analyses of union membership trends have produced
few surprises over the last twenty years, merely reinforcing the
popular and widely held view that inflation, and to a lesser extent
changes in unemployment, can chart the upturns and downturns in
trade union membership. But the statistical work associated with
the estimation of these aggregate series has changed dramatically.
Using techniques popularized by Hendry and Mizon (1978) and
Davidson *et al.* (1978), recent work on the so-called 'dynamics' of
union growth has not sought to address the processes of joining or
leaving trade unions but has concentrated on an elaborate curve-
fitting exercise which has little to do with the central issue—is
inflation the principal factor underlying trends in union membership, or does it act as a proxy for a more fundamental process?

On the evidence presented here, it must be concluded that the
case in favour of inflation as a principal causal factor begins to
look a little shaky. Obviously, there are weaknesses in the current
study, notably the fact that the data are derived from residents in
six localities, not from a nationally representative sample. But
this is not a critical weakness. The localities concerned cover a
mix of area types—traditional manufacturing, new high-technol-
ogy, high unemployment, recent employment growth, oil boom-
town, etc.—yet the results presented in this study show a
remarkable consistency across the areas. Like the time-series
models, refinement of the analysis of these longitudinal data has
produced a model of the dynamics of union membership which is
parsimonious in terms of the variables it embodies. A few factors, particularly knowledge of whether or not a person worked
in the public or private sector, the size of the establishment that
they joined or left at any point in their working life, the broad
industry sector in which they worked, knowledge of whether the
type of work was manual or white-collar, and access to internal
labour markets—these are sufficient to predict with a high degree
of certainty whether or not a person joined or left a trade union
in each of the 100,000 years of individual employment histories
that have been examined in detail in this study. The model
involves no elaborate curve-fitting involving multiple-lagged

variables. Despite this simplicity, there is no room for a variable describing inflation in this longitudinal analysis.

This important result cannot be deemed symptomatic of the difference between time-series and cross-sectional analysis. Time-series and cross-sectional analysts have often found different relationships in their data, often disregarded given the impossibility of replicating dynamic effects within a cross-section. But the advent of these detailed work histories, and on a scale large enough to create a virtual time-series of data, does not attract such ambivalence. One possible explanation is that inflation acts as a proxy for the structural influences on membership that are evidenced in this paper. But, if it acts as a proxy, how has it remained a good proxy over such a long period of time? As yet, this question is unanswered. The work history information used in this study covers the previous twenty years on average, whereas the secular trends in trade union membership have been studied over a period of almost 100 years. Hopefully, the availability of national longitudinal information on trade union membership will help to resolve this issue.

ACKNOWLEDGEMENTS

This chapter has benefited from many helpful comments and criticisms made on earlier drafts. In particular, I wish to thank David 'Danny' Blanchflower, Angela Dale, Duncan Gallie, Brian Main, David Oldman, Roger Penn, John Purcell, and Peter Sloane. Special thanks go to Christine Jones for her invaluable help with the complex computing and statistical estimation used in this study. Finally, I wish to acknowledge the initial help and encouragement given to me by George Bain.

6

The Union Relative Wage Gap

BRIAN G. M. MAIN

1. INTRODUCTION

The ability of a trade union to influence the wages of its members has long been a subject of interest to social scientists. Initially the focus was on whether or not a trade union could exert any appreciable influence at all, but gradually with the development of theory and the accumulation of empirical evidence, attention switched to a discussion of what is sometimes called the trade union mark-up on wages.[1] The empirical magnitude of this effect has an important bearing on certain explanations of Britain's current high level of unemployment and on recent government policy towards trade unions. This chapter utilizes data from the Social Change and Economic Life Initiative to produce estimates for 1986 of the union–non-union wage gap in Britain.

Early commentators were handicapped by inadequate theoretical models of wage determination, such as the wages fund, and saw little prospect of unions securing any long-term gains for their members.[2] This pessimistic outlook was enforced by the social and political considerations of the day, which gave much power to the employers and little to the workers or their combinations. In the words of Adam Smith (1976: 74–5):

The masters, being fewer in number, can combine much more easily; and the law, besides, authorises, or at least does not prohibit their combinations, while it prohibits those of workmen.

Many workmen could not subsist a week, few could subsist a month, and scarce any a year without employment. In the long-run the workman may be as necessary to his master as his master is to him, but the necessity is not so immediate.

The Combinations Law Repeal Act of 1824 marked the beginning of a slow change in the balance of industrial power. And, during the late nineteenth century, the emergence of the marginalist revolution in economic thought permitted Marshall (1920) to produce the first modern analysis of the effects of trade unions in his Laws of Derived Demand. Marshall's discussion in terms of demand and supply elasticities of the employment effects of any union-induced wage premium retains much of its validity and relevance to this day. In 1932 Hicks (1963) went on to provide a full integration of the trade union into the neoclassical analysis of wages, but it was the work of Dunlop (1944a) and Ross (1948) that provided the stepping-off point for much of the subsequent empirical analysis of trade unions. Both Dunlop and Ross placed the trade union at the centre of their analyses, with Ross laying emphasis on the social and political forces that circumscribe the actions of trade union leaders and Dunlop projecting the union as a rational economic entity. But as Dunlop[3] was later to claim, 'The critical question is how much difference do unions make?'

If the impact of monopoly power on product prices is empirically modest then there will be little concern over the inefficient allocation of resources in the product market. So too in the factor markets will a modest distortion of wages cause little concern over trade union power. But a very large union–non-union wage gap suggests that from society's point of view, welfare could be improved by a transfer of labour from the non-union into the union sector. As will be discussed in the following section, there are substantial difficulties in providing an unbiased measure of the union–non-union wage gap. Not least among these difficulties is that the very existence of a wage premium may attract workers of superior quality into union jobs. Any failure to measure such quality differences would lead to an exaggeration of the union–non-union wage gap. Other difficulties exist in the treatment of fringe benefits, stability of employment, hours of employment (rationing), and the union membership–collective bargaining coverage issue.

Section 2 of the chapter describes how it is possible to address some of these issues by using data from SCELI. Results are presented in Section 3 and a policy discussion and general conclusions follow in Section 4. Throughout the chapter the emphasis is placed on measuring the extent to which union wages can be claimed to be higher than the non-union wages of similar individuals. It is not possible within the scope of this chapter to examine the productivity enhancing consequences that have been claimed for trade union organization by Freeman and Medoff (1984). These consequences flow from lower turnover and from increased worker satisfaction and co-operation that come through union-operated grievance procedures and union-influenced pay scales and promotion mechanisms.[4] It will be important to bear such effects in mind when interpreting the results produced below.

In the terms of Freeman and Medoff, unions have two faces—the monopoly face associated with the power to raise wages, and the collective voice–institutional response face associated with the efficient internal human resource management of any enterprise. This chapter looks only at the monopoly power face.

2. MEASUREMENT ISSUES AND DATA SPECIFICATION

2.1. Measurement

There are several measurement issues that must be confronted before any progress can be made towards estimating the union–non-union wage gap. The first concerns what is meant by union–non-union. There is a clear distinction that must be drawn between union membership and union coverage. In 1986 around half of all employees in employment in Britain were trade union members, but a higher proportion (around 70 per cent for full-time workers) enjoyed wages that were subject to collective bargaining agreements.[5] In this sense some individuals who were not members of trade unions enjoyed the free-rider benefit of having their wages negotiated by a trade union and may, therefore, have benefited from any trade union monopoly power. As Hirsch and Addison (1986) make clear, the extension of the measure of union influence to coverage need not lead to an increase in the estimated union–non-union wage gap. This is due to the fact that covered non-members are unlikely to add to a union's bargaining power. In addition, the coverage descriptor is thought to be more prone to measurement error.

While much of the previous work in this area, which is discussed below, has concentrated on membership, it will be possible in this study to investigate coverage effects also. A related issue is the question of bargaining level. Single employer versus multiple employer and firm-level versus plant-level bargains have been found to produce different levels of mark-up, but these details will not be addressed here.

The next measurement problem that must be confronted concerns the choice of outcome variable. In measuring the economic impact of trade unions on their members, is it best to focus on basic hourly wage rates, average hourly earnings, annual earnings, or earnings including fringe benefits and all forms of deferred compensation? It may well be that the price of labour is most directly measured in the basic hourly wage rate. But agreements concerning overtime rates and overtime working would be better captured in average hourly earnings. In a similar vein, any impact of trade union activity on restricted hours, lay-off, or unemployment might be better captured in annual earnings. Finally, it is well known that trade unions take a keen interest in fringe benefits such as sick pay, holidays, pension plans, etc. and a truly comprehensive measure of union power would incorporate all such elements. Due to data limitations, this chapter will focus on the basic hourly wage rate, but the results will be checked against those obtained using average hourly earnings.[6]

As has already been mentioned in note 1, all that can be measured in a study of this nature is the size of the gap between union and non-union wages rather than the actual mark-up of union wages over the competitive level. This is illustrated in Figure 6.1 where W_o is the wage that would prevail for the standard worker in the absence of unions. The use of union power in the union-jobs market forces wages above this level to W_u, so displacing workers from jobs. If these workers do not leave the labour market but all find jobs in the non-union market, the net effect is to depress non-union wages to W_n. The observed wage gap, $W_n - W_u$, therefore exaggerates the mark-up of wages above the competitive level.

In addition to the spillover effect of higher labour supply depressing wages in the non-union sector, there is also the threat effect whereby some non-union firms raise their wages to deter union entry. There are also effects working through the demand

Brian G. M. Main

side, as demand shifts away from the relatively high-cost union sector to the non-union sector thereby raising wages in the non-union sector. The general equilibrium modelling that would be necessary to embrace all of these effects is beyond the scope of this chapter.

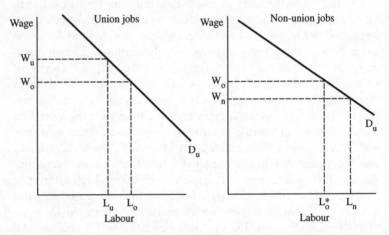

Fɪɢ. 6.1. The union mark-up and the union–non-union wage gap

Finally, there is the choice of average employee characteristics with which to make any comparison between union and non-union wages. One could ask two distinct questions. What would the average union member be paid if treated as a non-union member (the move from W_u to W_1 in Figure 6.2)? Or, what would the average non-union member be paid if treated as a union member (the move from W_n to W_2 in Figure 6.2)? There is clearly a potential for ambiguity present in this index number problem. The approach adopted below is to measure the wage gap at the average characteristics of all workers of that type (i.e. manual, non-manual, full-time, and part-time). This base seems to be consistent with the general econometric approach of removing selectivity bias. Results are also offered, however, measured at the average characteristics of trade union members. This second measure suggests the wage gap currently enjoyed by those holding union jobs.

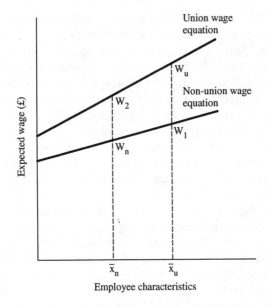

Fɪɢ. 6.2. Decomposition of union and non-union wages

2.2. Estimation

The availability of large microdata surveys of individuals and their earnings has permitted a great deal of work to be conducted in this area. The simplest approach involves regressing some measure of wages on a large range of descriptors of each individual's labour market characteristics including union status. The coefficient on union status then offers a crude measure of the union–non-union wage gap. Such an approach, however, forces the rewards to education, employment experience, etc. to be the same in the union and non-union sectors. This is clearly improbable. Nor does the use of separate wage equations, one for the union sector and one for the non-union sector, entirely remedy matters.

Union status, unlike gender or race, is not exogenous. If union jobs are indeed high-paying, then they can be expected to attract high productivity individuals. Given that no survey can ever hope to capture every productive characteristic of the respondents, there is then the real possibility that unmeasured productivity characteristics will be proxied by trade union status. Even with separate wage equations, estimation difficulties arise in the sense that the stochastic error terms in each equation are unlikely to have means of zero if the generally more productive workers end up in the union sector and the generally less productive workers end up in the non-union sector. One way around these estimation difficulties has been devised by Lee (1978). Lee's approach involves modelling the union membership phenomenon in an explicit manner, and then using these estimates to purge the respective wage equations of possible bias. The method has much in common with that of Heckman (1979) in dealing with selectivity bias.

The best-known examples of the use of microdata surveys to estimate the union–non-union wage gap in Britain are to be found in Stewart (1983), Shah (1984), and Green (1988). These authors found an average union–non-union wage differential of 7.7 per cent, 10 per cent, and 4–12 per cent respectively. Blanchflower (1984) utilized establishment data to produce estimates that were consistent with these magnitudes. Such estimates are much lower than the 20–30 per cent that had previously been produced on the basis of aggregate data (e.g. Mulvey (1976) and other work surveyed in Parsley (1980)).

2.3. Data Specification

The SCELI data set offers not just information on the labour market characteristics and wages of some 6,000 individuals,[8] but also extremely detailed information which covers not only the current employment situation but also provides a detailed life and work history. It is clear from the work of Stewart (1983) and others that the greater the detail available the less the chance of trade union status being incorrectly credited for wage effects that are in fact due to innate productive characteristics. The most obvious weakness of the data for the current purpose is that they do not represent a national sample but come from six distinct geographic areas.

The basic structure of the wage equations estimated below follows the human capital prescriptions of Mincer (1974) but with detail added to accommodate the institutional features of the labour market. In this sense current marital status (CMAR) is included. So too are details of education in the form of the number of years of post-compulsory education (EDUC).

In terms of labour market experience, the number of years of employment (EMP) and the number of years of non-employment (UNEMP), (covering both unemployment and out of the labour force for males but separated for females) are calculated on the basis of each individual's work history.[9] These are entered in both linear and quadratic form as suggested by Mincer and Polachek (1974).

A particular virtue of the data is the wealth of detail available on the current job. This includes whether the job has supervisory responsibility (SUP); whether it is in the public sector (PUBLIC); whether any training is required to do the job (CURTRAIN); whether the job is done exclusively or mainly by men (EXCMALE); if the job took at least six months to learn (TDUR); the size of the establishment (SIZE);[10] and whether the job was permanent (PERM) (as opposed to temporary or fixed term).

The data also allowed the attitude of unions of the father (FATHUN), and the current partner (PARTUN), to be described. Self-classification as working class (WCLASS), and Conservative voting intention (CONSERV), were also available. Conflict in employer–employee relationships at work (CON-FLICT), and the employer's attitude to unions[11] (EMPUN), were also utilized. A working partner (PARTEMP), and the age structure of children (PRESCH), (PRIMSCH), and (SECSCH) complete this class of descriptors.

It was also possible to identify in some detail the occupational and industrial classification of each job. For the purposes of this study, an eight-way occupational categorization and a ten-way industrial categorization were employed. In the wage regressions the dummy variables are 'unskilled manual' and 'other services'. In an attempt to control for the particular geographic distribution of the sample, dummy variables are utilized for residence in each area, with the omitted dummy being 'Swindon'. A listing of the variables used in this study is available in Table 6.5 at the end of this chapter.

3. EMPIRICAL FINDINGS

In the analysis that follows, males and females are dealt with separately. In addition, males are divided into manual and non-manual,[12] and females are divided into part-time and full-time.[13] Table 6.1 provides an introduction to the wage differences to be examined. Here the average basic hourly wage[14] for union members and non-members is presented. For males, average wages among union members are clearly higher than among non-members. A similar result holds for females but to a greater extent, with the average wage among female union members being around 25 per cent higher than the average wage among non-union members.

Such results, while useful in setting the context of the study, do not allow for the substantial differences in labour market attributes that may exist between union and non-union members. The use of multivariate techniques allows us to control for measured differences. Table 6.2 summarizes the results of multiple regressions where the logarithm of the basic hourly wage is regressed on a comprehensive list of personal and labour market descriptors including a dummy variable to capture trade union membership.[15] It is an interpretation of the estimated coefficient on trade union membership that is offered in Table 6.2.

It can be seen in Table 6.2 that, allowing for a comprehensive

TABLE 6.1. *Average basic hourly wage (£)*

	Union member	Non-member	Wage difference (%)	Union members (%)
Males				
Manual	3.88	3.45	12.5	60
Non-manual	5.47	5.28	3.6	50
Females				
Full-time	3.67	2.95	24.4	50
Part-time	2.89	2.30	25.6	27

Note: The percentage difference between the two averages, not the average percentage wage difference.

TABLE 6.2. *Union–non-union wage gap using ordinary least squares*

	Percentage	t-stat	Mean wage (£)	N
Males				
Manual	7.2	(2.64)	3.71	743
Non-manual	3.7[a]	(1.12)	5.37	594
Females				
Full-time	5.5	(2.02)	3.31	752
Part-time	9.8	(2.84)	2.45	602

[a] Not statistically significant.

range of personal and labour market descriptors,[16] trade union membership leaves the average manual male on a basic hourly wage that is 7.2 per cent higher than it would be in the absence of membership. For non-manual workers the figure is 3.7 per cent, but is statistically insignificant. The second part of the table suggests that union membership enhances the basic hourly wage of the average female full-time worker by some 5.5 per cent, and for the average part-time worker by some 9.8 per cent. This last figure is of interest as it shows that although only 27 per cent (see Table 6.1) of female part-time employees in the sample are members of trade unions, union membership is associated with a substantial wage premium in what is generally a low-wage employment sector. This result holds after allowing for a wide range of characteristics and circumstances, including public sector employment.

As has been explained earlier, ordinary least squares estimation is not entirely satisfactory in this context. Before moving on to a more sophisticated analysis, however, it is convenient to utilize this simple framework to investigate the effects of modifying the specification of the analysis. Table 6.3 offers alternative estimates of the union–non-union wage gap to those presented in Table 6.2 under three changes in specification.

In Column 1 of Table 6.3 the impact of performing the estimation with a curtailed or limited set of personal and labour market characteristics is displayed. Here the omission of details of the current job (specifically: training required for job, skill of job, length of training on the job, size of establishment, supervisory capacity, public sector, work done mainly or exclusively by men, and permanence of job) acts to raise the estimate of the union mark-up in all cases except the non-significant non-manual males. Presumably union membership correlates with the wage-enhancing aspects of these characteristics. This goes some way to explaining why some earlier estimates of the union–non-union wage gap for males have been higher than those produced in this chapter. This is particularly relevant for the Sloane and Murphy (1989) estimates which utilized the same SCELI data base as the present study.[17]

Column 2 of Table 6.3 illustrates the impact of utilizing average hourly earnings.[18] By comparison with Table 6.2 it can be seen that there is little difference in any of the cases. This seems to suggest that overtime working is not the particular province of either union members or non-members. Finally, Column 3 of Table 6.3 illustrates the impact of utilizing trade union coverage[19] or representation rather than trade union membership as a measure of trade union influence. This measure does make a difference to the estimated union–non-union wage gap but comparison with Table 6.2 suggests that the difference is modest. In the more sophisticated analysis that follows, results will be presented using both the basic wage and average hourly earnings, and trade union membership and trade union representation.

The OLS results in Tables 6.2 and 6.3 are imperfect in the sense that there is a failure to allow for the fact that trade union

TABLE 6.3. *Union–non-union wage gap using ordinary least squares with various alternative specifications*

	Wage gap as a percentage of non-union wage		
	Restricted range explanatory variables	Average hourly earnings	Trade union coverage
Males			
Manual	10.2	6.8	8.7
Non-manual	2.6[a]	4.1[a]	1.1[a]
Females			
Full-time	14.9	5.4	5.7
Part-time	22.0	9.5	7.2

[a] Not statistically significant.

membership is endogenous. Thus, unlike such attributes as gender and race, the descriptor of trade union membership is an outcome of a social process in which the very relationship we are trying to measure (the union–non-union wage gap) may play a part. If unions had no independent impact on wage levels then those ending up as trade union members could, for the purposes of this study, be regarded as having been randomly chosen. If, on the other hand, union membership results in a substantial wage premium then we can assume that the agents involved are influenced by this wage gap. There may, presumably, be some competition for union jobs. And in this competition the more productive workers may win out. Failure to allow for this possible correlation between trade union membership and innate productivity threatens to produce biased estimates of the union–non-union wage gap. As has been explained above, Lee (1978) offers a way by which the estimated probability of each individual being a trade union member[20] can be used to purge the subsequent wage equations[21] of any possible bias.

A summary of the results of this procedure is available in Table 6.4.[22] Here, two distinct questions are answered. The first, covered by the left-hand side of the table, is what would be the impact on the entire group (all manual males, all non-manual males, etc.) of being paid as union members versus being paid as

TABLE 6.4. *Estimates of the union–non-union wage gap allowing for endogeneity of union membership (percentage mark-up)*

	Base of calculation					
	All individuals			Trade union members[a]		
	Basic wage	Average hourly earnings	Union coverage	Basic wage	Average hourly earnings	Union coverage
Males						
Manual	9.0	7.5	13.1	6.2	5.0	12.6
Non-manual	0.1	0.1	8.6	8.1	7.7	11.4
Females						
Full-time	15.7	16.0	10.7	18.7	19.0	9.6
Part-time	8.0	5.7	15.2	13.5	11.7	14.5

[a] Except in the last column where, for consistency, trade union coverage is used.

non-members. The second half of the table describes the impact on the current union members in each group of being paid as union members versus non-members.[23] The first method of presentation offers a certain ease of interpretation in terms of the average person and is consistent with the econometric approach adopted, while the second reflects the extent of wage mark-up that was actually occurring in 1986. Table 6.4 also presents each measure for basic hourly wages, average hourly wages, and union coverage or representation (versus union membership).

As with the more naïve OLS results discussed above, basic hourly wages and average hourly earnings produce broadly similar results. On the other hand, the issue of trade union membership versus coverage makes a substantial difference. For full-time females, membership brings a larger mark-up than coverage or representation (15.7 per cent versus 10.7 per cent for the average female full-time employee). The opposite effect is seen for female part-timers (15.2 per cent by coverage versus 8.0 per cent by membership), thus suggesting that it is working in a trade-union-organized environment that is important. In the case of males, differences also appear. The wage gap appears to be larger for manual males when measured by coverage or representation (13.1 per cent versus 9.0 per cent). The effect is particularly noticeable for the average non-manual male where the union mark-up by the coverage or representation measure becomes 8.6 per cent. These results suggest clear free-rider benefits available to non-union members.

In terms of the basic wage, using trade union members as the basis of calculation of the wage gap makes a substantial difference to the computation of the mark-up. Except in the case of non-manual males, the mark-up seems higher, when based on current trade union member average characteristics—this is particularly clear for non-manual males. This suggests that among these groups of workers those who are trade union members or work in a trade-union-organized environment have more to gain from such representation than the average non-manual worker. This process of self-selection by comparative advantage does not seem to operate among manual males.

4. POLICY DISCUSSION AND CONCLUSIONS

From the results presented above it would seem that, based on the average characteristics of each worker type, the union–non-union wage gap in 1986 was of the order of 9.0 per cent for manual males, 0.1 per cent for non-manual males, 15.7 per cent for female full-time employees, and 8.0 per cent for female part-time employees. Measured at the average characteristics of current trade union members, the union wage gap was found to be 6.2 per cent for manual males, 8.1 per cent for non-manual males, 18.7 per cent for full-time females, and 13.5 per cent for part-time females. These results are dimensionally similar to those produced by Stewart (1983), who found a wage gap of 7.7 per cent for the average male manual trade union member. They are also consistent with similar microdata estimates by Shah (1984) and Green (1988).

One noteworthy result is the size of the female union–non-union wage gap. In a previous study that utilized aggregate data, Nickell (1977) had found evidence that trade unions raise the wages of women by more than those of men. Nickell also pointed out, however, that this result did not mean that trade union organization was unambiguously good news for women. Before this conclusion could be reached, it would be necessary to examine the role of trade unions in moderating the access of women to high-paying jobs. The present study confirms, however, that a trade union job is valuable to a woman in relative wage terms.

Policy interest in the union–non-union wage gap has traditionally centred on the consequent inefficient allocation of resources implied by the successful exploitation of trade union power in driving union wages above the market clearing level. From this perspective the larger the wage gap the worse the implications for lost output and lowered economic welfare. In one sense, the amount to be gained by any government setting out to weaken trade union power can be measured by the union–non-union wage gap. Estimates produced above suggest that even after the Employment Acts of 1980 and 1982 and the Trade Union Act 1984, the union–non-union wage gap in 1986 was still of substantial proportions. It showed no evident signs of plummeting from the 7.7 per cent level for 1975 produced by Stewart (1983).[24] On the other hand, these estimates are far from the 20 per cent and higher results produced by authors utilizing aggregate data.

More recently, estimates of the trade union mark-up have come to figure in discussions of the equilibrium rate of unemployment[25] as economists have attempted to explain the high levels of unemployment recorded in Britain during the 1980s. Central to such explanations is the construct of wage pressure. In addition to notions of replacement ratio and labour market skill mismatch, wage pressure is generally characterized as a function of union power, and union power can be represented in terms of the mark-up of trade union wages. As it is generally the change in the mark-up and, hence, the change in trade union power that is of interest, cross-section time-series estimates are used. But such estimates have been scaled by Layard and Nickell (1986) around the microdata estimates of Stewart (1983). The particular estimate referred to from Stewart (1983) is the 7.7 per cent mark-up for manual males in trade unions.[26] The figure produced above of 6.2 per cent for manual males is dimensionally consistent with Stewart's estimates but does not support the generally upward-moving time trend of the trade union mark-up assumed in this work.[27] It should be noted, however, that the results presented above do not have the same force as Stewart's as they are not based on a national sample.

Estimates of the union–non-union wage gap of the order of 10 per cent for males do seem to undermine one of the arguments put forward by Minford (1985) for Britain's high unemployment. Minford argues that a high trade union mark-up, which he tentatively estimates to be of the order of 70 per cent, displaces individuals into the non-union sector where the consequent labour supply increase causes wages to fall so low (relative to benefit levels) that many of the unemployed are not prepared to accept such work. This argument rests heavily on the assumed elasticity of supply of labour, but also on the extent of displacement from the union sector and, hence, on the size of the union mark-up and the elasticity of demand for labour in the union sector. With a union–non-union wage gap of the order of 10 per cent, this approach ceases to have the same empirical significance.[28]

As was emphasized in the introduction, this chapter has focused on the monopoly power face of trade unions to the neglect of their more positive second face—that of the efficiency-producing collective voice and institutional response mechanism by which management and workers achieve mutually profitable communication and change. An examination of this face of trade unionism can be found in Nickell *et al.* (1989). But what can be concluded here with regard to the monopoly power of trade unions in Britain in 1986 is that trade union membership may create a union–non-union wage gap of some 6–8 per cent for unionized males and of some 14–19 per cent for unionized females.

NOTES

1. As Greg Lewis (1986) makes clear, the computation of a trade union mark-up on wages would require the computation of a non-observed and counterfactual competitive wage that would exist in the absence of trade unions. What is generally available is the union–non-union wage gap. The existence of a significant unionized sector ensures that the non-union wage cannot be taken as representative of wages that would prevail in a world without unions.
2. An interesting account of the development of economic thought on this and other topics of labour economics can be found in McNulty (1984) from which some of the discussion below is taken.
3. The quote appears in McNulty (1984: 191) and is taken from the 1950 preface of the reprint of Dunlop (1944*a*).
4. Much of the thinking in this area can be traced to Hirschman (1971).
5. See Layard and Nickell (1987: 155–7) for further discussion.
6. All measures of wages will be made in gross rather than net (after tax and national insurance contributions) terms.
7. See Maddala (1983: ch. 11) for a general discussion.
8. The 6,000 individuals come in roughly equal proportions from six areas of Britain: Aberdeen, Coventry, Kirkcaldy, Northampton, Rochdale, and Swindon. The data used here were collected in June, July, and August 1986.
9. Computer programs for data analysis were originally developed by Peter Elias and Christine Jones, Institute for Employment Research, University of Warwick, Coventry, and by Steven Kendrick, Research Centre for Social Sciences, University of Edinburgh.
10. To facilitate the analysis, a series of dummy variables is used to represent what was in fact a range response. Thus 'works alone' or with

24 or less people is the omitted class; S25/500 works in establishment with 25–500 people; with 500 or more people is S500+; and no size reported is SNA.

11. A strong argument exists for the treatment of an employer's attitude to unions as endogenous. Though this point is well taken, a similar charge could be pressed against some other variables in the union attachment equation. For the purposes of this study the potential endogeneity of an employer's attitude to unions is ignored.

12. The definition of manual is somewhat arbitrary and is defined here as unskilled manual, semi-skilled manual, skilled manual, and foremen and supervisors. Non-manual is, therefore, management, professionals, intermediate non-manual, and junior non-manual.

13. Part-time versus full-time depends on a self-categorization rather than any hours of work cut off.

14. The basic hourly wage is computed by dividing the reported gross wage in the last pay period by the number of hours worked in that period. Overtime hours are assumed to have been paid at time and a half and are boosted accordingly to provide a measure of the basic hourly wage.

15. Tables 6.6 and 6.7 at the end of this chapter present the full details of these regressions.

16. See Section 2.3 and Table 6.5 for a fuller description.

17. Another important difference between the two studies lies in the wide range of identifying restrictions utilized here in the trade union membership probit. This compares with the use by Sloane and Murphy (1989) of only two identifying restrictions: namely working class membership; and number of dependent children.

18. Average hourly earnings are computed by dividing the reported gross earnings in the previous pay period by total hours worked with no attempt to distinguish overtime hours.

19. Trade union coverage or representation is measured by the response to the question, 'Where you work are there any trade unions representing people who do your kind of work?'

20. Or, alternatively, in terms of the trade union coverage descriptor, of working in a trade union environment.

21. The use of separate wage equations for union members and non-members allows for trade union membership interacting with other labour market characteristics such as educational qualifications or work experience.

22. Estimated wage effects are 'unconditional', i.e. they predict the experience of an individual chosen at random from the relevant worker type. Under certain conditions, particularly if wage premiums attach to jobs rather than workers, it may make sense to use 'conditional'

estimates, i.e. the expected wage a person with given characteristics can expect conditional on being in a union job versus conditional on being in a non-union job.

23. There is clearly an index number problem here and a certain amount of arbitrariness over which base is used for comparison purposes. Yet another, but less interesting, possibility is to compute the impact as the wage difference that would be enjoyed by non-members if they were treated as union members.

24. It should be emphasized here that Stewart's results were produced on the basis of a truly national sample (the 1975 National Training Survey) while the present results are based on data from six distinct areas of Britain.

25. Usually termed the 'natural' rate of unemployment or the non-accelerating inflation rate of unemployment (NAIRU).

26. See Layard and Nickell (1987: 156) where a figure of 11 per cent is also mentioned.

27. See Layard and Nickell (1985) and, in particular, Layard and Nickell (1987: 157).

28. See Nickell (1984) for a full critique of Minford's arguments.

TABLE 6.5. *Variables used in the analysis*

Variable	Description	Sample average	
Wage equation		Males	Females
EMP	Years of employment	20.611	16.210
EMPS	$(EMP)^2$	564.41	352.19
UNEMP	Years of unemployment	0.5149	0.3473
UNEMPS	$(UNEMP)^2$	1.4142	1.6527
OLF*	Years out of labour force	—	5.7078
OLFS	$(OLF)^2$	—	65.71
EDUC	Years of post-compulsory education	1.2727	1.1624
CMAR	= 1 currently married 0 otherwise	0.7075	0.7326
ABERD	= 1 if lives in Aberdeen	0.1862	0.2001
KIRK	= 1 if lives in Kirkcaldy	0.1675	0.1728
COV	= 1 if lives in Coventry	0.1750	0.1344
ROCHD	= 1 if lives in Rochdale	0.1616	0.1787
NORTHN	= 1 if lives in Northampton	0.1630	0.1632

TABLE 6.5 (*cont.*):

Variable	Description	Sample average	
Wage equation		Males	Females
SKILL	= 1 if regards job as skilled	0.7330	0.5340
TDUR	= 1 if took at least 6 months to learn	0.5729	0.2991
PERM	= 1 if believes employer regards job as permanent	0.9252	0.9202
CURTRAIN	= 1 if training undertaken since leaving FT education for type of work done	0.5639	0.3678
SUP	= 1 if has supervisory responsibility	0.4114	0.2518
PUBLIC	= 1 if job in public sector	0.3231	0.4284
S25/500	= 1 if size of establishment is 25–499 employees	0.4540	0.4195
S500+	= 1 if size of establishment is 500+ employees	0.2812	0.1529
SNA	= 1 if size of establishment is not reported	0.0112	0.0125
EXCMALE	= 1 if job done exclusively or mainly by men	0.8467	0.0591
IND1**	= 1 Agriculture	0.0067	0.0000
IND2	Energy	0.0583	0.0148
IND3	Basic industries	0.0322	0.0148
IND4	Engineering	0.2446	0.0702
IND5	Other manufacturing	0.1271	0.1004
IND6	Construction	0.0718	0.0089
IND7	Distribution/Hotels	0.1189	0.2349
IND8	Transport and communication	0.0853	0.0332
IND9	Finance	0.0755	0.0820
OCC1***	Management	0.1436	0.0576
OCC2	Professional	0.0725	0.0118
OCC3	Intermediate non-manual	0.1234	0.1854
OCC4	Junior non-manual	0.1047	0.4889
OCC5	Foremen and supervisors	0.0419	0.0111
OCC6	Skilled manual	0.2977	0.0495
OCC7	Semi-skilled manual	0.1713	0.1034

Variable	Description	Sample average	
Wage equation		Males	Females
	Probit identifying variables		
PARTUN	Partner is very or quite favourable to unions	0.2147	0.3272
FATHUN	Father was very or quite favourable to unions	0.3762	0.3538
WCLASS	Regards self as working class	0.2386	0.1972
PRESCH	Children 0–4 years old	0.1877	0.1078
PRIMSCH	Children 5–12 years old	0.2513	0.2356
SECSCH	Children 13–18 years old	0.1877	0.3456
PARWORK	Partner is in employment	0.4966	0.7061
CONSERV	Would vote Conservative in election tomorrow	0.1885	0.1617
CONFLICT	Employer/employee relations perceived as very or somewhat difficult	0.2977	0.1780
EMPUN	Employer encouraging or accepting unions	0.6335	0.5185
	Other variables		
WAGE	Basic hourly earnings	4.45	2.93
PT	Part time (females)	—	0.4446
MANUAL	Manual (males)	0.5557	—
TUMEMB	Trade union member	0.5475	0.3973
N		1,337	1,354

* For males unemployment experience and out of the labour force experience are combined and reported as UNEMP.
** The omitted industrial classification is Other Services.
*** The omitted occupational classification is unskilled manual for females and for manual males, and Junior non-manual for non-manual males.

Note: N = sample size. A straightforward description of probit techniques can be found in such sources as Norusis (1985).

TABLE 6.6. *Ordinary least squares regressions for male wages (dependent variable is log of basic hourly wage)*

Variable	Manual		Non-manual	
	Coefficient	(*t*-stat)	Coefficient	(*t*-stat)
TUMEMB	0.070	(2.64)	0.037	(1.12)
CONST	0.719	(7.68)	0.502	(5.31)
EMP	0.013	(3.50)	0.039	(7.04)
EMPS	−0.0002	(3.16)	−0.0007	(5.99)
UNEMP	−0.057	(2.92)	−0.079	(2.74)
UNEMPS	0.006	(1.76)	0.011	(1.87)
EDUC	0.053	(4.75)	0.052	(8.40)
CMAR	0.031	(1.20)	0.072	(1.88)
ABERD	−0.034	(0.84)	0.000	(0.01)
KIRK	−0.076	(1.95)	−0.039	(0.79)
COV	−0.012	(0.31)	−0.112	(2.30)
ROCHD	−0.095	(2.37)	−0.137	(2.81)
NORTHN	−0.036	(0.89)	−0.022	(0.48)
SKILL	0.060	(2.39)	0.069	(1.72)
TDUR	0.036	(1.51)	0.091	(2.92)
CURTRAIN	0.061	(2.68)	0.084	(2.67)
PERM	0.079	(2.01)	0.025	(0.42)
SUP	0.015	(0.57)	0.075	(2.39)
PUBLIC	−0.015	(0.50)	0.008	(0.19)
S25/500	0.028	(1.01)	0.092	(2.61)
S500+	0.111	(3.34)	0.213	(5.31)
SNA	0.129	(1.41)	0.106	(0.70)
EXCMALE	0.032	(0.62)	0.116	(3.56)
R-squared	0.262		0.440	
F-statistic	8.756		14.713	
Standard deviation of dependent variable	0.321		0.433	
Standard error of regression	0.275		0.324	
N	743		594	

Note: Nine industry and three occupational dummies were also included in the specification. *N* = sample size.

TABLE 6.7. *Ordinary least squares regressions for female wages (dependent variable is log of basic hourly wage)*

Variable	Full-time		Part-time	
	Coefficient	(*t*-stat)	Coefficient	(*t*-stat)
TUMEMB	0.054	(2.02)	0.093	(2.84)
CONST	0.510	(5.17)	0.389	(4.39)
EMP	0.026	(5.48)	0.009	(1.61)
EMPS	−0.0006	(5.36)	−0.0002	(1.14)
UNEMP	−0.019	(0.91)	−0.018	(0.90)
UNEMPS	−0.001	(0.49)	0.0009	(0.65)
OLF	−0.019	(2.93)	−0.011	(1.63)
OLFS	0.0006	(1.51)	0.0003	(0.87)
EDUC	0.056	(8.92)	0.032	(3.32)
CMAR	0.025	(1.00)	0.008	(0.21)
ABERD	0.031	(0.81)	−0.026	(0.60)
KIRK	−0.009	(0.22)	−0.058	(1.30)
COV	0.011	(0.26)	−0.121	(2.57)
ROCHD	−0.007	(0.17)	−0.051	(1.14)
NORTHN	0.011	(0.27)	−0.057	(1.28)
SKILL	0.016	(0.61)	0.071	(2.32)
TDUR	0.065	(2.51)	0.064	(1.49)
CURTRAIN	0.029	(1.22)	0.070	(1.98)
PERM	0.033	(0.71)	0.131	(3.03)
SUP	0.063	(2.32)	−0.040	(0.95)
PUBLIC	0.078	(2.20)	0.108	(2.83)
S25/500	0.127	(4.73)	0.093	(3.31)
S500+	0.159	(4.65)	0.194	(3.64)
SNA	0.026	(0.26)	0.127	(1.13)
EXCMALE	−0.047	(1.98)	0.002	(0.08)
R-squared	0.410		0.350	
F-statistic	15.117		9.760	
Standard deviation of dependent variable	0.387		0.375	
Standard error of regression	0.297		0.302	
N	752		602	

Note: Six industry and seven occupational dummies were also included in the specification. *N* = sample size.

TABLE 6.8. *Equations to estimate the union–non-union wage gap for manual males*

| Variable | Probit on TUMEMB | | Wage equations* | | | |
| | | | Members | | Non-members | |
	Coefficient	(*t*-stat)	Coefficient	(*t*-stat)	Coefficient	(*t*-stat)
CONST	0.066	(0.90)	1.018	(6.96)	0.519	(3.53)
EMP	0.011	(2.11)	0.008	(1.59)	0.016	(2.69)
EMPS	−0.0002	(1.79)	−0.0002	(1.60)	−0.0003	(2.03)
UNEMP	−0.029	(1.13)	−0.077	(1.92)	−0.046	(1.76)
UNEMPS	0.000	(0.00)	0.011	(1.00)	0.006	(1.36)
EDUC	−0.012	(0.83)	0.036	(2.32)	0.059	(3.75)
CMAR	−0.033	(0.73)	0.012	(0.38)	0.055	(1.35)
ABERD	−0.009	(0.17)	−0.109	(2.14)	0.022	(0.36)
KIRK	0.024	(0.47)	−0.119	(2.53)	−0.020	(0.32)
COV	0.135	(2.65)	−0.038	(0.82)	−0.014	(0.19)
ROCHD	0.078	(1.47)	−0.151	(3.07)	−0.024	(0.38)
NORTHN	0.004	(0.08)	−0.042	(0.80)	−0.035	(0.60)
SKILL	—	—	0.037	(1.25)	0.107	(2.55)
TDUR	—	—	0.053	(1.89)	0.014	(0.35)
CURTRAIN	—	—	0.053	(1.91)	0.082	(2.20)
PERM	—	—	0.066	(1.07)	0.077	(1.49)
SUP	—	—	0.006	(0.18)	0.052	(1.20)
PUBLIC	—	—	−0.041	(1.15)	0.040	(0.49)
S25/500	—	—	−0.002	(0.06)	0.034	(0.91)
S500+	—	—	0.077	(1.61)	0.148	(1.88)
SNA	—	—	0.215	(1.61)	0.060	(0.50)
EXCMALE	—	—	0.044	(0.59)	0.003	(0.04)
CONFLICT	0.245	(1.98)	—	—	—	—
PARTUN	0.047	(0.31)	—	—	—	—
FATHUN	0.061	(0.51)	—	—	—	—
EMPUN	1.866	(15.72)	—	—	—	—
CONSERV	−0.432	(2.49)	—	—	—	—
WCLASS	−0.056	(0.44)	—	—	—	—
UNEMP	0.181	(1.28)	—	—	—	—
PRESCH	0.185	(1.08)	—	—	—	—
PRIMSCH	−0.077	(0.50)	—	—	—	—
SECSCH	0.003	(0.03)	—	—	—	—
WAGE DIFF.	−0.440	(0.87)	—	—	—	—
UNION SELECTION	—	—	−0.050	(1.11)	−0.014	(0.29)
Chi-squared	374.40		—		—	
R-squared	—		0.209		0.273	
F-statistic	—		4.474		4.258	

| Variable | Probit on TUMEMB | | Wage equations* | | | |
| | | | Members | | Non-members | |
	Coefficient	(*t*-stat)	Coefficient	(*t*-stat)	Coefficient	(*t*-stat)
Standard deviation of dependent variable	—		0.298		0.337	
Standard error of regression	—		0.254		0.270	
N	743		447		296	

* Nine industry and three occupational dummies were also included in the specification. N = sample size.

TABLE 6.9. *Equations to estimate the union–non-union wage gap for non-manual males*

| Variable | Probit on TUMEMB | | Wage equations* | | | |
| | | | Members | | Non-members | |
	Coefficient	(*t*-stat)	Coefficient	(*t*-stat)	Coefficient	(*t*-stat)
CONST	3.070	(8.51)	0.486	(2.86)	0.515	(4.08)
EMP	0.066	(2.51)	0.032	(4.26)	0.041	(5.48)
EMPS	−0.001	(1.89)	−0.0005	(3.49)	−0.0008	(4.81)
UNEMP	−0.196	(1.30)	−0.027	(0.87)	−0.145	(2.80)
UNEMPS	0.029	(0.96)	0.004	(0.71)	0.022	(1.86)
EDUC	−0.007	(0.25)	0.047	(6.14)	0.052	(5.76)
CMAR	−0.271	(1.12)	0.037	(0.76)	0.106	(1.91)
ABERD	0.750	(3.48)	−0.047	(0.71)	0.003	(0.04)
KIRK	1.031	(4.43)	−0.073	(1.13)	−0.034	(0.44)
COV	0.814	(3.71)	−0.115	(1.77)	−0.169	(2.29)
ROCHD	1.011	(4.30)	−0.107	(1.62)	−0.204	(2.71)
NORTHN	0.614	(2.72)	−0.088	(1.33)	−0.014	(0.22)
SKILL	—	—	0.058	(1.16)	0.070	(1.17)
TDUR	—	—	0.121	(3.09)	0.049	(1.09)
CURTRAIN	—	—	0.069	(1.78)	0.101	(2.20)
PERM	—	—	0.178	(2.02)	−0.097	(1.22)
SUP	—	—	0.090	(2.40)	0.076	(1.60)
PUBLIC	—	—	0.062	(1.05)	−0.021	(0.28)
S25/500	—	—	0.032	(0.69)	0.127	(2.51)
S500+	—	—	0.138	(2.66)	0.259	(4.39)
SNA	—	—	−0.007	(0.04)	0.163	(0.65)

TABLE 6.9 (*cont.*):

| Variable | Probit on TUMEMB | | Wage equations* | | | |
| | | | Members | | Non-members | |
	Coefficient	(*t*-stat)	Coefficient	(*t*-stat)	Coefficient	(*t*-stat)
EXCMALE	—	—	0.132	(3.36)	0.109	(2.20)
CONFLICT	0.574	(3.81)	—	—	—	—
PARTUN	−0.096	(0.60)	—	—	—	—
FATHUN	−0.045	(0.32)	—	—	—	—
EMPUN	2.207	(11.96)	—	—	—	—
CONSERV	−0.630	(4.10)	—	—	—	—
WCLASS	−0.519	(2.91)	—	—	—	—
PARWORK	0.410	(2.57)	—	—	—	—
PRESCH	0.707	(3.66)	—	—	—	—
PRIMSCH	−0.051	(0.31)	—	—	—	—
SECSCH	−0.158	(1.03)	—	—	—	—
WAGE DIFF.	2.945	(4.94)	—	—	—	—
UNION SELECTION	—	—	0.090	(1.72)	−0.050	(0.82)
Chi-squared	290.94		—		—	
R-squared	—		0.400		0.449	
F-statistic	—		6.576		8.384	
Standard deviation of dependent variable	—		0.370		0.482	
Standard error of regression	—		0.268		0.337	
N	594		285		309	

* Nine industry and three occupational dummies were also included in the specification. N = sample size.

TABLE 6.10. *Equations to estimate the union–non-union wage gap for females in full-time employment*

| Variable | Probit on TUMEMB | | Wage equations* | | | |
| | | | Members | | Non-members | |
	Coefficient	(t-stat)	Coefficient	(t-stat)	Coefficient	(t-stat)
CONST	−2.143	(8.18)	0.561	(3.70)	0.521	(3.94)
EMP	0.064	(2.59)	0.027	(4.15)	0.019	(2.84)
EMPS	−0.001	(1.60)	−0.0006	(4.14)	−0.0005	(2.90)
UNEMP	−0.189	(1.76)	0.014	(0.43)	0.034	(0.81)
UNEMPS	0.022	(1.48)	−0.004	(1.17)	−0.013	(1.61)
OLF	−0.027	(0.77)	−0.026	(3.00)	−0.011	(1.24)
OLFS	0.0007	(0.36)	0.001	(2.36)	0.0001	(0.12)
EDUC	0.072	(2.43)	0.061	(8.03)	0.035	(3.64)
CMAR	−0.009	(0.05)	0.020	(0.63)	0.019	(0.54)
ABERD	0.111	(0.54)	−0.043	(0.77)	0.091	(1.87)
KIRK	0.462	(2.20)	−0.047	(0.84)	−0.017	(0.30)
COV	0.487	(2.17)	−0.002	(0.03)	0.015	(0.26)
ROCHD	0.614	(2.91)	0.023	(0.42)	−0.070	(1.33)
NORTHN	−0.023	(0.11)	0.007	(0.12)	0.012	(0.24)
SKILL	—	—	0.012	(0.34)	0.020	(0.58)
TDUR	—	—	0.121	(3.50)	0.008	(0.22)
CURTRAIN	—	—	0.063	(1.92)	−0.008	(0.25)
PERM	—	—	0.101	(1.61)	−0.043	(0.68)
SUP	—	—	0.033	(0.91)	0.123	(3.29)
PUBLIC	—	—	0.063	(1.18)	0.037	(0.72)
S25/500	—	—	0.049	(1.28)	0.160	(4.62)
S500+	—	—	0.037	(0.79)	0.275	(5.30)
SNA	—	—	−0.060	(0.47)	0.216	(1.44)
EXCMALE	—	—	−0.027	(0.84)	−0.041	(1.23)
CONFLICT	0.335	(2.42)	—	—	—	—
PARTUN	0.111	(0.77)	—	—	—	—
FATHUN	−0.103	(0.83)	—	—	—	—
EMPUN	1.858	(14.80)	—	—	—	—
CONSERV	−0.345	(2.17)	—	—	—	—
WCLASS	0.209	(1.34)	—	—	—	—
PARWORK	0.035	(0.18)	—	—	—	—
PRESCH	−0.058	(0.20)	—	—	—	—
PRIMSCH	−0.073	(0.39)	—	—	—	—
SECSCH	−0.034	(0.25)	—	—	—	—
WAGE DIFF.	−0.259	(0.68)	—	—	—	—
UNION SELECTION	—	—	−0.051	(1.08)	−0.072	(1.60)
Chi-squared	398.75		—		—	

TABLE 6.10 (*cont.*):

| Variable | Probit on TUMEMB | | Wage equations* | | | |
| | | | Members | | Non-members | |
	Coefficient	(*t*-stat)	Coefficient	(*t*-stat)	Coefficient	(*t*-stat)
R-squared	—		0.449		0.334	
F-statistic	—		9.316		6.053	
Standard deviation of dependent variable	—		0.383		0.361	
Standard error of regression	—		0.269		0.279	
N	752		378		374	

* Six industry and seven occupational dummies were also included in the specification. N = sample size.

TABLE 6.11. *Equations to estimate the union–non-union wage gap for females in part-time employment*

| Variable | Probit on TUMEMB | | Wage equations* | | | |
| | | | Members | | Non-members | |
	Coefficient	(*t*-stat)	Coefficient	(*t*-stat)	Coefficient	(*t*-stat)
CONST	−1.874	(3.56)	0.541	(2.39)	0.442	(4.53)
EMP	0.038	(1.06)	0.008	(0.70)	0.005	(0.75)
EMPS	−0.0008	(0.99)	−0.0001	(0.54)	−0.0001	(0.36)
UNEMP	0.121	(0.46)	0.041	(0.39)	−0.026	(1.21)
UNEMPS	−0.056	(0.82)	−0.015	(0.44)	0.001	(0.97)
OLF	−0.022	(0.51)	−0.002	(0.13)	−0.013	(1.78)
OLFS	−0.0006	(0.28)	0.0001	(0.08)	0.0003	(0.94)
EDUC	−0.054	(1.14)	0.039	(2.51)	0.036	(3.21)
CMAR	−0.080	(0.25)	−0.021	(0.28)	0.022	(0.51)
ABERD	−0.170	(0.59)	−0.175	(2.01)	0.004	(0.09)
KIRK	0.268	(0.97)	−0.113	(1.32)	−0.073	(1.41)
COV	0.067	(0.24)	−0.086	(0.98)	−0.141	(2.66)
ROCHD	0.215	(0.80)	−0.091	(1.06)	−0.076	(1.48)
NORTHN	−0.080	(0.28)	−0.264	(2.91)	−0.012	(0.24)
SKILL	—	—	0.039	(0.67)	0.067	(1.95)
TDUR	—	—	−0.017	(0.21)	0.098	(2.02)

Variable	Probit on TUMEMB		Wage equations*			
			Members		Non-members	
	Coefficient	(t-stat)	Coefficient	(t-stat)	Coefficient	(t-stat)
CURTRAIN	—	—	0.019	(0.30)	0.085	(2.10)
PERM	—	—	0.270	(2.67)	0.104	(2.21)
SUP	—	. —	0.146	(2.07)	−0.096	(1.95)
PUBLIC	—	—	−0.030	(0.31)	0.072	(1.68)
S25/500	—	—	0.061	(1.23)	0.067	(2.00)
S500+	—	—	0.148	(2.17)	0.228	(3.02)
SNA	—	—	0.136	(0.52)	0.124	(1.02)
EXCMALE	—	—	0.023	(0.35)	−0.005	(0.15)
CONFLICT	0.399	(1.90)	—	—	—	—
PARTUN	0.365	(2.30)	—	—	—	—
FATHUN	−0.290	(1.88)	—	—	—	—
EMPUN	2.099	(11.19)	—	—	—	—
CONSERV	−0.586	(2.46)	—	—	—	—
WCLASS	0.151	(0.87)	—	—	—	—
PARWORK	−0.070	(0.25)	—	—	—	—
PRESCH	−0.102	(0.43)	—	—	—	—
PRIMSCH	−0.063	(0.35)	—	—	—	—
SECSCH	0.055	(0.35)	—	—	—	—
WAGE DIFF.	−0.193	(0.46)	—	—	—	—
UNION SELECTION	—	—	0.044	(0.80)	−0.113	(2.33)
Chi-squared	289.06		—		—	
R-squared	—		0.436		0.272	
F-statistic	—		4.318		5.459	
Standard deviation of dependent variable	—		0.365		0.361	
Standard error of regression	—		0.240		0.294	
N	602		160		442	

* Six industry and seven occupational dummies were also included in the specification. N = sample size.

7

The Experience of Trade Unions in Rochdale During the 1980s

ROGER PENN AND HILDA SCATTERGOOD

This chapter deals with the experience of trade unions in Rochdale during the 1980s. The present analysis draws upon two sets of data: structured interviews conducted at thirty-two establishments in Rochdale during the period between June 1987 and February 1988; and a series of semi-structured interviews undertaken with local trade union officers between July 1988 and January 1989, supplemented by additional information acquired in the summer of 1989. These two sets of data provide a unique opportunity to assess the experience of trade unionism across an entire locality in the latter years of the 1980s. Initially the chapter presents the general parameters of what had come to be seen by commentators as the nature of the crisis faced by unions in Britain during the 1980s. This is followed by an examination of the two dominant interpretative models developed to explain this apparent crisis. These general explanations are then examined in the context of their applicability to the various data collected in Rochdale between 1987 and 1989. Rochdale was of particular relevance for the salience of such general theories of trade union crisis since it had experienced a period of mass unemployment and redundancies unprecedented since the early 1930s (Penn, 1989a). This rendered Rochdale rather different in its local employment from the two other localities examined in depth in this volume. Both Swindon (see Chapter 2) and Aberdeen (see Chapter 8) presented trade unionism with their own specific challenges during the 1980s, but these were manifestly different from the challenge to trade unions presented by mass unemployment in Rochdale during the 1980s.

1. THE CRISIS OF TRADE UNIONISM IN BRITAIN IN THE 1980S

There remains a pervasive air of crisis surrounding the contemporary British trade union movement. The long post-war period of rising union membership and increasing union density went into reverse during the 1980s. In 1979, there were 13.3 million trade union members in Britain and union density stood at 54.2 per cent. By 1982 membership had fallen to 11.6 million and density to 47.9 per cent. In 1987, union membership stood at 10.4 million and density at 42.0 per cent (Winchester, 1988; Towers, 1989; DoE, 1989). It has continued to fall, albeit at a slower rate since that time (Bird *et al.*, 1993). Part of the explanation for this fall, certainly in the early 1980s, was the sharp rise in unemployment after 1979. In that year unemployment in Britain stood at 1.2 million, whereas only three years later, by 1982, unemployment had risen to 3.1 million. However, even as unemployment fell after 1985, trade union membership continued to fall (Kelly and Bailey, 1989). Such a decline in membership had a serious effect on the finances of many unions, particularly smaller unions in private sector manufacturing industry, long before the end of the decade.

This fall of membership was overlaid with a significant decline in trade union political influence, which continued into the 1990s. This took two forms. First, the continued electoral failure of the Labour Party meant that national trade union leaders no longer possessed a natural entrée into the corridors of Whitehall power. However, this conjunctural political problem was compounded by the demise of tripartite and corporatist forms of governance which had occurred under the Thatcher Governments. The general attempt by successive previous British governments since 1945 to secure a national consensus among the institutions representing capital and labour with those of the state was abandoned and with it any real leverage that trade union leaders might have had upon policy planning and implementation (Longstreth, 1988). The degree of national trade union impotence was to be revealed by both the scale and scope of the 1980, 1982, and 1988 Employment Acts and the Trade Union Act 1984. These pieces of legislation limited the scope of trade disputes and restricted union immunities to situations where a majority vote had been secured in a secret ballot held no more than four weeks before any planned action. Failure to comply with these pieces of legislation left unions and their officials open to civil actions in the form of injunctions, fines, sequestration, receivership, and ultimately imprisonment. The history of the 1980s became littered with the case histories of various unions like the NGA, NUM, NUS, and the TGWU, who finally discovered the effects of this political sea-change upon the conduct of major industrial disputes in a series of hard shocks.

However, if the fall of union membership and the demise of national trade union leaders as a 'fifth estate' (Taylor, 1980) could be seen as consequences of a series of unfavourable exogenous variables, the same could not be said of the third aspect of the continuing crisis within British trade unions: the political conflicts between internal union factions. There occurred a series of well-publicized, damaging internal feuds throughout the 1980s, which seemed to stretch the notion of union solidarity well beyond the bounds of credibility. Of course, inter-union hostility was not a new phenomenon in Britain. The ASE, for instance, left the TUC after 1898 over the role of the Congress and the Boilermakers' Union during the 1897–8 engineering lock-out (Penn, 1983). However, the intensity of inter-union hostility at a national level during the 1980s was almost certainly unprecedented historically.

These disputes centred around a wide range of issues. They first surfaced significantly over the issue of Solidarity in Poland. The TUC General Council voted to accept an invitation from the Polish Government to send a delegation to Poland in 1980 at a time when Solidarity was challenging the state. This issue caused tremendous difficulties for those British union leaders who had always found it difficult to understand worker hostility to socialist institutions in Eastern Europe. The minority of unions who opposed acceptance of the invitation included the EETPU and the AUEW. These unions featured time and time again in the forefront of ideological conflict within the TUC over how to cope with the deteriorating political and economic environment after 1979. Indeed, the first major industrial example of serious friction between both the EETPU and the AUEW and other major unions involved the Isle of Grain power station dispute, which also took place in 1980.

This conflict centred upon twenty-seven laggers, members of the GMBATU, who had been suspended by the CEGB for refusing to accept that their bonus payments should have been limited to levels commensurate with incentive earnings of other skilled workers at the site. The EETPU and AUEW, in defiance of the Bridlington Principles, allowed their own members to be retrained in order to fill the vacant lagging jobs and then to work at the same bonus ceiling as other craftsmen at the Isle of Grain site. This dispute culminated in mass picketing, including the ubiquitous presence of Arthur Scargill and his Yorkshire mine workers. As a result, the new EETPU and AUEW laggers were accompanied across these picket lines by their own union officials, including the future leader of the EETPU, Eric Hammond. Ultimately, both unions were threatened with suspension by the TUC.

Another example of this split within the trade union movement involved the decision by the EETPU, the AUEW, and BALPA to accept Government financial assistance towards the costs of conducting postal ballots (a provision of the Employment Act of 1980). This ran counter to TUC policy as laid down at the millenarian 1982 Wembley Special Conference. This meeting had advocated non-co-operation with all aspects of Thatcher Government employment legislation. Eventually, both the EETPU and the AUEW accepted such monies and in 1985 the General Council attempted to discipline both unions based upon the 1982 Wembley decision. The AUEW successfully balloted its membership three times on the question of accepting such financial assistance from the Government and eventually the issue was allowed to die away. However, it left a considerable residue of inter-union acrimony.

Lack of common purpose among unions was seen again during the miners' strike of 1984–5. Executives of five transport unions (ASLEF, NUR, TSSA, NUS, and TGWU) and the ISTC recommended a blockade of all coal movements by their members. However, executives of the three power unions (EETPU, GMBU, and EPEA) advised their members to cross miners' picket lines. None the less, the former expression of solidarity did not last long, even at the national official level, since the ISTC soon began to co-operate with British Steel management in receiving coke by rail at the major steelworks.

Perhaps the most significant political split was seen when the NGA was fined £525,000 by the courts in 1983 and had its entire assets sequestrated. The Employment Policy Committee of the TUC agreed to support the NGA in its opposition to the fine, but this was immediately repudiated by the General Secretary of the TUC on the steps of Congress House in full view of the assembled television cameras. Mr Murray stated that 'only lawful support could be given to unions in dispute', a decision endorsed a few days later by the full General Council of the TUC by 31 votes to 20.

These deep-laid fissures within the British trade union movement came to a head in a series of battles over membership prerogatives. Probably the best known centred on the proposed Ford Dundee electronic components plant, which eventually was relocated to Spain after a bitter dispute between the AEU and the TGWU, MSF, and GMB. However, there also occurred a whole succession of inter-union feuds over recognition rights at such places as the UPM paper mill at Shotton, the Coca-Cola bottling plant at Wakefield, the Nissan plant near Sunderland, and in Fleet Street. As trade union membership levels fell and an increasing proportion of trade union members were located in ever fewer large conglomerate unions, the traditional basis for membership allocation was called ever deeper into question.

If union solidarity often appeared dubious at a national level during the 1980s, there was also evidence of a declining inclination by union members to obey either the calls of their union executives or of their local shop steward committees for industrial action. The first major example of this 'rank-and-file revolt' occurred in 1980 when Welsh members of the NUM voted against a strike called over job losses in Wales during the bitterly fought national steel strike (Docherty, 1983). At about the same time, members of the AUEW at BL overwhelmingly voted against strike action, as recommended by the Executive of the AUEW, in support of the reinstatement of Mr Derek Robinson (formerly shop steward convener at Longbridge). In April 1984, various areas of the NUM refused to support strike action and some of these areas, notably in Nottinghamshire, continued to work throughout the long miners' strike. Indeed, a significant proportion of the union in the Midlands left the NUM and formed a rival union: the UDM (Adeney and Lloyd, 1986).

Dockers, in the main, failed to support either of the two national dock strikes called as a result of the long-running coal strike in 1984–5. In November 1984, BL workers at Cowley and Longbridge voted to return to work against the advice of their shop stewards, once again signalling a revolt by the shop floor against their own local union leaders.

It was clear that unprecedented internal turbulence was occurring within the ranks of organized labour during the 1980s. In 1988, the EETPU was expelled from the TUC for failing to comply with Congress directives. The AEU succeeded in pre-empting the TGWU in its single-union deal with Cadbury Schweppes at the Wakefield Coca-Cola bottling plant, but this remained subject to continuing bitter recriminations between the two unions. At one stage there was considerable talk of the formation of a rival to the TUC and the emergence of two ideologically distinct trade union federations in a fashion parallel to the divided unionism of France and Italy (Penn, 1985*b*). Whilst this did not happen, it was the case that a major union—the EETPU—remained outside the TUC until 1993. This expulsion represented a danger to orderly collective bargaining in Britain at the time of the fieldwork in Rochdale.

A final element in the ongoing crisis of British unions was the rise of conglomerate unionism. This resulted from a series of mergers between unions (Buchanan, 1981). The causes of this merger movement were partly financial and partly political. As membership fell in many unions, revenues also decreased. Both smaller and larger unions were pressed towards amalgamation in order to provide a reasonable level of services. However, the form of mergers was often determined more by political factors than by purely economic contingencies. The various amalgamations that led to the emergence of the MSF during the 1980s demonstrated this point as did the decision of the boilermakers to amalgamate with the GMWU rather than the AUEW. During the 1980s there was an increasing concentration of union membership in a small number of large conglomerates. Winchester (1988) revealed that 50 per cent of trade unionists were contained in the membership of eight large unions. Such developments were to overlay the political factionalism between these large unions. In particular, the advent of conglomerate unionism put enormous pressure upon the traditional conventions surrounding inter-union jurisdiction. The political divisions meant that the moral legitimacy of these institutional arrangements was increasingly questioned by a wide range of unions.

2. TWO MODELS OF THE CRISIS OF TRADE UNIONS IN CONTEMPORARY BRITAIN

Two models have been developed to interpret the significance of the crisis of trade unionism in Britain. The pessimistic model suggested that the 1980s witnessed a profound and fundamental structural transformation in the central parameters of British political, legal, economic, and social institutions and that these changes represented a significant and irreversible change in the position of trade unions in Britain. Leadbetter (1987), for instance, announced that 'British trade unions are in a state of structural paralysis unable to find a role in a society which has moved away from them in a fundamental sense'. Membership decline was seen as the result of major structural changes that made it highly unlikely that trade unions would ever recapture the historically high levels of union density achieved in the period prior to 1979. Indeed, Lloyd (1988) announced that 'the unions are on the decline: numerically, socially, industrially' and that this decline was almost certainly permanent. This pessimistic model had various inter-related causal elements. First, the decline of manufacturing industry and the precipitous fall of employment in nationalized industries like coal, steel, shipbuilding, and cars and the subsequent privatization of many of these nationalized industries were all seen to have profoundly weakened the core of the traditional union movement. Second, technological change was thought to be eliminating a wide range of manual skills, both in production and maintenance, with the consequence that craftworkers, who formed the militant core of many unions historically, were being progressively eliminated in the 1980s (Armstrong, 1988). Third, employment patterns themselves were seen to be subject to a major structural transformation. The growth of part-time, casual, marginal, and peripheral employment located predominantly in the service sector and often employing women and/or ethnic minorities was seen as antithetical to union membership (Atkinson and Meager, 1986; Hakim, 1987*a* and 1987*b*). Such prophets of doom saw the typical

modern worker as a check-out attendant at Sainsburys or a
server at McDonalds rather than the traditional miner, composi-
tor, or engineering worker (Beynon, 1992). According to this
model—which became the dominant orthodoxy—unions were
finding it more difficult to organize such 'peripheral' workers
both as a result of their precarious position in the labour market
and the hostility to unionization displayed by their employers.
The pessimistic model also suggested that neither the new labour
relations legislation nor the high levels of unemployment in the
1980s were particularly significant in explaining the underlying
processes of structural change. Rather it suggested that the historic rise of union density in the post-war period was a conjunctural contingency and it had been succeeded by an inexorable
decline.

The alternative model was far less gloomy in its prognoses. It
suggested that the fall in union membership was both far less
than that between 1926 and 1935 (Rose, 1986) and was a short-
term, conjunctural deviation from the general trend since 1945.
The decline in trade union membership and power was explained
primarily in terms of the rise in unemployment and the negative
effects of labour legislation. For instance, Mortimer (1988)
argued vehemently against any notion of a secular decline in
union membership in Britain. He stated boldly: 'There will be
recovery in the future. Indeed, despite the problems, the unions
have so far weathered the adversities rather better than on some
previous occasions.' Whilst Mortimer acknowledged the rise of
peripheral forms of work, these were seen as representing an
additional challenge to unions, which could be overcome either
by an appropriate recruitment strategy or through economic
reflation. Mortimer was unequivocal and stated: 'In every trade
depression for the last 100 years workplace trade union activity
has tended to decline. Nevertheless, it has always recovered when
trade revives. It will do so again.' Other exponents of this more
optimistic model emphasized the stability of everyday industrial
relations in British workplaces in the 1980s (Batstone, 1984;
Millward and Stevens, 1984), the lack of any managerial assaults
on union recognition (Rose and Jones, 1985) comparable with
those that had taken place in the USA during the 1980s (Wrenn,
1985), and the continued influence of unions in the workplace,
particularly through the extensive shop steward system. As Kelly

(1987) put it, in his discussion of the Department of Employment's 1984 Industrial Relations Survey, 'the data convey an overall sense of institutional stability and testify to the resilience of trade unionism and collective bargaining through the recession'. This model also emphasized the historic tradition of union membership in Britain and the widespread culture of labourism, with its attendant emphasis on the need for collective representation at the place of work.

Clearly, there were two radically divergent interpretations of the situation of trade unions in contemporary Britain. However, much of the commentary was at a high level of generality. Explanations were developed about British trade unions at a *national* level. Such macro-level explanations ignored the local variations in trade unionism which have been such a longstanding feature of British labour relations (Turner, 1962; Burgess, 1975; Clegg, 1979). Furthermore, much analysis combined high-level theoreticism, such as an alleged structural shift from Fordism to post-Fordism (or some similar eschatological binary opposition), with the crudest appropriation of data.

3. THE QUESTIONS ADDRESSED IN THIS ANALYSIS

This section examines data on the situation of trade unions in Rochdale in the 1980s. It combines materials from intensive case studies of thirty-two establishments in Rochdale across a wide range of sectors of employment undertaken in 1987 and 1988, with evidence from the officials of thirteen trade unions collected in 1988 and 1989. The research was designed to assess the situation of trade unions in the later years of the 1980s, how this had changed during the 1980s, and the response of trade unions *qua* local organizations to such developments.

The thirty-two case studies were selected from a random sample of 177 establishments analysed in a telephone survey in 1986. Interviews were conducted at these thirty-two establishments that involved a further series of questions addressed to a representative of the management. At larger establishments this was often the personnel manager but at smaller organizations it was generally a senior managerial representative. The questions were posed

by a member of the Lancaster team and the questionnaire completed by the researcher on the spot. Some interviews involved
return visits and in a few instances additional data were supplied
by letter and/or telephone to the researchers. The team assessed
the level and scope of union recognition in the establishment,
both for manual and non-manual workers. We also ascertained
whether there were union members but no union recognition
within the establishment. We asked directly about the existence
of a closed shop and also about the existence of shop stewards
(or their equivalent). Questions were posed concerning relations
between management and both shop stewards and local trade
union officials. Further questions were posed concerning the
nature of collective bargaining within these establishments. We
also asked for management's views about any changes in the
influence of trade unions within their establishment since 1980
and about their attitudes to such influence. Information was collected about industrial disputes, absenteeism and labour turnover,
and an assessment of the effects of trade union legislation during
the 1980s.

The team also conducted twenty-five interviews with various
trade union officials who dealt with the Rochdale membership of
their union. These interviews were semi-structured. The questions
dealt with the structure of the union and the nature and size of
the membership in Rochdale. We asked detailed questions about
how collective bargaining functioned in the locality and their
views about their union's relationships with employers in the
town. We asked specifically about collective bargaining in the
thirty-two establishments where this was pertinent. Questions
were also asked about the strength of the union in Rochdale and
each official's perception of the general strength of unions in the
town. The team also asked about the development of new work
regimes in Rochdale, the impact of technological change, the situation of women and ethnic minorities within each union, and
the official's beliefs about why people did not join their particular
union. Given the period of our fieldwork we also probed for their
views about the conflict between the EETPU and TUC in 1988.
All these questions were posed within the general context of perceived changes during the 1980s.

Overall, our data allowed us to provide strong arguments
about the degree and nature of changes to trade unions in

Rochdale during the 1980s, and thereby to address the wider issues of the form and content of the crisis of British trade unions within a specific locality: Rochdale.

4. THE CONTEXT

4.1. The Structure of Trade Unions in Rochdale in 1980

The trade union movement in Rochdale displayed certain general characteristics in 1980.[1] There was a high level of union density in manufacturing industry. The historic nodes of employment in the town since industrialization in the early nineteenth century were textiles and engineering. Both sectors were strongly unionized in Rochdale throughout the twentieth century (Penn, 1985a). However, the sharp decline in textile employment in Rochdale in the latter years of the 1970s had already put considerable strain on this classic pattern of textile unionism. Traditionally textile unionism was occupationally centred and powerfully rooted in each locality (Turner, 1962; Penn, 1983 and 1985a). By 1980 most textile workers in Rochdale were members of the ATWU, although three small skilled unions persisted—the Overlookers, the Tapesizers, and the Beamers, Twisters, and Drawers. Likewise, engineering unionism retained a strong local identity in 1980. Rochdale remained a separate District of the AUEW (the local Engineering Employers were also a distinct part of the EEF at that time). Furthermore, most collective bargaining was focused at the plant level and conducted primarily by locally elected shop stewards in the classic pattern of engineering industrial relations (Marsh, 1965).

However, since 1945 a new centre of union power had developed, concentrated in the public services. In particular, unions representing local authority, health, and public utility workers (water, gas, electricity, telecommunications, postal services) had become far more prominent. By 1980, there was a clear bifurcation within the union movement in Rochdale between predominantly industrially based manufacturing unions with powerful localized systems of collective bargaining and a series of large public services trade unions where collective bargaining was undertaken predominantly away from the locality at a national level (particularly negotiations over pay and conditions).

4.2. The Transformation of Employment Patterns in Rochdale During the 1980s

The 1980s witnessed a major transformation of employment patterns in Rochdale. Between 1979 and 1982 unemployment rose from 6.0 per cent to 18.7 per cent (Penn, 1989a). Absolute numbers of the registered unemployed rose from 3,125 to 9,420 over the same period. This growth of unemployment involved a massive number of redundancies, particularly in the years 1980, 1981, and 1982 (see Table 7.1). As is clear from Table 7.1, there had been 4,702 confirmed redundancies in textiles and 2,280 within mechanical, electrical, and instrument engineering between 1980 and 1987. Such a collapse in employment within the two core areas of manufacturing was unprecedented, at least since the early 1930s. The Censuses of Employment in 1981 and 1984 revealed a similar picture (see Table 7.2). Such changes within specific sectors of employment were paralleled by changes in the pattern of hours in employment.

However, although part-time employment had increased during the period between 1981 and 1984, the rise was not dramatic. Indeed, part-time employment has been a long-standing feature of economic relations in Rochdale (Penn, 1985a; Penn et al., 1991) and the major structural change in hours of work in Rochdale predated the 1980s. In the period between 1850 and 1970 most female part-time employment was concentrated in textiles, whereas by the 1970s and 1980s, most was concentrated in retailing, public administration, and health care. In 1984, the latter two sectors accounted for around 40 per cent of all female part-time employees in Rochdale whereas textiles accounted for less than 1 per cent.

4.3. Conclusions

By 1980 Rochdale had become a strongly unionized town. Union strength was concentrated in textiles, engineering, and public services. It was also clear that there was a major deterioration in employment within the town, particularly in the period between 1980 and 1982, when both the textile and engineering industries were ravaged by recession. The form of economic crisis was more acute in Rochdale than in many areas of Britain, particularly

TABLE 7.1. *Confirmed redundancies in Rochdale local authority district: 1980–1987*

Standard industrial classification	Industry	1980	1981	1982	1983	1984	1985	1986	1987 to July	Totals
	Manufacturing Industry									
2	Chemical	44	52	108	44	10	—	50	—	308
32	Mechanical engineering	307	286	266	18	75	87	129	93	1,261
34–37	Electrical engineering and instruments	283	105	81	40	170	143	175	22	1,019
31	Metal manufactured goods	43	27	32	40	—	—	—	—	142
41–42	Food, drink, and tobacco	—	—	—	—	50	278	—	—	328
44–45	Leather footwear and clothing	125	400	188	485	58	140	26	45	1,467
43	Textiles	2,426	987	560	243	113	43	324	6	4,702
46	Timber and furniture	81	—	14	—	111	178	115	—	499
47	Paper, printing, and publishing	24	463	70	—	211	—	42	—	810
48–49	Other manufacturing	252	76	54	—	16	—	—	—	398
	Others (balancing)	166	81	123	37	24	23	—	23	477
	TOTAL All manufacturing	3,751	2,477	1,496	907	838	892	861	189	11,411

										Total
50	Construction	81	171	53	76	40	53	—	—	474
	Service Industries									
61–63	Wholesale distribution	—	—	—	—	81	54	56	26	
64–65	Retail distribution	—	—	—	—	112	106	172	38	
67	Repair consumer goods and vehicles	—	—	—	—	—	—	—	20	
71–77	Transport	—	—	—	—	33	36	65	—	
79	Telecommunications	—	—	—	—	—	—	—	61	
81–85	Insurance, banking, etc.	—	—	—	—	—	—	22	—	
91–94	Public administration and defence	—	—	—	—	12	19	—	—	
96–99	Other services	—	—	—	—	11	—	—	—	
	TOTAL All service industry	535	251	506	177	249	215	315	145	2,393
	GRAND TOTALS	4,367	2,899	2,055	1,160	1,127	1,160	1,176	334	14,278

Source: Carter (1987).

TABLE 7.2. *Employment patterns in Rochdale, 1981–1984 (selected sectors)*

	1981	1984	% change
Mechanical engineering	4,758	4,079	−14.2
Textiles	4,622	3,452	−25.3
Retail	4,767	5,188	+8.8
Insurance, banking	1,858	2,179	+17.3
Public administration	9,249	9,725	+5.2
Health	3,195	3,232	+1.2

Source: Penn (1989*b*).

TABLE 7.3. *Gender and hours of work in Rochdale, 1981–1984*

	1981	1984	% change
Male full-time	29,122	28,537	−2.0
Male part-time	1,370	2,358	+72.1
Female full-time	13,961	14,049	+0.6
Female part-time	9,969	10,652	+6.9
Overall	54,422	55,587	+2.1

Source: Penn (1989*b*).

when measured in terms of registered levels of unemployment or notified redundancies. Consequently, Rochdale provided an excellent site to undertake an examination of the local response by trade unions to the general crisis identified earlier.

5. THE STRUCTURE OF TRADE UNIONISM IN CONTEMPORARY ROCHDALE: A SECTORAL ANALYSIS OF THIRTY-TWO ESTABLISHMENTS

As part of the Lancaster team's research into changing patterns of economic life, an investigation into trade unionism in thirty-two establishments was undertaken. The establishments were selected from an earlier telephone survey conducted by the PSI in Rochdale in 1986. Establishments were selected for subsequent interviews with a view to achieving a reasonable coverage of the major sectors of employment in the town. As is clear from Table 7.4, the establishments themselves covered 5,345 employees and were representative of the major employment sites in the town. For details of the sectoral spread of contemporary employment in Rochdale see Penn (1989*b*).

TABLE 7.4. *Comparison of the numbers of employees in the thirty-two establishments with the 1984 Census of Employment*

Sector	No. employees in the establishments in the 1988 sample	No. employees in Rochdale in 1984
Textiles	1,947	3,452
Engineering	871	6,434
Other manufacturing	310	not available
Financial services	14	2,179
Professional services	20	not available
Public services	788	12,957
Retail and distribution	1,329	6,215
Transport	66	2,304

Source: 1984 Census of Employment and data from the thirty-two establishment firms.

Table 7.5 provides a summary of the results from these interviews. As is clear from these data, unions were recognized in twelve of the seventeen manufacturing plants. All but one textile plant were unionized, as were six of the eight engineering plants. As we have seen, textiles and engineering had been the two core spheres of twentieth-century manufacturing industry in the town. They had also been the dominant nodes of trade unionism in Rochdale during that period. These results reveal that this remained the case in the contemporary period. However, most textile and engineering workers were now represented by four large unions: the GMWU, the AEU, the EETPU, and the MSF. This was partly a function of recent union mergers which had led to the Sheetmetalworkers Union, ASTMS, and TASS forming the conglomerate union MSF. Non-manual workers were more likely to be recognized in textiles than in other industrial sectors within manufacturing and there was only one plant where unions

TABLE 7.5. *Trade union membership: data from the thirty-two establishment study in Rochdale*

	Manufacturing			Other
	Textiles	*Manufacturing*	*Engineering*	*Other*
Trade unions	√ √ √ x √	√ √ √ √ x x	x √ √ √ √ √	x √ x √ √ — x
Recognized: manual	GMB · AEU · GMB · GMB AEU EETPU · AEU GMB UCATT EETPU	AEU EETPU SMU · SMU · AEU GMB · x · x · AEU	AEU · AEU EETPU SMU · AEU EETPU UCATT · x · x · AEU	x · SOGAT AEU · x · AEU · x · — · x
Recognized: non-manual	x · x · MATSA ASTMS · MATSA · MATSA TASS APEX	√ · x · x · x · x · x	x · TASS · x · x · x	x · √ · x · √ · — · √
Members but not recognized	— — — — —	— — — — x AEU TASS APEX	— — — x	x — — — —
Closed shop	x x x x √	√ x √ x x √	x x √ x x	x x x √ √ — x
Shop stewards	√ x √ √ √	√ √ √ x x √	x √ √ √ √	√ √ x √ √ — x
Relations with stewards	H — H H H/U	H H H — — H	U H H H H	H — H — —
Contacts with local officials	√ x √ √ √	— x √ x √ √	√ √ √ √ √	x √ x √ √ — x

Relations with officials	U	—	—	—	H	H	—	—	H	—	H	—	H	—	H/U	—
Negotiations over pay	Multi	Co.	Co.	Plant	Multi	Plant	P/Multi	Plant	Plant	Plant	P/Multi	P/C	P/Multi	Plant	Co.	Plant
Non-pay negotiations	Many	None	—	None	Many	Many	Many	Many	Many	None	None	Many	Some	None	Many	None
TU influence since 1980	—	—	—	—	△	—	▽	—	—	—	—	—	—	—	▽	—
Policy to TUs	C	C	—	C	C	C	C	C	C	C	C	C	C	C	C	C
Relationship management and TUs	C	C	—	—	C	C	C	C	—	—	C	C	C	C	C	—
Attitude to union influence	H	—	H	—	U	H	U	H	H	H	H	H	H	H	H	H
Effects of TU legislation	Large	—	—	—	Large	Little	Little	None	Little	None	Little	—	Little	None	—	—
Disputes	✓	x	x	x	x	✓	x	x	x	x	✓	—	x	x	x	x
Absenteeism	C	△	▷	C	△	▽	C	C	C	C	△	—	C	C	C	▷
Turnover	C	▽	◁	C	◁	C	◁	◁	◁	◁	C	—	◁	C	◁	◁

(cont.)

TABLE 7.5 (cont.):

Services

	Financial		Professional		Public							Retail and distribution			Transport
Trade union	x	√	√	x	√	√	√	√	√	√	√	√	x	x	√
Recognized: manual	NA	NA	NA	NA	NUPE	NUPE	NUPE	NUPE	TGW GMB	NA	NA	GMB	x	x	TGW
Recognized: non-manual	x	BIFU	ACTSS	x	NALGO NUT NASUWT NAHT	NALGO NUT NASUWT NAHT	NALGO NUT	NATFHE NALGO NUT	NALGO	CPSA SCS	MATSA	MATSA	x	x	x
Members but not recognized	—	—	—	x	—	—	—	—	—	—	—	—	x	—	—
Closed shop	x	√	x	x	x	x	x	x	√	x	x	√	√	x	x
Shop stewards	x	√	√	x	√	√	√	x	√	√	√	√	x	x	x
Relations with stewards	—	H	H	—	H/U	H	—	—	H	H	H	H/U	—	H	—
Contacts with local officials	x	√	√	x	x	√	√	x	√	x	√	√	x	√	x
Relations with officials	—	H	H	—	—	—	—	—	H	—	H	H/U	—	H	—
Negotiations over pay	Estab.	Co.	Co.	Estab.	LA	LA	LA	LA	LA	National	Multi	Co.	Plant	Wages Council Rates	None

Table: The 32 establishment interviews in Rochdale.

Non-pay negotiations	None	Some	Hols.	None	LA	LA	LA	Wkng. practices (rest LA)	—	Some	Some	—	None	None
TU influence since 1980	—	C	—	—	△	—	—	▽	—	—	C	—	—	—
Policy to TUs	—	C	C	C	C	C	C	C	C	C	C	—	C	C
Relationship management and TUs	—	C	C	C	C	C	C	C	C	—	—	—	C	C
Attitude to union influence	H	H	H	H	H	H	H	H	H	H	H	H	U	U
Effects of TU legislation	None	None	None	—	Little	Little	Little	Little	None	Little	Little	—	Little	None
Disputes	x	x	x	x	✓	✓	✓	x	x	x	x	x	✓	x
Absenteeism	C	C	C	▽	△	C	C	C	C	C	C	C	—	△
Turnover	C	C	C	C	▷	C	C	▷	C	C	C	▷	—	—

Key

H = Helpful
U = Unhelpful (relations with shop stewards and officials)

Multi = Multi-employer
Co. = Company
P = Plant
LA = Local authority (levels at which negotiations over pay take place)

△ = Increasing
▽ = Decreasing
C = Constant

Source: The 32 establishment interviews in Rochdale.

had members but no recognition. This firm had involved a management buy-out during the 1980s. There was little evidence of any sustained pattern of union derecognition in Rochdale during this period. This confirmed the picture of very limited union derecognition in Britain during the 1980s as portrayed both by Millward and Stevens (1986) and Claydon (1989).

Most unionized manufacturing plants had elected shop stewards. This was not a great surprise in the engineering industry, which had featured a long-standing tradition of shop steward organization. However, it was of considerable interest that four textile plants had shop stewards given that there had been a widespread hostility by the textile unions traditionally towards the development of such an institution within their industry (Turner, 1962; Penn, 1985*a*). A major factor in this transformation of labour representation within textiles had been the amalgamation of the dominant textile workers' union, the ATWU, with the GMB in 1986. Since that time the GMB had devoted considerable efforts towards the construction of an extensive shop steward system within the local textile mills in Rochdale.

Management in most manufacturing plants reported that their relations with shop stewards had been helpful. A similar attitude towards relations with trade union officials was expressed but it was clear from the interviews that direct dealings with local union officials had been infrequent and certainly not sought regularly by management. Closed shops were said to be in force at five manufacturing plants despite their lack of any continued legal basis. Our interviews suggested that this was a historic pattern that suited those managements that enforced such closed shops. There was little evidence that these arrangements were sustained by formal external union pressure. Rather they continued as the result of a symmetry of interests between local managements and their local workforces.

Almost all manufacturing establishments negotiated pay with their workforces. In engineering, all firms reported significant plant bargaining. This has been a general feature of the post-war British engineering industry whereby the employers (EEF) and unions (CSEU) negotiate national *minimum* rates, and local deals, beyond these minima, are struck at specific workplaces (Marsh, 1965). The situation in textiles was more complex. Industrial textile firms undertook company-level bargaining, as did the subsidiary of Courtaulds since the latter was no longer a member of the British Textile Employers Association (BTEA). The other two consumer textile plants were part of the overall multi-employer negotiation with the BTEA. Nevertheless, at twelve of the seventeen manufacturing plants there was significant local wage bargaining. Indeed, four of the five non-unionized manufacturing establishments utilized this system of bargaining with their workforces.

Half the manufacturing establishments also negotiated over issues beyond payment levels and wage systems. In some cases such negotiations were extensive but they rarely involved local trade union officials; rather they were conducted for the most part by local managements and local shop stewards. Such results confirmed the claim made by Bassett (1987) that consultation between management and worker representatives had survived the 1980s recession in Britain.

There was little evidence that managements felt that the influence of trade unions had changed significantly during the 1980s. Only two managements suggested any significant weakening of the power of unions during this period. All unionized manufacturing establishments reported that there had been no significant change in either their policy towards trade unions or in the general relationship of unions and management. Almost all managements reported satisfaction with the *status quo* within their plants in relation to trade union influence, whatever that *status quo* actually entailed. Again, few managements in manufacturing felt that the trade union and employment legislation passed successively during the 1980s had significantly affected their situation. Indeed, most managers were unaware of the main features of that legislation.

There was little evidence of significant industrial disputes in these seventeen Rochdale manufacturing plants during the 1980s. Interestingly, none of the three reported to the team was over issues of pay. One concerned health and safety (fumes in the workshop), one concerned the sub-contracting of security personnel, and the third was over time off for Asian workers for prayers during Ramadan. Such results provided empirical support for Edwards's (1987) conclusion that strike action fell significantly within private manufacturing industry during the 1980s. Absenteeism was felt to have risen at four plants and to have fallen at two. However, nine plants reported significant rises in labour turnover. This was consistent with the changing nature of the local labour market where skill shortages increased sharply and unemployment fell steadily after 1985.

Nevertheless, the overall impression of industrial relations within these manufacturing plants was one of localized bargaining between managements and shop stewards. Trade union officials were distant from, and had little purchase on, the everyday workings of this system of collective bargaining. There was only one example of attempts to de-unionize plants or to bypass the localized, plant bargaining system. This generalized pattern of mutual accommodation pre-dated the 1980s and represented the culmination of a long historical process involving the institutionalization of bargaining within manufacturing plants in Rochdale (Penn, 1983).

Indeed, there had been a growing homogenization of such patterns during the 1980s, primarily because textile mills had become more like engineering plants with respect to their industrial relations systems. Pay remained the central issue for negotiation in most plants but union officials were at some distance from much of the everyday bargaining. There was no evidence of major industrial disputes over pay during this period. Such results, therefore, disconfirmed Brown's (1987) claim that there had been a generic tendency for pay bargaining to become removed from the plant level during the 1980s. These results suggested an increasing focus on plant level bargaining within manufacturing industry in Rochdale during these years.

Interestingly, immediately after our interviews were completed in the textile mills, two of them were involved in the first national stoppage within the textile industry since the titanic struggle of 1932. The 1988 conflict centred upon a clash between the BTEA and the GMB over proposed increases in basic rates of pay. In April 1989, the team returned to these two plants and questioned management and workforce representatives further on these issues. At one plant, collective bargaining had changed from the pre-existing national bargaining pattern to a local plant-based system. This provided further evidence of a generic tendency in the 1980s towards a standardized pattern of collective bargaining within Rochdale manufacturing establishments.

The pattern of industrial relations in the fifteen service sector establishments was more complex than within manufacturing. Two of the four financial and professional services firms recognized non-manual unions. All the establishments in the public services—a primary and a secondary school, the technical college, a department of the local authority, a branch of a government department, and a publicly funded hostel—also recognized trade unions. In most cases, they dealt with a multiplicity of large public sector unions. Manual workers were predominantly represented by NUPE; and non-manual workers by NALGO and the various teaching unions. Only one of the firms in retailing and distribution recognized a union. This firm effectively ran a closed shop with the GMB for all manual and non-manual grades. The one transport firm in the sample recognized the TGWU but did not negotiate with it. Recognition was the result of pressure from local customers who had insisted on unionized lorry drivers.

Trade union influence in unionized places of work was not seen generally as having changed significantly during the 1980s and no service sector establishment reported any change in the relationship with local trade unions, whether they afforded such unions recognition or not. Nobody reported any major effects of the 1980s trade union and employment legislation. However, industrial disputes within the public service establishments were reported in most cases. These centred primarily upon pay and conditions, with the teachers' dispute of 1987 being the most widely cited instance. Absenteeism had risen in two of the three educational establishments in the sample. Only one service sector firm reported any increase in turnover and it was an unusual firm in so far as most of its employees were either part-time or casual, working as caterers.

Shop stewards or workforce representatives were recognized in five public service establishments, in two large retailing organizations, and at a bank. In all cases relations with these stewards were described by management as helpful, although in two cases this was the dominant rather than the universal experience. Seven establishments dealt with local trade union officials, although very infrequently. These relations were generally felt to be helpful by management. Within the local authority establishments almost all local bargaining was conducted at the authority rather than the establishment level. In the large retailing organization and the bank, bargaining was conducted at company level remote from

Rochdale. Local bargaining within an establishment only occurred at three small service sector establishments. These were located in financial and professional services.

Overall, only ten of the thirty-two establishments did not recognize trade unions. Recognition was concentrated in textiles, engineering, and public services. Seven of the twenty-two unionized establishments recognized only one union, but seven large unions featured in forty-three of the fifty-seven union recognitions. Indeed, if we add the various teaching unions to these seven (GMB, TGWU, EETPU, AEU, NUPE, NALGO, and MSF), only six of the fifty-seven union recognitions were unaccounted for. It is clear, therefore, that most effective union power in Rochdale resided with the seven large conglomerate unions whose membership was concentrated in manufacturing plants and the public services. It should also be noted that this number of conglomerate unions has continued to fall since the SCELI research.

At manufacturing plants most bargaining was undertaken within the factory between local managements and local shop stewards. Most bargaining concerned pay but there was also a small arena for wider discussion about the use of managerial prerogatives. In the service sector most collective bargaining was undertaken away from the place of work in either national or wider company-level negotiations. There was little evidence from the thirty-two establishments surveyed of any significant onslaught by managements upon traditional collective bargaining arrangements nor of a widespread breakdown of the patterns of accommodation and institutionalization of such industrial relations that have evolved during the post-war period.

Indeed, most managements expressed a pragmatic acceptance of union power within their establishments. A managerial respondent at the largest manufacturing site in Rochdale asked, 'how else would workers be represented?' Another managerial respondent stated that 'we accept it as a fact of life' in a fashion akin to the local weather and the seemingly permanent position of the football club near the bottom of the Football League. Other respondents were rather more enthusiastic in their comments. One claimed that 'we are not against unions. It is in our interests.' Another told us that it was 'beneficial to have lines open through shop stewards rather than each problem having to be discussed individually. It reduces anomalies and makes day-to-day running smoother.'

However, there was little evidence that local union officials remained powerfully placed within any other environment than the local authority. Rather, it was mainly workforce representatives who exercised most power within the majority of non-local authority unionized establishments in both manufacturing and services in Rochdale by the late 1980s.

6. THE SITUATION OF TRADE UNIONS IN ROCHDALE IN THE 1980s

6.1. *Union Structure* (see Table 7.6)

On the basis of the team's interviews with local officials of twelve trade unions, it was evident that there had been a series of changes to the dominant historical pattern of unions identified earlier in this chapter. These changes centred upon three separate processes. First, the AEU had dissolved its Rochdale District in the mid-1980s upon the retirement of its former District Secretary and amalgamated it with Oldham. The office of the new Oldham and Rochdale District was located in Oldham. This had been prompted by the financial difficulties of the AEU and had resulted in a significant distancing of the union from its Rochdale membership. Second, the Sheetmetalworkers' Union had combined with TASS and become part of the craft section of the newly formed MSF conglomerate. This also had led to increasing distance between the Rochdale membership and the officers of the MSF craft section in Salford. However, the most significant change involved the amalgamation of the ATWU in Rochdale with the GMB to form part of the textile section of that union. The new GMB textile section was headquartered in Rochdale as a result of its taking over the headquarters building of the ATWU in the town.

This amalgamation had radically altered the union structure for most unionized textile workers in Rochdale. The ATWU itself had been a federated union, with no shop stewards and controlled by local union officials who made decisions about wage bargaining directly with local employers (Turner, 1962).

TABLE 7.6. *Trade union structure in Rochdale during the 1980s*

Union	Union structure	Membership			Occupations	Gender	Bargaining	Strength of union	Relations with employers	Relations with other unions	Relations with EETPU
		Numbers	Change								
			Numbers	Density							
AEU	Rochdale used to be a separate District. Now amalgamated with Oldham. Offices in Oldham	@ 3,000	Falling	Constant	Mainly manual	Over-whelmingly Male	Plant	Strong, except numbers falling	Deteriorating. 30 external conferences in last year. Series of ballots on wages	Generally good	Cautious support
EETPU	Mixture of Geographic and Industrial Branches. Offices in Manchester	Unknown	Static	Constant	Mainly craft-workers	Over-whelmingly Male	Plant/ National	Strong	Good	Generally good. Few indications of hostility in Rochdale	—
MSF (Craft section)	Workplace branches	Unknown	Static	Constant	Craft-workers. Technicians	Over-whelmingly Male	Plant	Average	No untoward difficulties. No ballots on wages	Lack of friction. Clear jurisdiction	—
COHSE	Rochdale District Branch	500	Increasing	Increasing	Nurses	—	Health Authority	Strong	Quite good	Generally good	EETPU have sought to recruit nurses unsuccessfully

	Branch	Number			Type	Gender	Level	Strength			
NUT	Branch in every school	Unknown	Static	Increasing	Professional	Predominantly Female	—	—	Good	Good	No dealings with them
NALGO	Local Authority	2,000	Static	Constant	White-collar	51% Female	National/Employer	Average	Good	Good apart from FUMPO. Jurisdiction agreement in Local Authority	—
NUPE	3 branches in Local Authority. 1 branch in Health Authority	2,900 in Local Authority. 700 in Health Authority	Rising in Local Authority. Falling in Health Authority	Increasing in Local Authority. Decreasing in Health Authority	Non-skilled Manual	Male and Female	National/Employer	Strong formally. Weak in practice	Poor in Health Authority. Good in Local Authority	—	Hostile to EETPU in Health Service
TGWU	Trade groups for manual workers. Separate section for all non-manual workers	@ 2,000	Falling	Constant	Mainly manual workers	Male and Female	Plant/Company/National	Weaker	—	Poor: GMB, NUPE, AEU	—
GMBU	General branch in Rochdale. Officials now elected every 2 years	2,000	Static	Constant	Mainly non-skilled manual	Male and Female	Local Authority/Company/Plant	Strong	Some good, some bad	Poor: TGWU, NUPE, EETPU	—

(Cont.)

TABLE 7.6 (*cont.*):

Union	Union structure	Membership			Occupations	Gender	Bargaining	Strength of union	Relations with employers	Relations with other unions	Relations with EETPU
		Numbers	Change								
			Numbers	Density							
GMB (Textiles)	Textile branch in Rochdale. Officials now elected every 2 years	1,800	Increasing	Increasing	Manual workers. Concentrated among non-skilled	60% Female	Plant/ Company/ Industry	Strong	Fraught	Good:: Overlookers, Tapesizers, Beamers, Twisters, & Drawers. Poor: TGWU	'Open war'
Beamers, Twisters and Drawers	Rochdale part of a wider District	Very few	Falling	Constant	Skilled manual workers	Over-whelmingly Male	Plant/ Company/ Industry	Almost all beamers, twisters, & drawers are unionized	Co-operative	Good with all the other small textile unions	Merger discussions with AEU
Tape-sizers	Rochdale part of a wider District based in Bury	Very few	Falling	Constant	Skilled manual workers	Male	Plant/ Company/ Industry	100% unioniz-ation	Co-operative	Poor: GMB	Merger discussions with AEU
Over-lookers	Autonomous Rochdale branch	60	Falling	Constant	Technicians	Male	Plant/ Company/ Industry	100% unioniz-ation. Very strong strategic position in	Co-operative	—	Merger discussions with AEU

The GMB both represented a far more centralized union and had encouraged the development of an extensive shop steward network in textiles. Instead of the historic pattern whereby bargaining had been undertaken overwhelmingly by local officials, it was being conducted partly by local shop stewards and partly by GMB officials by the end of the 1980s. Paradoxically, such a new pattern closely mirrored the historic structures of union organization in the local engineering industry.

On the other hand, the three small skilled textile unions—the Tapesizers, the Overlookers, and the Beamers, Twisters, and Drawers—all retained the classic pattern of textile unionism. In each case the Rochdale membership formed a District within the wider Lancashire textile union. The Rochdale District formed a part of the wider, highly autonomous, federated union structure. Despite a range of merger discussions, both among themselves and with various larger conglomerate unions, these small skilled textile unions continued very much as they had done throughout the twentieth century, albeit with dramatically fewer members. To some external observers, they might appear to have become somewhat anachronistic but their survival remained a testimony to the strength of occupational consciousness, particularly among groups of skilled textile workers (Turner, 1962; Penn, 1983 and 1985*a*).

The structure of the main public services unions had not changed significantly during the 1980s. NUT, NALGO, NUPE, and COHSE all had local branches of considerable size. The AEU, EETPU, TGWU, and GMB also maintained smaller branches in both the local authority and the health authority. In formal terms, these structures of representation within what were the two largest employers in the town had remained remarkably stable during the 1980s. Clearly, the fall of union membership in manufacturing industry, which had been associated with high levels of unemployment and redundancies in local textile and engineering plants, had affected trade union structures in Rochdale to a far greater extent than had been the case within the public services, where levels of employment had fared far better during the 1980s.

6.2. Union Membership

The pattern of union membership was complex. Officials of the EETPU, MSF, and NUT could not provide estimates of numbers for their membership in Rochdale. In the former two cases, this partly reflected the structure of the union and the existence of small numbers of members in a large number of plants across Greater Manchester. Lack of precise knowledge about membership was not, however, confined to these unions. Both the AEU and GMB (textiles) officials were unaware that they had members at some of our thirty-two establishment case studies. These findings confirmed the picture presented by Kelly and Heery (1989) concerning the difficulties that full-time union officers were experiencing in the 1980s. Kelly and Heery catalogued the long hours worked by such officials and the fact that they were heavily overloaded in terms of the competing demands put upon them. Our data confirmed this picture and, given such circumstances, it was hardly surprising if union officials, particularly those newly elected and somewhat distant from the locality, should be unaware of the whereabouts of all their members. Perhaps more surprisingly, these officials were unaware of the existence of some of the plants where managements had reported that their particular union was recognized. We shall return to this issue when membership recruitment is examined later in the chapter.

Membership numbers had fallen in the AEU, NUPE (health branch), the TGWU, and among all three small skilled textile unions. Membership had risen within COHSE and the GMB textile section. These falls in membership were due to a variety of factors. The AEU, the TGWU, and the three small textile unions put their respective membership losses down to losses of employment in their areas of organization in Rochdale during the 1980s. However, they did not feel that there had been any fall in overall union density locally. NUPE had experienced a fall both in membership and in density within the Rochdale health authority as a result of deteriorating conditions of employment and demoralization among the groups of predominantly non-skilled health workers that they represented. COHSE, on the other hand, agreed that working conditions in health care had deteriorated but stated that this had galvanized union recruitment and increased union density among nurses. As a COHSE official graphically put it, 'Pay alone would not have got them to this pitch.' Of the other unions, only NUPE (local authority branch) and the GMB (textiles section) reported rising union membership and increasing union density. All the others reported broadly stable membership levels.

There was also a static picture with regard to the occupational and gender characteristics of most unions' memberships, with the exception of MSF and GMB. The latter two sets of changes were exclusively the results of recent amalgamations. There was little evidence of any significant expansion by any of the other unions outside their classic spheres of occupational representation. Likewise, the pattern of bargaining reported by each union in Rochdale had been broadly stable during the 1980s, with the important exception of the relative decline of national bargaining within local textile plants.

All the unions felt that they remained strong within the locality, with the exceptions of NUPE and the TGWU. In these two cases, officials felt that the position of the union in Rochdale had been weakened during the 1980s as a result of the increasingly hostile climate for the kinds of workers that they traditionally represented. Relations with local employers were reported to be good in most instances. The exceptions were NUPE's negative perception of relations with the health authority and the situation reported by the GMB (textiles section) and the AEU. In the case of textiles, relations had deteriorated as a consequence of the 1988 national strike, and in engineering there had been increasing disagreement over levels of pay. Clearly, wages remained a core arena for local conflict within both textile and engineering plants. *Plus ça change!*

Relations between unions were generally reported to have been good, although there had been some friction between the large conglomerates within the local authority. Generally, though, there had been a lack of friction and a clear mutual understanding of jurisdictional boundaries. It appeared to have been in nobody's interests to have engaged in large-scale membership battles which would, in all probability, have simply left all the unions involved with fewer members. A similar picture emerged over the issue of the EETPU's suspension and expulsion from the TUC. Attitudes towards the EETPU varied predictably. The

AEU was quite supportive, whereas NUPE and the GMB were hostile. Nevertheless, since the expulsion of the EETPU from the TUC in September 1988, there had been no major membership wars locally. An attempt had been made to exclude the EETPU from union meetings with the health authority in Rochdale but the motion had been defeated. Most EETPU members in Rochdale existed in small clusters in a large number of separate manufacturing plants. The main potential threat to this membership came therefore from either the AEU or MSF. However, the much larger AEU was not at all hostile towards the EETPU. Indeed, the two unions were moving towards a merger. The MSF union, although hostile, had a similar pattern of membership to the EETPU in Rochdale, and any membership battle would have been fraught with dangers to the MSF union either from the EETPU or the AEU or both. Consequently little change of note happened after the EETPU's expulsion from the TUC. Such results confirmed the impression of Eric Hammond, the leader of the EETPU, when he stated that 'I do not think that there is an army of zealots on either side . . . willing to have a go at other unions' members' (quoted in *Marxism Today*, September 1988).

These data further suggested that it was not the Bridlington Agreement *per se* that maintained traditional union jurisdictions but rather the balance of mutual advantage and the organizational incapacity of unions to engage in sustained membership recruitment campaigns. As Kelly (1987) has shown, full-time officers were 'already burdened with large case-loads of organized plants'. In Rochdale, full-time officers had major difficulties in translating the various central union campaigns to recruit new members, particularly peripheral workers, into effective local action. Neither the TGWU's 'Living Wage' and 'Link-Up' campaigns nor the GMB's 'Fair Laws and Rights in Employment' (FLARE) campaigns to recruit peripheral workers had been particularly successful in Rochdale. As Lane (1987) and Waddington (1988) indicated, neither union had the organizational capacity to sustain such membership drives. The GMB did, in fact, recruit over 1,000 new members in the north-west during a three month period in 1988, but two-thirds of these recruits were textile workers, of whom only 50 were part-time workers. These new recruits represented the classic feature of a successful union membership drive—they resulted from a successful strike and involved the recruitment of formerly demoralized or disinterested core workers. They did not reflect a significant expansion into organizing peripheral workers.

As we have indicated, unions representing the workforce in Rochdale did not have the resources or the inclination to undertake inter-union membership battles. None the less, all was not rosy in the house of organized labour. During our fieldwork we uncovered a series of major attacks made by national union leaders on each other in the columns of their union journals.[2] Such high levels of vituperation were, in our estimation, unprecedented in the twentieth century.[3] However, it was unclear what effect, if any, these diatribes had on union members. What was clear, nevertheless, was that they had not led to any significant battles over union membership within Rochdale.

6.3. Unions and Social Change (see Table 7.7)

The team asked a series of questions concerning trade unions and social change. It was clear that, at least as far as the trade union officials in our sample were concerned, there was little perception of any major effects of technical change upon the union or its members. The MSF craft section felt that technical change had been incremental and had involved some degree of enskilling and some deskilling[4] and this was also the view of the Beamers, Twisters and Drawers. Such a view corresponded to the state of technical change in Rochdale during the 1980s (see Penn, 1994). In none of the sectors analysed as part of the SCELI research was there evidence of widespread technical change.

There was also little evidence of significant changes in the relationships of women and ethnic minorities to trade unions in Rochdale. The AEU, EETPU, MSF, and the three small skilled textile unions were all overwhelmingly male and white in terms of the social characteristics of their members. This reflected the general pattern of exclusion of women and ethnic minorities from skilled manual work in Rochdale (Penn, Scattergood, and Martin, 1990 and 1991). There was certainly no evidence of any pressure from the unions themselves to change this situation. Rather, they claimed that it was the responsibility of the employers.

The main area of Asian employment in Rochdale had always been in textiles (see Penn and Scattergood, 1992). The GMB

TABLE 7.7. *Trade unions and social change in Rochdale*

Union	Effects of technical change	Gender	Ethnicity	Training	Effects of industrial relations legislation	Reasons for non-unionism	Changes over the last decade
AEU	—	—	—	No change apart from general decline in apprentice-ships	Increased use of ballots. 8 in previous 6 months	—	—
EETPU	—	Few members	Few Asian members. Union does not recruit workers or apprentices	Apprenticeships have fallen. Union develop-ing its own training programmes	None	—	—
MSF (Craft section)	Incremental. Some deskilling. Some enskilling	Union favours female appren-tices. Members have never been tested	No Asian members	No changes	'Most employers do not know one end of the new legislation from another'	None could be given	—
COHSE	Widespread in Health Service	Women less active in the main	Few Asian members	Increased training for nurses	Need to learn about balloting. More legalistic environment	Unions not very good at listening	General increase in unionization in health care. This was the result of 'the politicization of health care'. 'Pay alone would not have got them to this

				talked about pupils not teachers	accommodate GCSE	—	teachers stay at work. More concerned about conditions. More activism
NALGO	Mainly word processors and computers. No loss of jobs caused	No change. Women concentrated in lower-paid jobs	Union favours Local Authorities employing same % of ethnic minorities as live in their area	More post-entry training now	None	—	Union more effective today. 'Less sleepy'. Less cosy relations with Local Authority
NUPE	—	Continued discrimination in ambulance service	Members are more racist. Local Authority officers also racist	Decline of trainee auxiliary nurses. Lack of cash	Election of officers. Ballot for action tied the hands of negotiators	—	Union is significantly weaker. Members demoralized. Harder to negotiate
TGWU	—	—	—	—	Weakened the power of the union. Ballot clauses inhibit industrial action	—	—
GMBU	No change	No change	Few Asian members	—	No real effects	—	Reorganization of GMB has led to greater internal union democracy

(cont.)

TABLE 7.7 (cont.):

Union	Effects of technical change	Gender	Ethnicity	Training	Effects of industrial relations legislation	Reasons for non-unionism	Changes over the last decade
GMB (Textiles)	No change	Increasing proportion of female shop stewards and branch secretaries	Strong supporters of the union	—	The provisions of the legislation caused serious difficulties over picketing and secondary action during the 1988 strike	—	Reorganization of GMB has led to greater union democracy. The amalgamation with the Textile Workers Union has led to increasing shop floor representation and new bargaining structures. Increasing shop floor militancy over wages
Beamers, Twisters and Drawers	Deskilling and enskilling	No female branch secretaries or shop stewards	Employers reluctant to take them on	No change	No impact	—	No significant changes
Tape-sizers	No change	Continued barriers to entry. Employers'	Employers' reluctance blamed	No change. 'Dead men's shoes'	No significant effect	—	Amalgamation with Preparatory Workers Union. Fewer Districts

reported that Asian textile workers—almost all of whom were male—had been their most 'solid' supporters during the 1988 textile strike. However, there were few Asian shop stewards in textiles. On the other hand, the GMB reported increasing interest by female textile workers in the union and an increasing number of female shop stewards. The large public sector unions indicated that there were few Asian members and that both ethnic and sexual discrimination were deep-set within the employing organizations in which their members worked. Most unions admitted that ethnic monitoring within the local authority was little more than a charade, although most preferred to say this 'off the record' (see Penn, Scattergood, and Martin, 1990). They also claimed—again 'off the record'—that other unions were racist. Only NUPE were prepared to admit that some of their own members in Rochdale were racist.

There was little evidence of significant changes in training provision for trade unionists in manual work within manufacturing industry in Rochdale. Indeed, most unions pointed out the general decline in apprenticeships as being the *most* significant recent change. The main areas of reported changes were in professional work within the public services—most notably for nurses and teachers. In other areas the situation was reported as essentially unchanging during the 1980s. Overall, though, trade unions were being marginalized from training structures in Rochdale. They had little purchase on MSC schemes and were to be side-lined in the late 1980s when Rochdale TEC was formed with virtually no union representation.

However, the unions did report a series of significant effects of the industrial relations legislation passed during the 1980s. The AEU reported an increased use of ballots over action in relation to pay claims. Balloting was seen as a significant new constraint by the TGWU, COHSE, and NUPE. Generally most unions saw the new legislation as having created a more legalistic environment and as requiring greater caution in the pursuit of industrial action. However, as we saw in the previous section, industrial conflict had been rare in Rochdale during the 1980s. This partly reflected a general decline in strike activity during the 1980s in Britain and partly the mix of industrial sectors within the town. In this context, the effects of the new legislation upon union action during the 1988 textile strike were probably illustrative of increasing difficulties for trade unions.

The 1988 national textile strike had been the first in the industry since 1932. The conflict between the textile unions and the BTEA was complicated initially by the fact that Courtaulds— Europe's largest textile company—were not a party to the agreement and had settled separately with their unions. Courtaulds were a major customer of many BTEA member firms. When Courtauld's drivers—members of the TGWU—were confronted with GMB pickets at BTEA mills, they faced a serious dilemma. On the one hand, GMB's white-collar workers (members of MATSA) were not party to the dispute and they continued to work within the plants: for them to have done otherwise would have been illegal. On the other hand, Courtaulds instructed their own drivers to make their deliveries or else the firm might well have decided to contract out their transport functions. GMB textile strikers felt that the solidarity of labour should hold sway but, in the end, the drivers were instructed to cross the picket lines by their own union, the TGWU.

Such an episode was by no means unique during the 1980s. In a series of disputes, union members had to weigh the moral case for action in support of other union members against the legal and economic sanctions that could have been brought to bear upon them. In the case of the TGWU drivers, it was clear that they disliked the situation that they were faced with. Indeed, they refused to allow anybody without the appropriate health and safety credentials to unload or load their lorries. In our opinion, such moral dilemmas for trade unionists will persist whilst the present legislative constraints operate. Such a situation represented a major change for organized labour in Rochdale since 1980.

7. CONCLUSIONS

This paper has delineated the changing position of trade unions in Rochdale during the 1980s. The general conclusion from these data was that trade unions have held on to their position within the town during this period. *There occurred no major significant gains in union strength yet, conversely, there was no strong evidence of union decline.* No concerted effort was mounted by employers in the locality to weaken trade unions or to rearrange the fundamentals of collective bargaining. Such results confirmed the earlier results of Rose and Jones (1985). The general pattern of collective bargaining remained locally based within manufacturing and focused overwhelmingly on wages. The merger of the ATWU and GMB led to a *convergence of collective bargaining structures* across a wide spectrum of textile and engineering plants in the town. In the service sector, particularly within public services and administration, local collective bargaining was not concerned with wages directly but rather with disputes over the position of individuals and groups of workers within nationally negotiated pay grades.

There occurred no significant collapse of union membership and most trade unionists belonged to a small number of conglomerate unions. These unions had come to inhabit, and to maintain, a well-ordered environment between themselves. There was no evidence of jurisdictional disputes between these unions in Rochdale. Nor did such a development seem very likely for the future since, despite the national acrimony between rival union blocs, there was little local advantage to be gained from membership wars. Unions lacked either the resources or the cadres with which to sustain such a strategy. Indeed, they were finding it very difficult to extend their membership even within their own spheres of jurisdiction. The main exception was the GMB textile section, which had been able to recruit significant numbers of new textile members after the 1988 national strike. However, this success has to be seen within the context of declining union density within textiles during the last years of the semi-moribund ATWU. The success of the GMB in textiles, therefore, probably only represented a return to the historic norm of high union membership within the industry.

We uncovered no evidence of single-union deals or of the other, widely publicized panoply of the 'new collective bargaining' (Lloyd, 1988). We concluded that such developments were being, and continue to be, exaggerated and related to a small number of atypical examples—albeit widely cited by commentators. We also concluded that there were overwhelming dangers inherent in the anecdotal mode of data appropriation that had become popular among social scientists concerned with contemporary trade unionism.

We found little direct evidence of any effects of the new industrial relations legislation. However, it had affected the attitudes of trade union officials and had made them more cautious in the escalation of industrial grievances. We discovered evidence of advantages created by the balloting provisions within the engineering industry. A strong ballot in favour of industrial action in pursuance of a pay claim invariably produced an improved offer from employers. However, the inter-union difficulties caused by the legislation for the TGWU and GMB during the 1988 textile strike revealed the other side of the coin. Nevertheless, most employers and most unions reported that the new legislation had produced few significant changes in the conduct of everyday collective bargaining in Rochdale. It is worth reiterating that similar conclusions, using different data and methods of research for the other SCELI localities, are presented in Chapters 2 and 3 of this book.

Which of the two models of trade union crisis outlined earlier best approximates these complex data sets? We were forced to conclude that neither was appropriate. There was certainly no evidence of a terminal decline of trade unionism in Rochdale. The major employers in a wide range of sectors of employment continued to recognize and bargain with trade unions. Most local bargaining in manufacturing plants concerned wages, whereas most local bargaining in the service sector focused predominantly on anomalies within, and interpretations of, nationally agreed grading schemes. Ultimately, however, much of the force behind such grievances by trade unionists involved issues of payment. This economic focus of trade unions in Rochdale should not be a surprise. Economic issues were central to the early establishment of trade unionism in Rochdale from the mid-nineteenth century onwards (Penn, 1983 and 1985*a*) and have been integral to the continued development of trade unionism in the twentieth century, particularly since 1945. The contemporary emphasis of unionism on collective bargaining over pay and pay-related issues represents nothing more than a continuation of the long-standing historical tradition of collective economic instrumentalism in the town.

By 1980 a well-ordered, clearly demarcated pattern of relations between unions and employers and also between unions themselves had developed in Rochdale. These institutional arrangements were to weather the stormy climate of the 1980s remarkably well. If a crisis within local trade unionism had developed, it was not characterized by significant membership losses, increasing inter-union conflicts, or systematic de-unionization. Rather, it was manifested in the conservatism and traditionalism inherent within the institutional structures that 'held the line' during the 1980s. As a consequence of their preoccupation with collective economic instrumentalism, trade unions were poorly equipped to deal with such issues as gender and ethnic exclusion within the institutional nexus of which they formed a part. Nor were unions well prepared to deal with the evolving training system in Rochdale. Indeed, they had little input into either company training provision or the battery of Training Agency programmes. In our view, it was the relative success of unions in Rochdale during the 1980s that, paradoxically, revealed the real difficulties for trade unions in Rochdale (and, in all likelihood, elsewhere in Britain). The overwhelming focus of trade unions in the locality upon economic issues had rendered them ill equipped to deal with the wider parameters of social change in the town.

NOTES

1. For extensive analyses of the historical development of trade unionism in Rochdale, see Penn (1983 and 1985a).
2. See Towers (1988b). Union derecognition is not a general phenomenon in Britain at present. Its incidence is concentrated in shipping and publishing.
3. There were bitter recriminations between the TGWU and GMB and the AEU. See, for instance, *GMB Journal*, May 1988; *ACTSS Magazine*, June 1988; and the *AEU Journal*, June and July 1988.
4. The example of enskilling was CADCAM and of deskilling was CNC punching machinery. However, the MSF official stated that the effect of new computerized machinery upon skill levels was, in his view, more a function of managerial intentions than intrinsic to the equipment itself.

8

Trade Unionism in a Hostile Environment: An Account of Attempts to Organize the North Sea Off-Shore Oil Industry Between 1970 and 1990

JOHN SEWEL AND ROGER PENN

1. INTRODUCTION

The North Sea off-shore oil industry provides a relatively rare opportunity for examining the history of trade union organization in a new industry. Indeed, one of the reasons for choosing Aberdeen as one of the six localities for the SCELI research was that it served as the main on-shore base for the North Sea oil industry in Britain. The economic fortunes of the city itself, and much of the surrounding area, have been closely linked to oil since the pace of exploration quickened in the 1970s. This chapter looks at the development of trade unionism in this emergent industry since 1970 in the context of both economic and political change. In so doing, it also represents an implicit comparison with the challenges faced by trade unionism in Rochdale during the 1980s (see the previous chapter) and with those experienced in Swindon (see Chapter 3).

The off-shore oil industry has a number of distinctive characteristics that have helped shape the history of trade unionism. First, all oilfields go through a cycle of exploration, development, production, and eventual abandonment. Very different activities are associated with each stage in the cycle. During the exploration phase the dominant activity is drilling. Within the production phases the main emphasis is on controlling and monitoring the flow of oil. Within a larger oil province, a number of individual fields will be at different stages of the overall cycle, and individual field drilling will inevitably take place during the production phase as attempts are made to improve the overall efficiency of oil recovery.

The second distinctive, but not unique, characteristic of the off-shore oil industry is the prevalence of sub-contracting. The main oil companies, such as Shell and BP, constitute the field operators, but during all phases of the cycle most specialist activities, ranging from diving to construction work, from drilling to catering, are undertaken by sub-contractors. One consequence of such a client–contractor relationship is that it is not always clear who is ultimately responsible for working conditions and terms of employment off-shore. For instance, during the production phases maintenance work is predominantly sub-contracted, but contractors' employees may be engaged in similar activities to the core production workers employed by the oil companies, but with different terms and conditions of employment. There is also a seasonal element in that maintenance activities are concentrated over the summer months when weather conditions are relatively favourable.

A final, but important, contextual point in understanding the history of trade unionism off-shore is that, throughout the lifetime of the industry, successive British governments and the oil companies have shared a common interest in bringing oil on stream as quickly as possible and in trying to maximize output. Governments have relied upon the oil industry to save the economy from major balance of payments crises and to be a major source of revenue to the Exchequer. The oil companies have been concerned to bring viable and profitable fields on stream as quickly as possible in order to obtain a return on the extremely high level of capital investment necessary to develop a field.

A major factor inhibiting the trade unionization of the off-shore industry is not just the fact that an off-shore location imposes difficulties in undertaking recruitment activity and picketing in times of dispute, but that the workforce is drawn from a wide geographical area and has no on-shore residential focus. Many off-shore workers have traditionally been recruited from the north-east of England and west-central Scotland. The only contact these men have with Aberdeen is the railway station and the heliport, with perhaps a single-night stop-over. In the early days trade union recruitment drives were limited to leafleting workers as they arrived at the heliport to go off-shore, or as they arrived back in Aberdeen on the way south.

Geography also removed one other potent agent of trade unionization—the unfairly dismissed or aggrieved worker. Trade union officials have frequently drawn the comparison between organizing off-shore and on-shore. On-shore a worker who had been treated unjustly by his employers not only remained visible in the locality, but became a symbol inspiring solidarity and collective action among his fellow workers. Off-shore, a worker who fell foul of management was liable to instant dismissal and was immediately flown ashore and put on the first train south. Rather than providing a focus for solidarity, he simply disappeared. Alternatively, once home, he would be informed that his contract was not being renewed. Geography helped to remove an important basis of collective, solidaristic action.

The final factor of importance in the history of unionization off-shore is the general attitude of employers in the industry towards trade unionization. Here two sets of distinctions have to be made: first, between trade unions having representational rights and having collective negotiating rights, and, second, between the oil companies and the contractors as employers. In the account that follows it will be seen that these distinctions lie at the heart of attempts to organize the off-shore workforce. Although the formal position of both oil companies and contractors towards trade union membership tends to be one of neutrality, in reality neither have shown any enthusiasm and some contractors have been aggressively hostile to trade unions having collective negotiating rights. The oil companies have traditionally adopted the position that they are happy for their workers to belong to trade unions and to discuss virtually any matters with trade union officials, but they are opposed to granting trade unions negotiating rights, because such a move would be introducing a third party between the company and its workforce. Such an attitude is entirely consistent with the very strong emphasis placed on corporate identity and corporate membership by all the oil companies. The contractors are more likely, sometimes publicly but often informally, to oppose trade union negotiating rights from a 'macho' position. Trade unionization is seen by them as incompatible with the 'rough, tough', aggressive and dynamic nature of the oil industry.

Given this range of factors, organizing the workforce and obtaining representational and negotiating rights were unlikely to be achieved quickly or without difficulty in the oil industry. The following chronological account explores the emergence of various forms of collective action in the North Sea oil industry. Despite the lack of full negotiating rights, employers and trade unions have been drawn into relationships based upon expediency and pragmatism. Such relations have permitted minimal control and regulation of the off-shore workforce throughout most of this period.

2. EARLY DAYS

Exploration drilling started in the northern North Sea in the late 1960s, but it was not until the early 1970s that the oil industry began to have a significant impact on social and economic life in the north-east of Scotland. Early accounts portrayed the industry rather exotically, with wages and conditions beyond those normally experienced by workers in the north-east's indigenous industries.

In March 1972 the North East of Scotland Development Authority (NESDA), a local government development agency, estimated that there were 1,000 oil jobs in the Aberdeen area. The off-shore industry had reached a level at which a degree of regulation was necessary and from mid-1972 the first safety regulations controlling safety of rigs and drilling platforms came into force with the requirement that all off-shore installations had to register with the Department of Trade.

The first attempt to establish some sort of trade union organization occurred in February 1973 with the creation of the North Sea Oil Action Committee (NSOAC). This was an *ad hoc* body of local Aberdeen politicians and trade unionists, although the trade unions themselves were not heavily involved. The emergence of the NSOAC bore witness to the fact that there was no trade union organization in place at the time capable of representing the interests of the off-shore workers. The Committee hoped to exert influence not through its organizational strength, but through the prestige of those associated with it.

Robert Middleton, the Chairman of the Action Committee, acknowledged the difficulty of establishing trade union representation off-shore and appealed directly to the Government to intervene and standardize pay and working conditions. A specific demand was for the banning by the Government of a contracted rig upon which conditions were alleged to be particularly bad. All these early demands were phrased in terms of obtaining direct Government intervention: they were not expressed in terms of establishing trade union rights *per se*. Such approaches to Government were perhaps appropriate at that time given the Heath Government's greater preparedness to intervene and regulate wages and conditions in industries where trade union organization was low.

The NSOAC questioned the assumption that all off-shore workers were highly paid with a series of well-publicized strikes. The Committee's virtual plea was for the main trade unions to start organizing the oil workers themselves. The local Aberdeen evening paper approached the TGWU and the AEU to determine what they were doing and it came to the conclusion that they were too busy fighting an inter-union power struggle for control in the industry rather than doing battle for the men on the rigs. The newspaper story observed that the trade unions had taken few positive steps to try to negotiate either working conditions or pay on the rigs. Although the rigs had been operating since the mid-1960s, the trade unions had not requested an official visit off-shore.

However, the first steps towards more active involvement by the trade unions were taken later in 1973 during the annual conference of the Scottish Trades Union Congress in Aberdeen. As a result of a recommendation made at that conference, an exploratory meeting was held in Glasgow in June 1973 to discuss the possibility of the unions making a joint approach to the employers. The unions involved were the TGWU, UCATT, the EETPU, the GMBU, APEX, and the Boilermakers. From this initial and tentative first step, it became clear that the individual trade unions were prepared to discuss a joint approach. Clearly, however, there was no possibility of following Norwegian practice and having one union handle the interests of all North Sea oil workers.

The end of 1973 witnessed a fourfold increase in the oil price. This exerted a major influence on the development of industrial relations in the North Sea. The increase in the oil price significantly strengthened the hand of the oil companies and their contractors in negotiations with the incoming Labour Government. The rise in oil prices was to increase Britain's oil import bill in 1974 by £2,500 million. This made it imperative for the Government to ensure the speediest possible development of the North Sea oilfields. The rise in oil prices acted as a spur to both exploration drilling and field development. It also meant that the oil companies could look forward to a much greater return from their North Sea investment. From 1974 onwards the oil employers were in a much stronger position to resist any legislative constraints, whilst being able to buy out any industrial relations difficulties if that became necessary.

Given increasing levels of activity, the major problem the oil industry faced was one of shortages in labour supply. By early 1974 contractors were experiencing high turnover levels among their employees and difficulties in recruiting replacement staff. In some cases the oil companies themselves were becoming concerned about the quality of the work that the contractors were delivering. As a result, throughout the spring of 1974 significant changes were brought about in the conditions of crews on rigs throughout the North Sea. On some rigs the working pattern changed from two weeks off-shore and one week on-shore to one week off-shore and one week on-shore. Working hours were reduced from 56 to 42 per week. Such a solution to the high turnover problem was only possible with the agreement of the client oil companies. Indeed, it is likely the oil companies instigated, or at least encouraged, these changes in working practices as an attempt to secure stability of employment and to improve the quality of work on the rigs.

Conditions off-shore may have been improving, but the trade unions made little progress in their approaches to the oil companies and the contractors. With the election of a Labour Government in 1974, there was a significant change in political rhetoric. Bruce Millan stated, during a visit to Aberdeen, that 'It is always in the best interest of employees to be members of their appropriate trade union and have negotiations conducted by their trade union on their behalf.' Millan's Aberdeen visit coincided with two milestones in the industrial relations history of the off-shore oil industry. SEDCO, a drilling contractor, flew home 27 crew men who had refused to work because of a grievance over shift patterns. The cause of the dispute lay in the fact that

SEDCO were still working a two weeks off-shore, one week on-shore pattern, while other rigs had adopted a one week on, one week off pattern. SEDCO's response revealed a problem which was going to reappear time and time again in subsequent disputes. Who effectively controlled policy—the contractors or the oil companies?

The second industrial relations milestone was the formation of the Inter-Union Off-Shore Oil Committee in April 1974. The discussions between the national officers of the oil-related unions produced an agreement that recognition was best pursued through co-ordinated action. The Inter-Union Off-Shore Oil Committee was the local expression of that agreement. The Committee consisted of the local full-time officials of seven trade unions: TGWU, AUEW, ASTMS, the Boilermakers Society, EETPU, UCATT, and APEX. The objectives of the Committee were clearly stated: 'The trade unions are no longer prepared to countenance a situation of non-unionization in the country and particularly in the North Sea oilfields . . .'.

For the next sixteen years the Inter-Union Off-Shore Oil Committee was the vehicle through which individual trade unions sought recognition and negotiating agreements with both the oil companies and the contractors. It also became the main point of contact between the unions and the employers and the forum within which disputes were effectively resolved.

The early years of the British off-shore oil industry had, therefore, been marked initially by inaction and a degree of indifference on the part of the national trade unions towards the opportunities and difficulties created by the emergence of an entirely new industry. By April 1974, however, the unions had formed the Inter-Union Off-Shore Oil Committee, thereby creating an organization which would enable the individual unions to try and tackle recognition in a co-ordinated way.

3. ORGANIZATION, REPRESENTATION, AND DEFEAT: 1974–1979

The period between 1974 and 1979 saw an explosion in North Sea oil-related activity and the emergence of Britain as a major oil producer. In 1974 the Grampian Regional Council estimated

that 4,455 people were employed in the oil industry in the
Aberdeen and Buchan area. By 1981 the total estimate of oil
employment in the Grampian Region was over 39,000 with an
estimate of 26,000 working off-shore. The first oilfield to come
on stream was Argyll in July 1975, followed by the giant Forties
field in November of that year. By 1978 North Sea production
reached the level at which it had turned the balance of payments
into surplus.

Throughout much of this period the trade unions appeared to
be making steady progress in organizing the off-shore workforce.
Agreements were reached with the oil companies that enabled
trade union officials to visit rigs and platforms and to meet individual workers off-shore. Representational agreements were made
with a limited number of oil companies that allowed trade unions
to make representations over grievances, but excluded negotiating
rights over terms and conditions of employment. The off-shore
catering industry became subject to collective bargaining between
the catering contractors, the NUS, and the TGWU. As importantly, the construction and engineering unions negotiated an
agreement with the construction contractors covering employment on production platforms up to the moment they became
'live' (i.e. when the oil started to flow). Both these agreements
were made with either the active involvement or passive acceptance of the oil companies.

The progress of the trade unions off-shore took place within
the context of a more favourable legislative framework. Both the
repeal of the Heath Government's Industrial Relations Act and
the passing of the Labour Government's Employment Protection
Act provided a more positive milieu for trade unions.
Government ministers also indicated that one of the criteria
likely to be taken into account in future licensing rounds for
exploration blocks was a company's attitude towards trade
unions. Despite the progress made during this period towards
organizing the off-shore workforce, the period ended with the
defeat in 1979 of an unofficial strike by construction workers.
The impact of that defeat was to be far-reaching and represented
a major setback for the trade unions and their attempts to extend
trade unionism throughout the industry.

May 1974 saw the newly formed Inter-Union Off-Shore Oil
Committee deciding its tactics. On the one hand, it invited the

drilling companies and the oil companies to talks on union recognition. On the other, it indicated that despite a wish to behave reasonably and responsibly, it was prepared to put the off-shore installations 'under siege' by using its strength in the servicing side of the industry to cut off supplies to the rigs. The NUS claimed 100 per cent membership of British boats, many of whom had been recruited from trawler crews, which formed 70 per cent of the North Sea supply fleet.

The employers were reluctant to enter into discussion with the Inter-Union Committee. The drilling companies simply refused to discuss union membership and only BP and Shell of the oil majors attended the first meeting called by the Committee. Industrial action that brought the oilfields to a standstill would have been as unwelcome to the Government as to the oil companies. Nevertheless, although there was some sabre rattling from within the industry in the local press, there was never any real possibility that the oil companies would relocate because of any putative level of trade union activity. Of more importance to the oil companies was negotiating an acceptable tax regime with the new government.

The most significant product of this first round of co-ordinated union action was the Hook-Up Agreement between the construction unions and the contractors covering fitting-out and preparing the platforms prior to the commencement of oil flowing. The oil companies had studiously avoided entering into agreements with trade unions that gave them negotiating rights on behalf of their own employees. Why should the oil companies, therefore, have encouraged an agreement between the contractors and the unions which could set a possibly uncomfortable precedent for collective agreements within the industry? The most convincing explanation is that the oil companies saw different factors predominating in the hook-up and post-hook-up phases. It is in the interests of oil companies for a platform to be brought on stream as quickly as possible. In preparing a platform for production, small-scale disputes involving only a few workers could result in major and costly delays. In such a situation there is considerable advantage in having an agreement with trade unions involving procedures for resolving disagreements and disputes without a stoppage of work. Trade union negotiated rates are less of a problem during the hook-up phase, because relatively higher labour costs are more than compensated for by the savings involved in bringing the platform into production as soon as possible and without unnecessary, costly delays. The oil companies have always opposed post-hook-up construction agreements where cost, control, and impact on production considerations are quite different. Nevertheless, during the mid-1970s most platforms were only just coming into production. This meant that a significant proportion of the off-shore workforce were covered by a collective agreement at this time.

In early 1976, the Energy Secretary, Tony Benn, announced that, in the future licensing round, preference would be given to applicants who showed a willingness to allow trade union representatives on off-shore installations. As it was the oil companies themselves who applied for development licences, this constituted one of the first attempts to put pressure on the operators rather than the contractors. It had also become clear, as a result of an Industrial Tribunal decision, that the protection against unfair dismissal contained in the Trade Union and Labour Relations Act 1974 did not extend beyond territorial waters. The Labour Government announced that such provision would be extended in their forthcoming Employment Protection Bill.

The Labour Government's sympathetic attitude towards trade union recognition was further witnessed by Benn's direct involvement in establishing a Memorandum of Understanding between the Department of Energy, the United Kingdom Off-Shore Operators Association (UKOOA), and the Trades Union Congress, which formalized and regulated the access of trade union officials to off-shore installations. Under the terms of the Memorandum a request for a visit was to be channelled through the Inter-Union Off-Shore Committee and not made directly to an operator by an individual union. UKOOA agreed that the operators would provide transport and off-shore facilities including overnight accommodation, and that all workers would have free access to such trade union officials. UKOOA and the Inter-Union Off-Shore Committee further agreed that any requests for recognition off-shore would be made to the individual companies through the Committee. By August 1977 both the TGWU and ASTMS had made applications for union recognition. The first recognition agreement was made between the TGWU, the Association of Clerical, Technical and Supervisory Staffs, and

Shell, covering fifty-three workers on a semi-submersible drilling rig. The first recognition agreement covering men working on a production platform was between Occidental and ASTMS. The agreement gave the union recognition and representational rights, which allowed it to discuss disciplinary measures and conditions of employment, but it did not involve the granting of negotiating rights or the right to discuss salaries.

By 1978 the oil companies were becoming increasingly concerned that competition among catering companies was driving down wages to such a level that such companies were not able to provide the service at the standard required. As catering covered not only chefs, but also stewards, housekeepers, and cleaners, there were many opportunities for an inadequate standard of service to lead to dissatisfaction among other employees. There were reports of catering workers not turning up to go off-shore, of companies not being able to put a full crew together, and of companies who found themselves short of key workers poaching from other companies at Aberdeen airport. Organization and regulation was therefore in the mutual interests of both the oil companies and the unions.

The campaign to obtain a collective agreement covering the catering industry started in the spring of 1978, when the NUS demanded negotiating and bargaining rights for workers employed by Off-Shore Catering Services (OCS) on an accommodation barge, among whom the NUS claimed 98 per cent membership. The company's initial response was to suggest a ballot but this was rejected by the NUS on the grounds that union membership density was so high that a ballot was unnecessary. It was at this stage that the oil companies intervened and indicated to the catering companies that it was time to introduce a degree of regulation into the industry. They were advised to form an association to negotiate industry-wide rates with the trade unions. The oil companies also indicated that in order to bring about regulation and standardization they would not be prepared to accept tenders that were not based on the agreed rates. Following the intervention of the oil companies, OCS recognized the NUS for negotiating and bargaining purposes, agreed an immediate interim wage rise, and announced that it was calling a meeting with other catering firms to discuss the terms of the agreement. The outcome of that meeting was a decision to form an association of off-shore catering companies.

In September 1978 events were set in motion that were to cul-
minate in an unofficial strike, which was, at that time, the most
widespread and the longest industrial dispute that had affected
the industry. The defeat of the strikers and the circumstances of
the defeat were to have far-reaching implications for the future of
trade unionism off-shore. On 6 September 1978, 500 men
engaged on hook-up work on Chevron's Ninian oilfield (who
were covered by the Hook-Up Agreement) started industrial
action by downing tools and asking to be airlifted ashore. The
shop stewards recommended a return to work, following an
assurance from the contractors that they would be willing to
meet AUEW leaders in London. The offer of talks was dependent upon the men returning to work. By 14 September there
had not been a return to work and the contractors confirmed
that they were terminating the contracts of the 500 men who had
stopped work in breach of the agreed procedures and against the
advice of their shop stewards. The contractors expressed their
willingness to re-employ those men who undertook to honour
national agreements.

The Ninian construction workers ended their two-week strike
on 21 September when, at a mass meeting in Glasgow, they
accepted the recommendation of the full-time union officials from
London for a return to work. The return to work included the
reinstatement of the dismissed workers and there was an undertaking that shop stewards from rigs throughout the oilfield would
meet in November to air their grievances and seek a basis upon
which dissatisfaction over wages, conditions, and travel
allowances could be taken up in the annual renegotiation of the
Hook-Up Agreement.

The main grievance identified by the shop stewards was the
existing shift pattern of working one week off-shore and one
week's leave. The men wanted to move to a cycle of two weeks
off-shore and two weeks' leave. This led trade union officials to
enter negotiations with the Contractors' Association on a new
Hook-Up Agreement. The Contractors' Association offered a
wage increase to bring skilled salaries up to £4 an hour and a
working rota of three weeks off-shore and two weeks on-shore.
The offer was rejected by the national union negotiators, but,
before another meeting could be arranged with the contractors,
the men came out on unofficial strike. This time they had the

support of their shop stewards. As well as a change in shift rotas, the men were demanding increases in wages and allowances which would take their total earnings to £15,000 a year.

Initially ten platforms were affected when the strike began in the first few days of January 1979. By 25 January construction work had been stopped on fourteen platforms. Throughout the dispute about 4,000 men were on strike, which was organized through an unofficial strike committee in Glasgow, with a local committee based in Aberdeen. The strike had initially involved construction workers on platforms that were not in production. However, there were signs by late January that the strike was spreading to platforms in production. Sixty men on BP's Forties platform joined the strike on 25 January, followed by workers on the Thistle platform on 2 February. However, in neither case was production affected.

The AUEW District Secretary, Tom Lafferty, who had spent much of the previous few years trying to organize the off-shore workers and obtain agreements from the employers, opposed and criticized the actions of his own members. Quite how bitter relations had become between the trade union permanent officials and the shop stewards leading the unofficial action was to become apparent through exchanges in the local press. The shop stewards attempted to spread the dispute by picketing on-shore oil-related activities. Lafferty was reported as advising his members on shore to ignore such unofficial picket lines since there was no official dispute. Lafferty pointed out to the press that the union was not in disagreement with the shop stewards about progressing the claim. The difference arose over how the claim should be processed. Lafferty then proceeded to dismiss the claim made by the shop stewards that the employers had started to employ foreign replacement labour. One of Lafferty's central concerns was that the failure of the unions to prevent unofficial action removed one of the main attractions that a union negotiated agreement had for employers. There was little point in employers entering into agreements if they did not avoid costly delays. Relationships deteriorated when Lafferty accused the shop stewards of being more interested in the disruption of oil supplies than in improved pay and conditions for oil workers.

The first sign of an end to the dispute was an announcement that a meeting of eighty shop stewards in Glasgow had agreed the basis of a formula for a return to work. Following negotiations with the national unions and the intervention of the Junior Energy Minister, Dickson Mabon, a meeting of 2,000 strikers on 26 February agreed to a return to work. The main condition was the resumption of negotiations between the Contractors' Association and the national officials. A demand that five shop stewards should be present at any talks was dropped as a result of opposition from union officials. The employers made the concession that a ballot could be held among workers at the firms that did not recognize trade unions. The shop stewards demanded, but did not get, a TUC inquiry into the mishandling of the dispute. As the men returned to work, one of the contractors, Wimpey, declared 283 men redundant. Despite the claim by the shop stewards that this created an explosive situation, there was no further industrial action. The national union officials recommended acceptance of an offer on pay and conditions that fell far short of the original demands. The recommendation was defeated but the offer was none the less implemented.

Interviewed ten years later, Lafferty identified the circumstances of the 1979 strike as one of the most important factors in explaining the lack of trade unionism off-shore. According to Lafferty, the men saw it not only as a massive defeat, but as them being let down by their union. From then on it had become far more difficult to motivate the men to take an interest in trade unionism, at least until the late 1980s. This 'winter of discontent' brought to an end the steady progress that had been achieved in extending trade union influence off-shore. Mrs Thatcher's victory in the General Election of 1979 was to further change the legislative framework and the political climate.

During the period between 1974 and 1979, conditions were relatively favourable for the development of trade union organization in the off-shore oil industry. Government ministers made statements and intervened in disputes, indicating not only their support for the idea of trade union membership, but emphasizing the need to conduct disputes through official trade union structures. Similarly, legislation had removed the constraints of the Industrial Relations Act. Through the conciliation provisions of the Employment Protection Act, a mechanism was in place which allowed trade unions to test the degree of support among the workforce for trade unions obtaining representational rights.

Ministerial intervention had secured access for trade union officials to off-shore platforms and rigs. The Government was quite happy to facilitate the growth of trade unionism off-shore, even to the extent that it held out the prospect that the allocation of exploration licences was going to be influenced by the attitude of the oil companies towards trade union membership.

This legislative framework and wider political climate enabled the trade unions to gain recognition, but this was limited. Although a number of procedural or representational agreements were concluded with the oil companies as field operators, collective bargaining rights over wages and conditions were never generally conceded. However, the need to resolve disputes nevertheless drew the operators into discussions and negotiations with the Inter-Union Off-Shore Committee. Indeed, in the catering sector the problems of reliability and quality of service were so severe that the operators effectively imposed a collective bargaining framework upon the contractors.

Undoubtedly, the major success of the 1974–9 period for the trade unions was the construction Hook-Up Agreement. This was a conventional collective agreement negotiated between the national officials of the unions representing men engaged on pre-production work on the platforms and the representatives of the contracting companies. The Hook-Up Agreement only came into being with the approval of the client operators, who from the very beginning were strongly opposed to granting negotiating rights covering their own employees. Nevertheless, they accepted a collective bargaining agreement that covered a significant and strategic group of off-shore workers whilst resisting any attempt to unionize their own workforces on the production platforms.

There are three factors that help explain the paradoxical approach of the oil companies. The high levels of investment and borrowing that the development of the North Sea required of the oil companies made it imperative that the fields should be brought into production as quickly as possible so as to start generating income for the oil companies. The possibility of production being delayed because of time lost due to disputes between contractors and their employees was a real danger given the number and variety of off-shore contractors. Without the involvement of trade unions there was a danger that disputes would take a long time to resolve, because there were no accepted procedures for resolving grievances. The economics of oil exploration and production made the oil companies prepared to accept a collective agreement in this pre-production phase. However, by the end of the Labour Government's period of office in 1979 there was a classic confrontation between the rank and file and trade union leaders. The 'winter of discontent' in the North Sea paralleled events on-shore. The upshot was a residue of bitterness between the men, their shop stewards, and union officials that weakened the drive towards unionization on the production platforms in subsequent years.

4. FROM EXPLORATION TO PRODUCTION

The late 1970s and early 1980s saw a change in the type of activity that was taking place off-shore. Previously, the emphasis had been heavily in favour of exploration and development, but as more fields came on stream, off-shore activity became dominated by production and maintenance. The interests of the field operators also underwent a subtle and significant change in emphasis from seeking to get fields into production as quickly as possible to ensuring that production flows were not disrupted by stoppages. Throughout the early 1980s the North Sea oil industry performed in a way markedly different from the rest of the British economy. At a time when the British economy was undergoing a period of painful restructuring with massive job losses and very high levels of unemployment, the oil industry continued to boom. A high price, peaking in 1984 at over $34 per barrel, underpinned high levels of activity in exploration, development, and production. By 1981 the direct oil sector was estimated to be providing 39,200 jobs in the Grampian Region. The peak was achieved in 1985 when direct oil jobs stood at a level of 52,000, with an estimated 25 per cent of all employment in the Grampian Region depending directly or indirectly on oil.

As Britain endured a deep recession, oil and Aberdeen boomed. The early 1980s saw little concerted trade union activity. Local trade union officials now regard the early 1980s as a period when the interest of off-shore workers in trade unionism was at its lowest. The trade unions were discredited because of the failure of the 1979 unofficial dispute. Furthermore, in comparison with other sectors of the economy, the oil industry in Aberdeen offered an increasing number of relatively well-paid jobs.

Despite such unfavourable circumstances for unionization, two issues emerged at this time which were to increase in salience in later years. In 1981 the Inter-Union Off-Shore Committee and four Labour MPs produced a 'North Sea Charter'. Of the twenty points in the Charter, eleven dealt with various aspects of safety, including the demands that all responsibility for off-shore safety should be transferred from the Department of Energy to the Health and Safety Executive. They also demanded that health and safety inspectors should have a right of access to off-shore installations without prior notice. More conventionally, the Charter proposed that the member unions of the Inter-Union Off-Shore Committee should be recognized and granted negotiating rights by the oil companies. Unsurprisingly, no such agreements were forthcoming. However, the basis had been laid for a series of future demands affecting off-shore safety, which were to be central to later episodes of collective action.

In 1981 local trade union officials took the lead in attempting to extend the terms of the Hook-Up Agreement on Pay and Conditions to men employed on maintenance. The rise in the number of maintenance companies in the late 1970s had increased competition for skilled labour. Although there was no industry-wide agreement, the larger established companies had negotiated wage rates either formally or informally with the trade unions, but twenty-four predominantly smaller, newer companies had refused to be bound by this loose agreement. The entry of new companies that refused to negotiate agreements with the trade unions into the field of maintenance work opened up an increasing opportunity for price competition. According to the local union officials, competition had resulted in disregard for health and safety, an increase in the number of working hours, and the widening of the differential between men employed by companies with a union agreement, where the rate was £5.20 per hour, and those employed by firms without a union agreement, who were earning £3.50.

In an attempt to control 'unfair' competition, the Inter-Union Off-Shore Committee tried to obtain the agreement of the oil companies that maintenance contracts would only be awarded to companies with unionized employees. However, the oil companies refused to discuss the matter. Although the local officials were in favour of pursuing the issue of a standardized pay and working conditions package through industrial action, the national officers, taking perhaps a more realistic view of the probable difficulties of mobilizing the workforce at that time, drew back from direct action.

The period between 1985 and 1986 was the most traumatic period that the North Sea oil industry has so far experienced. Over a period of months the price of a barrel of oil fell from over $30 to under $10. The off-shore oil industry was now faced with the necessity of making the painful adjustments that much of British industry had made earlier in the decade. The immediate reaction of oil companies was to cut back on their exploration and development programmes. In addition, all the field operators embarked on extensive cost-cutting exercises. This led to increased pressure on the contractors as contract prices were driven down. In July 1985, fifty men refused to leave a platform in protest against declining wages and cuts in allowances covering leave payments, overnight allowances, and travel expenses. Throughout 1986 there were frequent reports of off-shore workers either being made redundant or being required to take wage cuts.

As the vulnerability of contractors' employees, many of whom were on limited contracts themselves, became more apparent, there was a further attempt to secure a standard set of conditions off-shore. The annual negotiation of the Hook-Up Agreement for 1986 broke down when the unions refused to continue with negotiations unless the contractors agreed to extend its provisions to those employed on production and maintenance. In February 1986 the unions refused to sign agreements on salaries and conditions for two new hook-up projects. The refusal of the unions to sign a new hook-up agreement was not aimed at the contractors but at the operators. The union officials believed that without an overall agreement the bringing of platforms into production would be delayed by many small disputes and that this would be sufficient for the oil companies to permit the contractors to negotiate standard terms and conditions throughout production and maintenance.

In June 1986, it appeared that the strategy of the unions had been successful when an agreement was signed with the Off-Shore Contractors Council which for the first time applied to production workers and laid down standard wage rates for a two-year period. The intention of the agreement was the elimination of competition among contractors over differential wages and conditions. This agreement was negotiated by the Contractors Council and the trade unions independently of the client oil companies. Since competition had become so fierce as a result of pressure from the oil companies, it was in the interests of both the trade unions and the contractors to introduce a degree of regulation. The response of the oil companies was to nullify the agreement by indicating to the contractors that they were not prepared to award any contract that had been drawn up on the basis of the new agreement, a response that was more effective because it was never made publicly explicit. Pressure on the contractors was maintained and the deterioration of wages and conditions continued throughout 1986–7.

Increased competition and the pressure to cut costs also put at risk one of the few effective collective agreements that had been negotiated in the North Sea oil industry. Since 1978 the wages and conditions of catering workers had been subject to a collective agreement. In 1986 Occidental awarded a two-year contract to Phoenix Catering under which stewards were to be paid £2,000 a year less than the agreed rate. On this occasion the operators were divided. While some thought that market conditions had created an opportunity to reduce costs, others were reluctant to run the risk of provoking a disruption to off-shore supplies. The implicit threat of embargoing supplies to all platforms where contractors were paying below the agreed rate led to an informal agreement being reached that any contracts which undercut the agreed rate would not be renewed. However, the success of the trade unions in preserving the catering agreement was little consolation to those unions who had their attempts to bring all off-shore construction work within a collective agreement decisively thwarted by the oil companies.

5. RESURGENCE AND DISASTER

Directly oil-related employment in the Grampian Region peaked at 52,400 in June 1985 and fell to a low of 40,700 in June 1987. The end of 1987 and the beginning of 1988 saw the first signs of a revival with employment in the industry rising by 3,400 in the last quarter of 1987. In the spring, Shell Expro revealed their commitment to develop eight new oil and gas fields in the North Sea. An early sign that recovery was under way was the reported difficulty of drilling companies in finding qualified rig crews.

The upturn in activity did not lessen the determination of the oil companies to implement cost-cutting measures throughout the industry. Inevitably this meant continued pressure on the contractors, who reacted by changing work rotas and altering pay structures. In the context of a tightening labour market, the oil companies felt that it was essential to prevent trade unions from establishing recognition and negotiating rights. An organized workforce might have been in a position to exploit conditions in the labour market and to frustrate the cost reductions that the oil companies were seeking. Rather than attempting to 'buy out' trade unionism, the objective was to resist attempts at recognition in order to implement economies.

It was during the early months of 1988 that the full implications of legislative changes affecting trade union recognition became most fully apparent. The resurgence in activity in late 1987 and early 1988 took place when labour market conditions favoured the trade unions, but attempts to organize the workforce were effectively frustrated by the unions' inability to secure ballots on recognition. During early 1988 local trade union officials experienced a simple refusal by employees in the industry to discuss recognition, even when in some cases the companies informally acknowledged that a majority of workers in a particular category wished to be represented by a trade union. There was now no statutory means by which the unions could pursue the matter.

Another major obstacle to the growth of trade unionism was the fact that despite many years of effort, the unions were external to the industry. Although nearly all the major trade unions had local officials and local officers in Aberdeen, these officials represented workers in a wide range of industries and no structure had developed that involved off-shore workers as a separate group within the trade unions. Even after nearly two decades none of the local officials had a background in the off-shore oil industry and among the local lay officers there were no off-shore workers. There was no identifiable trade union body rooted in the oil industry that could legitimately claim to speak for the workers in the industry.

6. THE LEGACY OF PIPER ALPHA

On 6 July 1988, Occidental's Piper Alpha production platform exploded with the loss of 167 lives. The immediate response of the trade union officials to the Piper Alpha disaster was to suggest a direct link between the differences in the pay and conditions of oil company and contractors' employees. The disadvantageous conditions experienced by the latter had, in their view, led to a demoralized workforce, which had resulted in a decline in safety practices and standards.

Following the Piper Alpha disaster, the local Aberdeen paper carried a series of articles which focused on the disadvantaged position of employees of the contracting companies. Not only were pay differences highlighted, but also differences in safety training provision, work rotas, travel expenses, and pensions. The first public meeting of off-shore workers following Piper Alpha was called by the Inter-Union Off-Shore Oil Committee on 31 August and was attended by over 200 people. The main theme to emerge from the meeting was that the constant pressure from the oil companies had made safety 'a sick joke'. The point was made by at least one speaker that the workers themselves had become part of a 'conspiracy on safety', knowingly engaging in unsafe practices. Representatives of UKOOA defended the use of sub-contractors on the grounds that they were necessary since oil companies could not be expected to carry out all the various support tasks off-shore.

A second public meeting of oil workers was held in Aberdeen in November at which not only were the oil companies and the contractors criticized, but dissatisfaction started to be expressed against the apparent inaction of the unions at national level. The meeting of 140 men from thirty-six different platforms focused its demands on the issue of obtaining an agreement for contracting sectors of the industry similar to the conditions that existed for off-shore operators' direct employees. In essence, it was a demand to reactivate the aborted post-hook-up agreement which had been negotiated with the contractors in 1986, but which the operators had effectively made inoperable. The lack of confidence in any agreement being possible through negotiation with the operators and the contractors produced a strong demand that the national officers of the unions should sanction strike action.

Throughout 1988 the local trade union officials had been successful in channelling the dissatisfaction of the off-shore workforce within conventional procedures. However, the failure of the national officers to agree to strike action in December led to a situation where the local officials were finding it increasingly difficult to contain the increasing militancy of some sections of the workforce. This intensified when, in early 1989, a ballot among catering workers produced an improved offer and settlement. Prospective strike action among off-shore construction workers presented the trade unions with numerous difficult organizational and legal problems. The workers were technically employees of over a hundred separate contractors. The geographical dispersion of the workforce made a pre-strike ballot difficult. Finally, union density was still relatively low and for most categories of workers fell well below 50 per cent.

As it became increasingly clear that the national unions were unwilling to take the risk of falling foul of the Government's trade union legislation, a new unofficial body of rank and file trade union members emerged who were increasingly committed to industrial action. Through the spring of 1989 this Off-Shore Liaison Committee was associated with a series of short strikes off-shore where the men stopped working and refused to leave the platforms. At one stage the industrial action involved 400 construction and maintenance workers on seven platforms. As the demand for co-ordinated strike action grew, the local officials were losing control. This new wave of industrial militancy hit the industry at a time when labour market conditions were beginning to tighten.

Dissatisfaction among off-shore trade unionists with existing trade union structures led to the announcement in June 1989 that the Off-Shore Liaison Committee was to found an entirely new union for off-shore workers. The initial reaction from local trade union officials and Labour MPs was entirely hostile. For them, any attempt to set up a new union was seen as divisive and likely to absorb energy that could be better spent directed against the oil companies. The new union did not start recruiting members, hoping that the existing trade unions would transfer their present members. However, the Liaison Committee was in the forefront of a series of large-scale rolling 24-hour strikes. On 5 June 1989, 1,000 construction workers on over a dozen platforms took part in a 24-hour stoppage. Through the tactic of the 24-hour stoppage the Liaison Committee had demonstrated that they were able to bring about industrial action on a scale not seen off-shore since the unofficial strikes of 1979. During June, platforms operated by Shell, BP, Conoco, Chevron, Texaco, and Mobil were all affected by the programme of rolling 24-hour stoppages.

In an attempt to deal with off-shore safety issues and thus deprive the unions of an argument which they had deployed to build up public support, the Energy Secretary announced new regulations for health and safety off-shore on 13 June. Under the new regulations each off-shore installation was to have an elected safety committee with a reporting procedure from the elected representatives through the installation manager to the Energy Department's inspectorate. These regulations fell well short of the unions' demands for trade union representation on safety committees, for the transfer of responsibility for off-shore safety from the Department of Energy to the Health and Safety Executive, and for the right of the inspectorate to make unannounced visits to off-shore installations.

The first sign that the operators were concerned to resolve some of the grievances over pay and conditions emerged towards the end of June with the leaking of an internal BP memorandum. The memorandum indicated that BP was prepared to increase the length of the average contract with sub-contractors from the present average of 1–2 years to anything between 3 and 5 years. It was hoped that this would lead to greater security and continuity for contract workers and increase familiarity with safety systems and routines. BP also indicated to the contractors that they should be looking at ways of increasing the amount of training given to staff, and of ensuring that their pay levels were sufficient to attract high-quality staff.

Once the operators had indicated a willingness to review contracts, a number of contractors started to have discussions with local trade union officials on pay and conditions. Despite the lack of a collective agreement and the absence of any formal negotiating procedures, a form of crypto-unionism came into operation, similar to that which had resolved disputes in the earlier period of development prior to the Hook-Up Agreement. Lafferty, the AUEW District Officer, now worked closely with Ronnie McDonald, the Chairman of the unofficial Liaison Committee. Both were involved in a meeting with the representatives of ten contracting companies. Although the meeting did not produce a solution, it was successful in identifying the possible components of a settlement and the problems of implementation.

However, the prospects for the talks between the unions and the contractors suffered a major setback when, in early July, BP flew Dutch workers on to one of their platforms to replace workers engaged in industrial action. This action brought an immediate response from McDonald, who promised that the strike would be 'right across the North Sea by the end of the week'. On the eve of the Piper Alpha anniversary, a day that the Liaison Committee had previously hoped to mark by a 24-hour stoppage across the North Sea, some 4,000 workers on twenty-six installations were confirmed as being on indefinite strike. The use of foreign labour by BP was in danger of turning sporadic off-shore action into an indefinite strike, unprecedented in the history of the industry.

The contractors had continued discussions with the local unions, and had given some indication that, if the industrial action was called off, a settlement might be possible. At this stage the contractors were giving the impression that a settlement might involve a collective agreement. At the height of the dispute on 6 July, McDonald and the Liaison Committee advised the men to return to work. The return to work was not achieved without difficulty, with McDonald recognizing that many of the men felt angry and let down, and that the votes to return had been very close on a number of platforms. The threat to resume action if their claim was not settled remained.

Discussions between the Off-Shore Contractors Council and the three major construction unions, AUEW, MSF, and the EETPU, broke down after a week. On pay the contractors had offered improvements ranging from 3 per cent to 20 per cent for different categories of workers, but on trade union recognition they had refused to concede. Any belief that it would be difficult to remobilize the workers once they had returned to work proved ill-founded. During the weekend following the breakdown of

discussions, twenty platforms were involved in 24-hour stoppages. Both operators and contractors now felt it necessary to
define their attitudes towards trade union recognition publicly.
An internal Shell report was leaked that appeared to spell out the
company's attitude on the dispute. Specifically, on the key issue
of recognition, it took up the position that it should be settled by .
an independent secret ballot so that the employees could make
their own decision. While denying that it represented a recommendation to the contractors, Shell indicated that it was the
approach they would take if the dispute did concern them.
Although the report could be interpreted as conceding the idea of
a ballot, in the context of the negotiation between the unions and
the contractors it was more probably an indication of Shell's
concern that the contractors would concede too great a degree of
union recognition without the test of a ballot.

A possible resolution appeared with the involvement of ACAS.
Following a meeting with Lafferty, ACAS put the demand for a
secret ballot on trade union recognition to the contractors.
ACAS involvement appeared to result in an agreement with the
contractors to introduce grievance and arbitration procedures
into new contracts. This, together with a 'model' agreement
negotiated with the John Wood Group, which also included wage
increases of between 3 per cent and 40 per cent depending on
skill level, was sufficient for the Liaison Committee to call off
what had become a 7-week period of rolling strikes.

McDonald and the Liaison Committee appeared to be controlling the course of the dispute through their ability to mobilize
off-shore workers to take action and, as importantly, to be able
to instruct them to return to normal working. The Liaison
Committee's tactics were based on exploiting the reference made
in the Shell internal memorandum that trade union recognition
should be decided by a secret ballot. The Liaison Committee also
fully appreciated that striking workers were unlikely to be
putting their jobs in danger because the contractors were finding
it difficult to recruit skilled construction workers.

Despite the earlier optimism, the end of July and the beginning
of August saw the breakdown in the ACAS talks. The stumbling
block remained union recognition. Lafferty claimed (a claim
never publicly disputed) that the Off-Shore Contractors' Council
had voted 13 to 2 in favour of negotiating a union agreement as

opposed to individual contracts of employment. All the indica-
tions were that the oil companies then intervened and made it
clear to the contractors that they were still not prepared to put
contracts out to tender in the context of an industry-wide wages
and conditions agreement.

The response of the Liaison Committee and the trade unions to
this defeat was immediate. The national officers of the five signa-
tory unions to the Off-Shore Construction Agreement on Hook-
Up operations gave the contractors three months' notice of
cancellation of the agreement. The cancellation of the agreement
by the unions increased their options for industrial action. The
involvement of construction workers in disputes during the pre-
production phase could result in the oil companies experiencing
costly delays in bringing platforms into production. The industrial
action that had occurred on the live production platforms had disrupted construction and maintenance programmes but no production had been lost. Although a nuisance, the rolling strikes held
during the summer of 1989 had not disrupted the flow of oil.

The Liaison Committee did not respond to the breakdown of
the ACAS talks by renewing the rolling strikes. This was perhaps
prudent, given the probable difficulties of remobilizing men for a
second time after action had been called off. In any case, the
approach of autumn meant that the most effective period for taking action, the summer months when maintenance programmes
were at their highest, was coming to an end. McDonald stressed
that the task of the Liaison Committee was to organize and
become stronger. Within the North Sea, every platform was
going to be represented on the standing committee of the Liaison
Committee. In order to overcome the problems of a dispersed
workforce, rallies were held in Aberdeen, Glasgow, Newcastle,
Middlesbrough, Hull, and Liverpool, the main areas from where
off-shore construction workers were recruited.

An indication of the Government's attitude to the issues of
trade union recognition and the application of the Health and
Safety legislation off-shore was given during the two-day visit
off-shore of Mr Morrison, the Junior Energy Minister. On
returning to Aberdeen, he announced that he had met 'a per-
fectly contented workforce', and that recognition was 'a matter
between the company and the workforce'. The Minister's statements produced letters and comments in the local paper to the

effect that petitions had been presented to him and that whenever any workers had tried to engage in discussion on union recognition or terms and conditions, he had tended to look at his watch and mumble something about the need to move on.

During the summer an effective working relationship had evolved between the local trade union officials and the Liaison Committee. The earlier dissatisfaction and frustration of rank-and-file trade union members with the activities of the official unions had been replaced by a recognition that the unions and the Liaison Committee were complementary. The leadership of the Liaison Committee, especially McDonald, undoubtedly enjoyed considerable authority among the off-shore workers. In addition, McDonald's knowledge of the industry and his closeness to the workers brought with it a tactical awareness that the shore-based union officials lacked. The strength of the Liaison Committee was that it could mobilize the off-shore workforce and legitimately claim to be the authentic representative of the organized off-shore workforce. The Liaison Committee had limited assets and could not, from its own resources, support a wide range of trade union activities. Its lack of resources was also its strength because it was not worth while for either the oil companies or the contractors to take legal action against it. Although working closely with the union officials, McDonald was not directly involved in negotiations with the contractors or the oil companies, and later the oil companies were to refuse to accept him as co-opted member of the Inter-Union Off-shore Committee. All negotiations were formally carried out between the contractors and the trade union officials, but the trade union officials were not directly involved in organizing industrial action. So close had the relationship become between the Liaison Committee and the official unions that by the autumn of 1989 the possibility of the Liaison Committee eventually forming itself into a new trade union had disappeared. For McDonald the way to union recognition, the extension of all aspects of the Health and Safety legislation off-shore, and a single industry-wide agreement was through co-operation between the unions and the Liaison Committee.

The winter of 1989–90 was used by the Liaison Committee to build up their organizational strength among the off-shore construction workforce in anticipation of a major attempt to gain their objectives during the summer maintenance period of 1990. Opportunities for disruptive action off-shore were significantly higher in 1990 because the oil companies had been required by Government, as a direct result of the Piper Alpha disaster, to install sub-sea cut-off safety valves by the end of 1990. A further difficulty for the contractors was the increasing shortage of skilled construction and maintenance workers. In 1990 there was another massive trial of strength between the unions and the oil companies off-shore. Nevertheless, no union recognition was achieved and by the end of 1991 oil workers were once more discussing the formation of a separate trade union. However, to date, no such union has emerged and union recognition has not been conceded for the mass of the off-shore workforce.

7. CONCLUSION

The history of trade unionism in the North Sea off-shore oil industry can only be understood if it is accepted that a consistent policy objective of the oil companies has been to prevent trade union organization of the post-production workforce. Furthermore, it is also necessary to recognize that through the client–contractor relationship the oil companies have been able to control the industrial relations policies of the contractors, especially in the areas of trade union recognition and collective agreements. The opposition of the oil companies to trade union involvement in the post-production phase is primarily based on their desire to avoid a situation where the entire North Sea industry could be brought to a standstill and production lost as a result of periodic disputes on pay and conditions. A subsidiary reason for opposing recognition and collective agreements in the contracting sector was the appreciation by the oil companies that such arrangements would have significantly modified competition between contractors. Furthermore, after 1986, collective agreements would have been a major obstacle to the oil companies' pursuit of cost reduction policies. The exclusion of trade union influence post-production also reduced the possibility that the oil companies' direct employees would experience a 'contagion effect'. The frequently stated views of the oil companies that they were neutral on the question of trade union recognition and that relations between contractors and trade unions were entirely a matter for mutual settlement represented a less than accurate statement of their actual policies. Throughout the history of the oil industry in the North Sea, trade unions have found that they have been trying to organize in a markedly hostile environment.

The opposition of the oil companies to collective agreements and trade union recognition among production and maintenance workers is fully consistent with their acceptance of collective agreements covering both catering workers and construction workers in the pre-production, commissioning phase. The pre-production Hook-Up Agreement served the objective of bringing platforms into production as quickly as possible. The difference in pay and conditions between pre-production and post-production bore witness to the willingness of the oil companies to pay the price of higher labour costs and a collective agreement in order to ensure that costly stoppages and delays were avoided during the limited but critical commissioning period. The agreement covering catering workers was brought about at the behest of the oil companies and was designed to regulate a sector of the industry where unrestrained competition was affecting the standards of service delivery and the morale of construction and production workers. A collective agreement in the catering sector helped remove the possibility that post-production activities would be disrupted as a result of workers' dissatisfaction with their conditions.

The opposition of the oil companies, the structure of the industry, and the geographical dispersal of the workforce both off-shore and on-shore meant that trade union organization in the oil industry was never going to be easy. In the early days of the industry there were no collective agreements and no trade union recognition. Two decades later the situation appeared, at least superficially, to be remarkably unchanged. The ability of the trade unions to make advances and the success of the companies in resisting their efforts has depended upon the interplay of changes in the political climate, legislation, and the labour and product markets. Additionally, a long period of time elapsed before trade union leaders and structures emerged which were themselves rooted in the off-shore industry. The early years of the off-shore oil industry were marked by indifference on the part of national trade union officials towards the problems and opportunities created by the emergence of the oil industry. Even when the trade unions became more aware, effective attempts to organize were frustrated by inter-union rivalry. In a traditionally less-developed region industrially, with a history of low wages and high out-migration, the arrival of North Sea oil offered wages beyond the experience of many local workers. The early years passed without any demand on the part of the workers themselves for trade union involvement. It was the locally based North Sea Action Committee that established the need for trade union intervention and virtually goaded the national unions into action, by highlighting the activities of some foreign drilling companies.

The beginning of serious attempts by the trade unions to organize the off-shore workforce coincided with the return of a Labour Government in 1974, and the fourfold increase in the oil price. A degree of co-ordination was achieved through the unions coming together under the umbrella of the Inter-Union Off-Shore Oil Committee. Government ministers not only expressed support for union recognition and collective agreements, but also intervened to secure access rights for trade union officials to off-shore installations. New legislation provided a formal means of securing recognition. Despite these favourable conditions, the unions were only successful in securing collective agreements covering the catering sector and construction activity prior to production. At the time of its negotiation, the Construction Hook-Up Agreement could fairly be presented as a major step forward by the unions, but it never became a model that the oil companies were prepared to accept once oil production had commenced. The escalation of the oil price during the second half of the 1970s enabled the oil companies and the contractors to offer very high levels of pay. This removed an area of potential grievance around which the unions could have hoped to mobilize the workforce. When unofficial industrial action took place in the context of the 'winter of discontent', its outcome was to severely reduce the credibility of the unions in the eyes of their own members.

The early years of the first Thatcher Government were not favourable for the growth of trade unions in the off-shore industry. The early 1980s was a period when the greatest contrast emerged between the bulk of British industry and the off-shore oil economy. While Britain was experiencing a deep recession, employment in the oil industry continued to increase and wages remained high. The legacy of the 1979 defeat in the North Sea meant that trade unions remained on the defensive. Even when the unions and the contractors negotiated a post-production collective agreement, it was effectively repudiated by the oil companies. The sudden and dramatic collapse in the oil price in the mid-1980s brought with it severe job losses and a deterioration in pay and conditions. For the first time the vulnerable position of many off-shore workers, particularly those engaged on short-term contracts with contractors, became explicit. Although grievances were widespread, the trade unions were rendered relatively powerless and ineffective by the adverse change in the product market and the lack of organizational strength.

The upturn of activity in the oil industry in 1987, followed by the Piper Alpha disaster in July 1988, created conditions favourable for trade union recruitment and collective action. Contractors were recruiting in a tightening labour market while facing downward pressure on costs from the oil companies. In such a situation attempts by the workforce to regain at least the losses that had been suffered during the oil price collapse were likely to lead to conflict. The Piper Alpha disaster and the subsequent inquiry under Lord Gullen enabled the unions to argue that off-shore safety would only be improved through the direct involvement of trade union representatives on safety committees. Initially, it appeared that the failure of the trade unions to make any substantial advance had led to them becoming so discredited in the eyes of the workforce that the new militancy would challenge and possibly replace the existing trade union structures. The concern of the trade unions to avoid sanctioning action that would expose them to penalties under the Government's trade union legislation strengthened the charge of ineffectiveness.

The Government's industrial relations legislation, by requiring trade unions to be exceedingly cautious in moving towards industrial action, contributed towards the dissatisfaction amongst rank-and-file trade union members with the policies of their union officials. An unintended consequence of this involved the emergence both of the Oil Industry Liaison Committee, the first trade union organization rooted in the industry, and of Ronnie McDonald, the first authentic trade union leader produced by the industry. It was the forging of an effective alliance between

McDonald and the OILC on the one hand, and the local trade union officials on the other, that sustained the most widespread and longest period of collective action that the industry had ever experienced. If legislation had been less than successful in inhibiting industrial action, it posed a significant obstacle to recognition. The removal of the right of trade unions to obtain recognition ballots was a major factor in frustrating the 1989 recognition campaign.

Throughout the history of the North Sea oil industry, trade unions have tended to target the contracting sector of the industry. Most unions accepted that the terms and conditions provided by the oil companies to their own staff have made recruitment unlikely. On occasions, some oil company employees voted in favour of representational agreements, but this was often after specific disciplinary incidents. Although these were seen by some unions concerned as the first step towards gaining negotiating rights, such a progression never actually occurred. Other unions remained extremely suspicious of the value of representational agreements. They feared that such agreements would lead to an increase in the expectations of the members that the union would be able to exert influence across a wider range of issues than the agreement allowed. So limited was the scope of representation agreements that some union officials believed that they would inevitably result in the disillusionment of members with the unions' ability to protect their interests.

The public conflict between the trade unions and the employers—both the oil companies and the contractors—has been fought out in terms of formal recognition and collective agreements. This should not obscure the extent to which the unions have, over the years, been implicitly involved in the management of industrial relations in the North Sea. From the mid-1970s, trade union officials had been involved in resolving off-shore disputes without formal agreements. Despite the opposition of the oil companies to a collective agreement between the contractors and the unions for post-production work, there is no doubt that on a number of occasions individual contractors discussed pay and conditions with local union officials.

The oil companies have always maintained that they were willing to discuss, as opposed to negotiate, a wide range of issues with local officials. Given sufficient evidence, oil companies have been prepared on occasion to take action against contractors who had failed to fulfil the terms of their contracts. In a number of cases, this enabled the unions to obtain remedies for their members. By 1989 the conflict between the unions and the companies was at its most intense, but this should not distract from the extent to which a degree of crypto-unionism had developed throughout many areas of the industry. However, the history of trade unionism in the North Sea oil industry remains one of exclusion and minimal official relations between employers and unions. One of the most dynamic sectors of the British economy remained essentially non-unionized throughout the period of its greatest economic impact.

METHODOLOGICAL APPENDIX

The Social Change and Economic Life Initiative

DUNCAN GALLIE

1. INTRODUCTION

The Social Change and Economic Life Initiative (SCELI) focused on six local labour markets—Aberdeen, Coventry, Kirkcaldy, Northampton, Rochdale, and Swindon. These were selected to provide contrasting patterns of recent and past economic change. In particular, three of the localities—Coventry, Kirkcaldy, and Rochdale—had relatively high levels of unemployment in the early and mid-1980s, while the other three had experienced relatively low levels of unemployment.

In each locality, four surveys were carried out designed to provide a high level of comparability between localities: the Work Attitudes/Histories Survey, the Household and Community Survey, the Baseline Employers Survey, and the 30 Establishment Survey. The interview schedules for these surveys were constructed collectively by representatives of the different teams involved in the research programme. In addition a range of studies was carried out that were specific to particular localities. These were concerned to explore in greater depth a number of themes covered in the comparative surveys.

A distinctive feature of the research programme was that it was designed to provide for the possibility of linkage between the different surveys. The pivotal survey (and the first to be conducted) was the Work Attitudes/Histories Survey. This provided the sampling frame for the Household and Community Survey and for the Employers Baseline Survey. The Baseline Survey in turn provided the listings from which organizations were selected for the 30 Establishment Survey.

The field-work for the Work Attitudes/Histories Survey and for the Household and Community Survey was carried out by Public Attitudes Surveys Research Ltd. The Baseline Employers Survey was a telephone survey conducted by Survey and Fieldwork International (SFI). The interviews for the 30 Establishment Survey were carried out by members of the research teams.

TABLE A.1. *The Work Attitudes/Histories Survey 1986: achieved sample*

	Aberdeen	Coventry	Kirkcaldy	Northampton	Rochdale	Swindon	TOTAL
Eligible addresses	1,345	1,312	1,279	1,400	1,350	1,321	8,007
Achieved sample							
Main sample	997	990	1,011	957	987	955	5,897
Booster sample	48	23	—	65	18	60	214
Total interviewed	1,045	1,013	1,011	1,022	1,005	1,015	6,111
Response rate (%)	78	77	79	73	74	77	76

2. THE WORK ATTITUDES/HISTORIES SURVEY

This survey was concerned primarily with people's past work careers, their current experience of employment or unemployment, attitudes to trade unionism, work motivation, broader socio-political values, and the financial position of the household.

Two pilot studies were carried out in the preparation of the Work Attitudes/Histories Survey, testing questionnaire items, the placing of the work history schedule, interview length, and the contact procedure. The main field-work was conducted between June and November 1986. The objective was to secure an achieved sample of 1,000 in each of the six localities. As can be seen in Table A.1, the target was marginally exceeded, providing an overall sample of 6,111.

The sampling areas were defined in terms of the Department of Employment's 1984 Travel to Work areas (TTWA), with the exception of Aberdeen. In Aberdeen, where the TTWA was particularly extensive and included some very sparsely populated areas, the Daily Urban System area was used to provide greater comparability with the other locations.

A random sample was drawn of the non-institutionalized population aged 20–60. The electoral register was used to provide the initial selection of addresses, with probabilities proportional to the number of registered electors at each address. A half open-interval technique was also employed, leading to the identification of a small number of non-registered addresses in each locality. Doorstep enumeration of 20- to 60-year-olds was undertaken at each address followed by a random selection using the Kish procedure of one 20- to 60-year-old at each eligible address.

To provide sufficient numbers for analysis, it was stipulated that there should be a minimum of 150 unemployed respondents in each locality. A booster sample of the unemployed was drawn in the localities where this figure was not achieved through the initial sample. The booster sample was based on a separate random sample of addresses, with a higher sampling fraction in the wards with the highest levels of unemployment. As with the main sample, addresses were selected from the electoral register. But, for the selection of individuals, only the unemployed were eligible for inclusion. This booster sample was implemented in five of the six localities, producing a total of 214 respondents. Response rates for the combined main and booster sample were approximately 75 per cent in each of the localities, ranging from 73 per cent in Northampton to 79 per cent in Kirkcaldy (see Table A.1).

Where appropriate, weights have been used to take account of the booster sample, using the estimates of the proportion of unemployed available from the initial sample. There are also weights to provide a Kish adjustment for household size and to correct for an over-representation of women in the achieved sample (3,415 women compared with 2,696 men). The sex weight assumes equal numbers of men and women in the relevant population, as is shown to be almost exactly the case by examination of census data.

The interview consisted of two major sections. The first was a life and work history schedule in which information was collected about various aspects of the individuals' labour market, family, and residential history over the entire period since they had first left full-time education. Information about family and residential history was collected on a year grid basis. Information about labour market history—including spells of unemployment and economic inactivity—was collected on a sequential start-to-finish date-of-event basis. In the case of 'employment events' further information was collected about *inter alia* the nature of the job, the employer, hours of work, number of employees, gender segregation, and trade union membership. The second part of the interview schedule was a conventional attitudinal schedule, with a core of common questions combined with separate subschedules designed specifically for employees, for the self-employed, and for the unemployed and economically inactive.

While the greater part of the questions in the schedules provides direct comparability between localities, some scope was given for teams to introduce questions that would be asked only in their own locality (or in a subset of localities). This usually involved teams introducing a broader range of questions for investigating one or more of the themes covered in the common questions.

3. THE HOUSEHOLD AND COMMUNITY SURVEY

In 1987 a follow-up survey was carried out involving approximately one-third of the respondents to the 1986 Work Attitudes/Histories Survey. This focused primarily on household strategies, the domestic division of labour, leisure activities, sociability, the use of welfare provision, and attitudes to the welfare state. The survey was conducted in each of the localities, with the field-work lasting between March and July. The survey produced an achieved sample of 1,816 respondents, of whom 1,218 were living in partnerships and 588 were living on their own. Where applicable a range of questions was asked of partners as well as of the original respondents.

The sampling lists for the survey were generated from computer listings of respondents to the Work Attitudes/Histories Survey who had agreed to being reinterviewed. To ensure that a sufficiently large number of the unemployed respondents from the Work Attitudes/Histories Survey were reinterviewed, it was decided to specify that, in each locality, approximately 75 of the households in the follow-up survey would be from households where the respondent was unemployed at the time of the Work Attitudes/Histories Survey. For sampling, the lists were stratified into four groups, separating the unemployed from others and people who were single from those with partners. The sampling interval was the same for those of different partnership status, but different sampling intervals were used for the unemployed and for others to obtain the target numbers of people who had been unemployed at the time of the first survey.

In the event, 87 per cent of respondents (ranging from 84.8 per cent in Coventry to 89.7 per cent in Aberdeen) had indicated that they were willing to co-operate in a further phase of the research. Since the sampling areas were once more defined in terms of local labour markets, there was a further attrition of the original eligible sample due to people leaving the area (between 7 per cent and 9 per cent, depending on the locality). Response rates (for those that had agreed to be reinterviewed and were still in the area) were 75 per cent or better in each locality, ranging from 75 per cent in Rochdale and Northampton to 77 per cent in Kirkcaldy. The structure of the achieved sample is given in Table A.2. It should be noted that the table describes respondents with respect to their characteristics at the time of the Work Attitudes/Histories Survey, 1986, since this was the relevant factor for the sampling strategy. The economic and partnership status of a number of respondents had changed by the time of the second interview. For instance, while 1,223 of these respondents were classified as having had partners in 1986, the number with partners at the time of interview in 1987 was 1,218.

The questionnaire for this survey consisted of three sections: an interview schedule including questions of both respondents and partners, a respondent's self-completion, and a partner's self-completion. There was a shorter separate schedule for single people. The questionnaires included an update of the life and work histories of the original respondent and a full work history was collected for partners interviewed. The self-completion for respondents and partners was used at different points in the interview to collect independent responses from partners where it was thought that issues might be sensitive or that there was a danger of contamination of responses. The respondents and their partners filled in the relevant sections of the self-completion in the presence of the interviewer, but without reference to each other. The great majority of questions were common to all localities, but, again, a limited number of locality specific questions were allowed.

The *Time Budget Survey*. The data available through the Household and Community Survey interview was extended through a linked time

TABLE A.2. *The Household and Community Survey 1987: achieved sample by characteristics at time of Work Attitudes/Histories Survey*

	Aberdeen	Coventry	Kirkcaldy	Northampton	Rochdale	Swindon	TOTAL
Total issued	390	400	399	404	402	394	2,389
Achieved sample							
Employed/non-active with partner in 1986	153	162	167	163	155	175	975
Employed/non-active, single in 1986	68	54	62	60	68	48	360
Unemployed with partner in 1986	42	42	40	40	45	39	248
Unemployed, single in 1986	41	44	40	38	32	38	233
Total interviewed	304	302	309	301	300	300	1,816
Response rate (%)	78	76	77	75	75	76	76

budget survey. This project was directed by Jonathan Gershuny. The final five minutes of the Household and Community Survey were devoted to introducing the time budget diaries to the individual or couple present. The diaries were designed to cover a full week starting from the day following the household interview. They required natural-language descriptions of the diarist's sequences of activities to be kept on a fifteen-minute grid, for the whole week, together with any secondary (i.e. simultaneous) activities and a record of geographical location and whether or not others were present during the activities carried out. Interviewers left behind addressed, reply-paid envelopes for return of the diaries at the end of the diary week.

Forty-four per cent of those eligible (802 of the original 1,816 respondents and 533 of their 1,218 partners) completed usable diaries for the whole week. This low rate of response, though not unexpected from a postal survey, raises the issue of the extent of non-response biases. In anticipation of this problem, a number of questionnaire items were included in the original Household and Community Survey interviews which were intended to 'shadow' or parallel evidence from the diaries (i.e. questions about the frequency of participation in leisure activities and about the distribution of responsibilities for domestic work). An analysis of the two sources of data showed that the distribution of frequencies of the questionnaire responses of those who failed to complete diaries was very similar to the distribution of questionnaire responses for those who did keep diaries. From this we may infer an absence of bias at least with respect to estimates of these leisure and unpaid work activities (for a fuller account, see Gershuny 1990).

4. THE EMPLOYER SURVEYS

The implementation of the Baseline Employers Survey, which was a telephone survey, was the responsibility of Michael White of the Policy Studies Institute. The schedule was drawn up in collaboration with a working party of representatives from the different teams involved in the SCELI programme.

The survey involved a sample of establishments. The major part of the sample was drawn from information provided from the Work Attitudes/Histories Survey about people's employers. Each of the 1,000 individuals interviewed in each locality was asked, if currently employed, to provide the name and address of the employer and the address of the place of work. The sample was confined to establishments located within the travel-to-work areas that formed the basis of the research programme. Approximately 12 per cent of establishments initially listed

TABLE A.3. *The Baseline Employer Survey*

	Aberdeen	Coventry	Kirkcaldy	Northampton	Rochdale	Swindon	TOTAL
Sample from survey	345	280	229	287	233	273	1,647
Booster sample	52	54	32	51	55	39	283
Out of area	1	30	16	27	11	4	89
Eligible	396	304	245	311	277	308	1,841
Interviews	308	203	174	209	177	240	1,311
Response rate (%)	77.7	66.7	71.0	67.2	63.9	77.9	71.2

could not be included in the sample because of insufficient information or closures. The sample covers all types of employer and both the public and the private sectors.

This method of generating a sample differs from a straight random sample drawn from a frame of all establishments. The latter would have resulted in a very large number of small establishments being included, while there was considerable theoretical interest in medium-sized and large establishments as key actors in the local labour market. The method used in SCELI weights the probability of an establishment's being included by its size: the greater the number of employees at an establishment, the greater its chance of having one or more of its employees included in the sample of individuals (and hence itself being selected).

The above method is closely related to sampling with probability proportional to size (p.p.s.); however, there are generally too few medium-sized and large establishments to generate a true p.p.s. sample. To increase the numbers of these medium-sized and large establishments, an additional sample of private sector employers with fifty or more employees was drawn from market research agency lists, supplemented by information from the research teams. The booster consisted of all identifiable establishments in this size range not accounted for by the basic sampling method. The sampling method, then, was designed to be as comprehensive as possible for medium-sized and larger employers. In practice, 70 per cent to 85 per cent of the sample by different localities were provided through the listings from the Work Attitudes/Histories data, while only 15 per cent to 30 per cent were from the booster sample. The structure of the achieved sample is presented in Table A.3. The sample so generated under-represents smaller, and over-represents larger, establishments, but provides adequate numbers in all size groups. It is also approximately representative of employment in each area, but it is possible to use weighting to achieve an even more precise representation of local employment. This was carried out using tables of employment by size group of establishment within industry group within each local labour market, from the 1984 Census of Employment (by courtesy of the Statistics Division, Department of Employment).

There were five stages of piloting over the summer of 1986, particularly concerned to develop the most effective contact procedure. The main field-work period was from October 1986 to February 1987. The overall response rate was 71 per cent, ranging from 64 per cent in Rochdale to 78 per cent in Aberdeen and Swindon.

The interview schedules focused particularly upon occupational structure, the distribution of jobs by gender, the introduction of new technologies, the use of workers with non-standard employment contracts, relations with trade unions, and product market position. Different questionnaires were used for large and small organizations, with fewer questions being asked of small organizations. There were also minor variations in the schedules for public and private organizations, and for different industries. The four industry subschedules were: (1) manufacturing, wholesale, haulage, extractive, agriculture; (2) retail/hotel, catering/personal, and other consumer services; (3) banks, financial and business services, and (4) construction. These were designed to provide functionally equivalent questions with respect to product market position for different types of organization.

In each locality, there were follow-up interviews in at least thirty establishments—the 30 Establishment Survey—designed in particular to explore the motivation behind particular types of employer policy. While steps were taken to ensure that cases were included across a range of different industries, the composition of the follow-up sample was not a random one, but reflected team research interests. In contrast to the other surveys, the data from this survey should not be assumed to be generalizable to the localities.

5. THE RELATED STUDIES

Finally, most teams also undertook at least one smaller-scale further enquiry in their localities, each being designed exclusively by the team itself and funded separately from the three main surveys. These Related Studies sometimes built upon previous fieldwork a team had undertaken in its locality, and upon the resulting network of research contacts. Adopting for the most part documentary, case-study, or open-ended interviewing techniques of enquiry, the Related Studies dealt with special issues ranging from local socio-economic history to present-day industrial relations trends.

In one sense, then, the Related Studies can be thought of as freestanding research projects. At the same time, however, in interpreting the findings from a related study, a team could take advantage of the extensive contextual data provided by the main surveys. What is more, thanks to their use of methodologies permitting enquiry in depth and over time, the Related Studies could throw more light on many of the quantitative (and at times somewhat summary) findings of the main surveys. Several Related Studies were of particular value in validating and extending core-survey findings.

REFERENCES

ADENEY, M., and LLOYD, J. (1986), *The Miners' Strike 1984–5: Loss Without Limit* (London: Routledge).

AMEMIYA, T. (1981), 'Qualitative Response Models: A Survey', *Journal of Economic Literature*, 19: 1483–536.

ANDERSON, M., BECHHOFER, F., and GERSHUNY, J. (1994), *The Social and Political Economy of the Household* (Oxford: Oxford University Press).

ANTOS, J. R., CHANDLER, M., and MELLOW, (1980), 'Sex Differences in Union Membership', *Industrial and Labor Relations Review*, 33/2: 162–9.

ARMSTRONG, P. (1988), 'Labour and Monopoly Capital', in R. Hyman and W. Streek (eds.), *New Technology and Industrial Relations* (Oxford: Blackwell).

ATKINSON, J. (1985), 'Flexibility: Planning for an Uncertain Future', in J. Atkinson (ed.), *Manpower Policy and Practice*, i (Aldershot: Gower).

—— and MEAGER, N. (1986), *Changing Working Patterns: How Companies Achieve Flexibility to Meet New Needs* (London: National Economic Development Office).

BAIN, G. S. (1970), *The Growth of White-Collar Unionism* (Oxford: Clarendon Press).

—— (ed.) (1983), *Industrial Relations in Britain* (Oxford: Blackwell).

—— and ELIAS, P. (1985), 'Trade Union Membership in Great Britain: An Individual Level Analysis', *British Journal of Industrial Relations*, 23/1: 71–92.

—— and ELSHEIKH, F. (1976), *Union Growth and the Business Cycle* (Oxford: Blackwell).

—— —— (1979), 'An Inter-Industry Analysis of Unionisation in Great Britain', *British Journal of Industrial Relations*, 17/2: 137–57.

—— and PRICE, R. (1983), 'Union Growth: Dimensions, Determinants and Destiny', in G. S. Bain (ed.), *Industrial Relations in Britain* (Oxford: Blackwell).

—— COATES, D., and ELLIS, V. (1973), *Social Stratification and Trade Unionism* (London: Heinemann Educational).

BASSETT, P. (1987), 'Consultation and the Right to Manage', *British Journal of Industrial Relations*, 25/2: 283–6.

BATSTONE, E. (1984), *Working Order: Workplace Industrial Relations over Two Decades* (Oxford: Blackwell).

—— (1988), 'The Frontier of Control', in D. Gallie (ed.), *Employment in Britain* (Oxford: Blackwell).

BEAUMONT, P. (1987), *The Decline of Trade Union Organisation* (London: Croom Helm).

BELL, D. (1974), *The Coming of Post-Industrial Society* (London: Heinemann).

BERNSTEIN, I. (1954), 'The Growth of American Unions', *American Economic Review*, 44/2: 301–18.

BEYNON, H. (1992), 'The End of the Industrial Worker', in N. Abercrombie and A. Warde (eds.), *Social Change in Contemporary Britain* (Oxford: Polity Press).

BIRD, D., BEATSON, M., and BUTCHER, S. (1993), 'Membership of Trade Unions', *Employment Gazette*, May.

BLANCHFLOWER, D. (1984), 'Union Relative Wage Effects: A Cross-Section Analysis Using Establishment Data', *British Journal of Industrial Relations*, 22/3: 311–22.

BOOTH, A. (1983), 'A Reconsideration of Trade Union Growth in the United Kingdom', *British Journal of Industrial Relations*, 21/3: 379–93.

—— (1986), 'Estimating the Probability of Trade Union Membership: A Study of Men and Women in Great Britain', *Economica*, 53/6: 41–61.

BROWN, W. (1987), 'Pay Determination', *British Journal of Industrial Relations*, 25/2: 291–4.

BUCHANAN, R. (1981), 'Mergers in British Trade Unions, 1949–79', *Industrial Relations Journal*, 12/3: 15–25.

BURGESS, K. (1975), *The Origins of British Industrial Relations* (London: Croom Helm).

CARRUTH, A. A., and DISNEY, R. (1988), 'Where Have Two Million Trade Union Members Gone?', *Economica*, 55: 1–20.

—— and OSWALD, A. J. (1987), 'On Union Preferences and Labour Market Models: Insiders and Outsiders', *Economic Journal*, 97: 431–45.

CARTER, R. (1987), *Rochdale Local Employers' Network: Commissioning Report* (Rochdale: Rochdale Training Association).

CLAYDON, T. (1989), 'Union Derecognition in Britain in the 1980s', *British Journal of Industrial Relations*, 27/2: 214–24.

CLEGG, H. A. (1979), *The Changing System of Industrial Relations in Great Britain* (Oxford: Blackwell).

COLE, R. (1979), *Work, Mobility and Participation: A Comparative Study of American and Japanese Industry* (Berkeley, Calif.: University of California Press).

COMMONS, J. R., and SUMNER, H. L. (1911), *A Documentary History of American Industrial Society* (Cleveland: A. H. Clark).

CRESSEY, P., ELDRIDGE, J., and MacINNES, J. (1985), *Just Managing: Authority and Democracy in Industry* (Milton Keynes: Open University Press).

CROUCH, C. (1977), *Class Conflict and the Industrial Relations Crisis* (London: Heinemann).

—— (1986), 'Conservative Industrial Relations Policy: Towards Labour Exclusion', in O. Jacob *et al.*, *Economic Crisis, Trade Unions and the State* (London: Croom Helm).

CSO (1991), *Social Trends* (London: HMSO).

DANIEL, W. W. (1987), *Workplace Industrial Relations and Technical Change* (London: Frances Pinter).

—— and MILLWARD, N. (1983), *Workplace Industrial Relations in Great Britain: The DE/PSI/ESRC Survey* (Aldershot: Gower).

DAVIDSON, J. E. R., HENDRY, D. F., SRBA, F., and YEO, S. (1978), 'Econometric Modelling of the Aggregate Time-Series Relationship Between Consumer Expenditure and Income in the United Kingdom', *Economic Journal*, 88: 661–92.

DAVIS, H. B. (1941), 'The Theory of Union Growth', *Quarterly Journal of Economics*, 55: 611–37.

Department of Employment (1989), 'Membership of Trade Unions in 1987', *Employment Gazette*, May.

—— (1990*a*), *Employment Gazette*, May.

—— (1990*b*), *Employment Gazette*, August.

DISNEY, R., and MUDAMBI, R. (1987), Modelling Trade Union Membership: Theory and Evidence for the UK 1953–85, Working Paper, University of Kent, Canterbury.

DOCHERTY, C. (1983), *Steel and Steelworkers: The Sons of Vulcan* (London: Heinemann).

DUNLOP, J. T. (1944*a*), *Wage Determination under Trade Unions* (New York: Macmillan).

—— (1944*b*), 'The Development of Labor Organization: A Theoretical Framework', in R. A. Lester and J. Shister, *Insights into Labor Issues* (New York: Macmillan).

EASTON, D., and DENNIS, J. (1969), *Children in the Political System* (New York: McGraw-Hill).

EDWARDS, P. (1987), 'Industrial Action, 1980–1984', *British Journal of Industrial Relations*, 25/2: 287–90.

ELIAS, P., and JONES, C. (1990), *IDEAS for SCELI Life/Work History Data: A Manual for Users* (Coventry: Institute for Employment Research, University of Warwick).

ELSHEIKH, F., and BAIN, G. S. (1980), 'Unionisation in Britain: An Inter-Establishment Analysis Based on Survey Data', *British Journal of Industrial Relations*, 18/2: 169–78.

ETZIONI, A. (1975), *A Comparative Analysis of Complex Organizations* (New York: The Free Press).

FLANDERS, A. (1964), *The Fawley Productivity Agreement* (London: Faber & Faber).

FOX, A. (1971), *A Sociology of Work in Industry* (New York: Collier Macmillan).

—— (1985), *History and Heritage* (London: Allen & Unwin).

FREEMAN, R. B., and MEDOFF, J. L. (1984), *What Do Unions Do* (New York: Basic Books).

GALLIE, D. (1978), *In Search of the New Working Class: Automation and Social Integration in the Capitalist Enterprise* (Cambridge: Cambridge University Press).

—— (1988), *Employment in Britain* (Oxford: Blackwell).

—— (1989), *Trade Union Allegiance and Decline in British Urban Labour Markets*, SCELI Working Paper No. 9, Nuffield College, Oxford.

GAMBLE, A. (1988), *The Free Economy and the Strong State* (London: Macmillan).

GERSHUNY, J. I. (1990), 'International Comparisons of Time Use Surveys: Methods and Opportunities', in R. von Schweitzer, M. Ehling, and D. Schafer (eds.), *Zeitbudgeterhebungen* (Stuttgart: Metzer-Poeschel).

GOLDTHORPE, J. H. (1987), *Social Mobility and Class Structure in Modern Britain* (Oxford: Clarendon Press).

GOLDTHORPE, J., LOCKWOOD, D., BECHHOFER, F., and PLATT, J. (1969), *The Affluent Worker in the Class Structure* (Cambridge: Cambridge University Press).

GREEN, F. (1988), 'The Trade Union Gap in Great Britain: Some New Estimates', *Economic Letters*, 27: 183–7.

GREENSTEIN, F. I. (1965), *Children and Politics* (New Haven, Conn.: Yale University Press).

GUEST, D. E., and DEWE, P. (1988), 'Why do Workers Belong to a Trade Union? A Socio-Psychological Study in the UK Electronics Industry', *British Journal of Industrial Relations*, 26/2: 178–93.

HAKIM, C. (1987a), 'Homeworking in Britain', *Employment Gazette*, February: 92–104.

—— (1987b), 'Trends in the Flexible Workforce', *Employment Gazette*, November: 549–60.

HARBISON, F., and MYERS, C. A. (1959), *Management in the Industrial World* (New York: Wiley).

HECKMAN, J. (1979), 'Sample Selection Bias as a Specification Error', *Econometrica*, 47: 153–61.

HENDRY, D. F., and MIZON, G. (1978), 'Serial Correlation as a Convenient Simplification, Not a Nuisance: A Comment on the Study of the Demand for Money by the Bank of England', *Economic Journal*, 88: 549–63.

HICKS, J. R. (1963), *The Theory of Wages* (2nd edn.) (New York: Macmillan).

HINES, A. G. (1964), 'Trade Unions and Wage Inflation in United Kingdom', *Review of Economic Studies*, 31: 221–52.

HIRSCH, B. T., and ADDISON, J. T. (1986), *The Economic Analysis of Unions* (Boston: Allen & Unwin).

HIRSCHMAN, A. O. (1971), *Exit, Voice and Loyalty* (Cambridge, Mass.: Harvard University Press).

HOFSTEDE, G. (1983), *Culture's Consequences: International Differences in Work Related Values* (London and Beverly Hills: Sage).

HYMAN, R., and ELGER, T. (1982), 'Job Controls, the Employers' Offensive and Alternative Strategies', *Capital and Class*, 15: 115–49.

Institute of Employment Research (1987), *Review of the Economy and Employment* (Coventry: University of Warwick).

KAVANAGH, D. (1987), *Thatcherism and British Politics* (Oxford: Oxford University Press).

KAVANAGH, P., and SELDON, A. (1988), *The Thatcher Effect* (Oxford: Clarendon Press).

KELLY, J. (1987), 'Trade Unions Through the Recession, 1980–1984', *British Journal of Industrial Relations*, 25/2: 275–82.

—— and BAILEY, R. (1989), 'British Trade Union Membership, Density and Decline During the 1980s: A Research Note', *Industrial Relations Journal*, 20/1: 54–61.

—— and HEERY, E. (1989), 'Full-Time Officers and Trade Union Recruitment', *British Journal of Industrial Relations*, 27/2: 196–213.

KERR, C., and FISHER, L. (1956), 'Plant Sociology: The Elite and the Aborigines', in M. Komarovsky (ed.), *Common Frontiers of the Social Sciences* (Glencoe, Ill.: The Free Press).

—— DUNLOP, J. T., HARBISON, F., and MYERS, C. A. (1960), *Industrialism and Industrial Man* (Cambridge, Mass.: Harvard University Press).

—— KNIGHTS, D., WILLMOTT, H., and COLLINSON, D. (1985), *Job Redesign* (Aldershot: Gower).

KOCHAN, T. A. (1980), *Collective Bargaining and Industrial Relations: From Theory to Policy and Practice* (Homewood, Ill.: Irwin).

Labour Research (1988), 'New Wave Union Busting', 77: 4.

LANE, T. (1984), 'The Unions: Caught on an Ebb Tide', *Marxism Today*, September.

—— (1987), 'Unions: Fit for Active Service?', *Marxism Today*, September.

LAWSON, N. (1992), *The View From No. 11* (London: Bantam Press).

LAYARD, R., and NICKELL, S. (1985), 'The Causes of British Unemployment', *National Institute Economic Review*, 111/1: 62–85.

LAYARD, R., and NICKELL, S. (1986), 'Unemployment in Britain', in C. Bean, R. Layard, and S. Nickell (eds.), *The Rise in Unemployment* (Oxford: Blackwell).

—— —— (1987), 'The Labour Market', in R. Dornbusch and R. Layard (eds.), *The Performance of the British Economy* (Oxford: Oxford University Press).

—— METCALF, D., and NICKELL, S. (1978), 'The Effect of Collective Bargaining on Relative and Absolute Wages', *British Journal of Industrial Relations*, 16/3: 287–302.

LEADBETTER, C. (1987), 'Unions go to Market', *Marxism Today*, September.

LEE, L. F. (1978), 'Unionism and Wage Rates: A Simultaneous Equations Model with Qualitative and Limited Dependent Variables', *International Economic Review*, 19/2: 392–415.

LEWIS, H. G. (1986), *Union Relative Wage Effects: A Survey* (Chicago: University of Chicago Press).

LLOYD, J. (1988), 'Parting of the Ways', *Marxism Today*, March.

LONGSTRETH, F. (1988), 'From Corporatism to Dualism? Thatcherism and the Climacteric of British Trade Unions in the 1980s', *Political Studies*, 36: 413–32.

MCCARTHY, W. E. J. (1966), 'The Role of Shop Stewards in British Industrial Relations', *Royal Commission on Trade Unions and Employers' Associations* (London: HMSO).

—— (1992), *Legal Intervention in Industrial Relations* (Oxford: Blackwell).

MCILROY, J. (1988), *Trade Unions in Britain Today* (Manchester: Manchester University Press).

MACINNES, J. (1987), *Thatcherism at Work: Industrial Relations and Economic Change* (Milton Keynes: Open University Press).

MCKAY, L. (1986), 'The Macho Manager: It's no Myth', *Personnel Management*, January: 24–8.

MCNULTY, P. J. (1984), *The Origins and Development of Labor Economics* (Cambridge, Mass.: MIT Press).

MADDALA, G. S. (1983), *Limited Dependent and Qualitative Variables in Econometrics* (Cambridge: Cambridge University Press).

MARGINSON, P., EDWARDS, P. K., MARTIN, R., SISSON, K., and PURCELL, J. (1988), *Beyond the Workplace: Managing Industrial Relations in Multi-Establishment Enterprises* (Oxford: Blackwell).

MARSH, A. I. (1965), *Industrial Relations in Engineering* (Oxford: Pergamon).

MARSH, D. (1992), *The New Politics of British Trade Unionism* (London: Macmillan).

MARSHALL, A. (1920), *Principles of Economics* (8th edn.) (London: Macmillan).

MILLWARD, N., and STEVENS, M. (1986), *British Workplace Industrial Relations 1980–84: The DE/ESRC/PSI/ACAS Survey* (Aldershot: Gower).

—— —— SMART, D., and HAWES, W. R. (1992), *Workplace Industrial Relations in Transition: The DE/ESRC/PSI/ACAS Surveys* (Aldershot: Gower).

MINCER, J. (1974), *Schooling, Experience and Earnings* (New York: Columbia University Press).

—— and POLACHEK, S. (1974), 'Family Investments in Human Capital: Earnings of Women', *Journal of Political Economy*, Special Supplement, 82/2: S76–S108.

MINFORD, P. (1985), *Unemployment: Cause and Cure* (Oxford: Blackwell).

—— (1988), 'Mrs Thatcher's Economic Reform Programme', in R. Skidelsky (ed.), *Thatcherism* (London: Chatto & Windus).

MORTIMER, J. E. (1988), 'Problems Facing the Trade Union Movement', *Work, Employment and Society*, 2/3: 535–45.

MULVEY, C. (1976), 'Collective Agreements and Relative Earnings in UK Manufacturing in 1973', *Economica*, 43: 419–27.

NICKELL, S. J. (1977), 'Trade Unions and the Position of Women in the Industrial Wage Structure', *British Journal of Industrial Relations*, 15/2: 192–210.

—— (1984), A review of *Unemployment: Cause and Cure* by Patrick Minford with David Davies, Michael Peel, and Alison Sprague, in *Economic Journal*, 94: 946–53.

—— WADHWANI, S., and WALL, M. (1989), 'Unions and Productivity Growth in Britain, 1974–86: Evidence from UK Company Accounts Data', Centre for Labour Economics Discussion Paper No. 353, London School of Economics.

NIELSON, H. G. (1983), *British Attitudes towards the Political Influence of Trade Unions*, Working Paper No. 9, London: London School of Economics.

—— (1985), 'British Attitudes toward Trade Unions', Working Paper No. 9, Institute of Political Studies, University of Copenhagen.

NORUSIS, M. J. (1985), *SPSSX Advanced Statistics Guide* (New York: McGraw-Hill).

PARSLEY, C. J. (1980), 'Labor Union Effects on Wage Gains: A Survey of Recent Literature', *Journal of Economic Literature*, 18/1: 1–31.

PAYNE, J. (1989), 'Trade Union Membership and Activism Among Young People in Great Britain', *British Journal of Industrial Relations*, 17/1: 111–32.

PENN, R. D. (1983), 'Trade Union Organization and Skill in the Cotton and Engineering Industries in Britain, 1850–1960', *Social History*, 8/1: 37–55.

PENN, R. D. (1985*a*), *Skilled Workers in the Class Structure* (Cambridge: Cambridge University Press).

—— (1985*b*), 'Britain in 1984: A Dual Crisis for Labor', *Berkeley Journal of Sociology*, 30: 611–30.

—— (1987), *Technical Change and the Division of Labour in Contemporary Rochdale*, Lancaster University Social and Economic Life Research Working Paper No. 38, University of Lancaster.

—— (1989*a*), *Unemployment in Rochdale between 1923 and 1988: Time Series Data*, Lancaster University Social and Economic Life Research Working Paper No. 49, University of Lancaster.

—— (1989*b*), *Changing Patterns of Employment in Rochdale 1981–84*, Lancaster University Social and Economic Life Research Working Paper No. 51, University of Lancaster.

—— (1994), 'Technical Change and the Division of Labour', in R. D. Penn, M. Rose, and J. Rubery (eds.), *Skill and Occupational Change* (Oxford: Oxford University Press).

—— and SCATTERGOOD, H. (1992), 'Ethnicity and Career Aspirations in Contemporary Britain', *New Community*, 19/1: 75–98.

—— MARTIN, A., and SCATTERGOOD, H. (1989), *The Changing Contours of Ethnic Incorporation and Exclusion: Employment Trajectories of Asian Migrants in Rochdale*, Lancaster University Social and Economic Life Research Working Paper No. 62, University of Lancaster.

—— ROSE, M., and RUBERY, J. (1994), *Skill and Occupational Change* (Oxford: Oxford University Press).

—— SCATTERGOOD, H., and MARTIN, A. (1990), 'The Dialectics of Ethnic Incorporation and Exclusion: Employment Trajectories of Asian Migrants in Rochdale', *New Community*, 16/2: 175–98.

—— —— —— (1991), 'Gender Relations, Technology and Employment Change in the Contemporary Textile Industry', *Sociology*, 25/4: 569–87.

PERLMAN, S. (1923), *A History of Trade Unionism in the United States* (New York: Macmillan).

Personnel Management (1981), Special Issue on Japanese Management, September.

PHILLIPS, A. W. (1958), 'The Relationship Between Unemployment and the Rate of Change in Money Wages in the United Kingdom, 1861–1957', *Economica*, 25: 283–99.

POLLERT, A. (1991), *Farewell to Flexibility* (Oxford: Blackwell).

PRANDY, K., STEWART, A., and BLACKBURN, R. M. (1983), *White-Collar Unionism* (London: Macmillan).

ROBERTS, B. (1988), 'Trade Unions', in P. Kavanagh and A. Seldon (eds.) (1988), *The Thatcher Effect* (Oxford: Clarendon Press).

Rose, M. (1986), *Integrative Employment Relations Policies: Trade Unionism and Social Change*, Bath University Social and Economic Life Research Working Paper No. 3, University of Bath.

—— (1993), 'Trade Unions—Ruin, Retreat, or Rally?', *Work, Employment and Society*, 7/2: 291–311.

—— (1994), 'Levels of Strategy and Regimes of Control', in J. Rubery and F. Wilkinson (eds.), *Employer Strategy and the Labour Market* (Oxford: Oxford University Press).

—— and Jones, B. (1985), 'Management Strategy and Trade Union Response in Plant-Level Reorganisation of Work', in D. Knights, H. Willmott, and D. Collinson (eds.), *Job Redesign* (Aldershot: Saxon House).

Ross, A. M. (1948), *Trade Union Wage Policy* (Berkeley, Calif.: University of California Press).

Routh, G. (1987), *Occupations of the People of Great Britain* (London: Macmillan).

Rubery, J., and Wilkinson, F. (eds.) (1994), *Employer Strategy and the Labour Market* (Oxford: Oxford University Press).

Saunders, P. (1981), 'Beyond Housing Classes: The Sociological Significance of Private Property Rights in the Means of Consumption', *International Journal of Urban and Regional Research*, 8: 207–27.

SAUS (1985 onwards), *Reports for the Changing Urban and Regional System (CURS) Research Initiative* (Bristol, School for Advanced Urban Studies).

Scoville, J. G. (1971), 'Influences on Unionisation in the USA in 1966', *Industrial Relations*, 10: 354–61.

Shah, A. (1984), 'Job Attributes and the Size of the Union/Non-Union Wage Differential', *Economica*, 51: 437–46.

Shister, J. (1953), 'The Logic of Union Growth', *Journal of Political Economy*, 61: 413–33.

Sisson, K. (ed.) (1989), *Personnel Management in Britain* (Oxford: Blackwell).

Sloane, P., and Murphy, P. D. (1989), *The Union/Non-Union Wage Differential Revisited: An Analysis of Six Local Labour Markets*, ESRC–SCELI Working Paper No. 8, Nuffield College, Oxford.

Smith, A. (1976), *An Inquiry into the Nature and Causes of the Wealth of Nations*, ed. Edwin Cannan (Chicago: University of Chicago Press).

Spilsbury, M., Hoskins, M., Ashton, D. N., and Maguire, M. J. (1987), 'A Note on the Trade Union Membership Patterns of Young Adults', *British Journal of Industrial Relations*, 25/2: 267–82.

Stevens, M., Millward, D., and Smart, D. (1989), 'Trade Union Membership and the Closed Shop in 1989', *Employment Gazette*, November: 615–23.

STEWART, M. B. (1983), 'Relative Earnings and Individual Union Membership in the United Kingdom', *Economica*, 50: 111–25.

STOREY, J. (1985), 'The Means of Management Control', *Sociology*, 19/2: 193–211.

—— (ed.) (1989), *New Perspectives on Human Resource Management* (London: Routledge).

TAYLOR, R. (1980), *The Fifth Estate: Britain's Unions in the Modern World* (London: Pan).

TEBBIT, N. (1989), *Upwardly Mobile* (London: Futura).

TOWERS, B. (1988a), 'Reorganizing British Trade Unions: Implications and Consequences', *Industrial Relations Journal*, 19/3: 7–14.

—— (1988b), 'Derecognising Trade Unions: Implications and Consequences', *Industrial Relations Journal*, 19/3: 181–5.

—— (1989), 'Running the Gauntlet: British Trade Unions under Thatcher, 1979–88', *Industrial and Labor Relations Review*, 42/2: 178–87.

TURNER, H. A. (1962), *Trade Union Growth, Structure and Policy: A Comparative Study of the Cotton Unions* (London: Allen & Unwin).

WADDINGTON, J. (1988), 'Business Unionism and Fragmentation Within the TUC', *Capital and Class*, 36: 7–15.

WARNER, M. (1983), 'Corporatism, Participation and Society', *Relations Industrielles*, 38/1: 3–29.

WARR, P. B. (1982), 'A National Study of Non-Financial Employment Commitment', *Journal of Occupational Psychology*, 55: 297–312.

WINCHESTER, D. (1988), 'Sectoral Change and Trade Union Organization', in D. Gallie (ed.), *Employment in Britain* (Oxford: Blackwell).

WRENN, R. (1985), 'The Declining Power of Labor', Berkeley, Calif.: University of California.

INDEX

Abercombie, N. 330
Aberdeen 9, 138 n., 231n.
  availability of well-paid employment in 302
  compared with Rochdale 243
  early growth of oil-related employment 292-3
  exceptionalism in 209
  history and character of labour-market in 319
  importance for SCELI research design 286
  poor union organization for oil industry in 305-6
  prevalence of sub-contractor work in 287
  response-rate in Baseline Employer Survey 326-8
  response-rate in Household and Community Survey 322
  response-rate in Work Histories/Attitudes Survey 320-2
  Travel to Work Area restricted for SCELI 321
  union membership fluctuation in 183
  union membership in 191
  union strength in 142
absenteeism 81, 267
  commitment to work and 88
  trends in Rochdale 265-6
ACAS (Advisory and Conciliation Service) 86
  role in settling 1989 North Sea oil dispute 310-11
actor approach, in SCELI research on trade unions 11-12
actor intentions 12
actor orientation:
  support for union and 168
* ACTSS (Association of Clerical, Technical and Supervisory Staffs) 262, 295-6

Addison, J. T. 217, 333
Adeney, M. 246, 329
Advisory and Conciliation Service, *see* ACAS
AEU (Amalgamated Engineering Union) 259, 268, 269, 290
alienation from unionism 21
amalgamation of unions 26-7
Amemiya, T. 189, 210, 329
American employers 28-30, 88, 133
  communications practice of 16, 79-80
  effect on regime of control 75
Anderson, M. 329
anecdotal method of social analysis 283
anti-unionism:
  amongst employers 14
  continuing strength of North Sea employers 313-18
  exaggeration of employer 134
  principled 171
  rarity of ideological 106, 282-5
  renewal of employers' in North Sea 305-6
  of servicemen's partners 111-12
  source of among employees 126
  weaknesses of evidence of 172-3
Antos, J. R. 192, 329
APEX (Association of Professional and Executive Staff) 260, 290, 292
area effects, *see* 'locality effects'
Argyll oilfield 293
Armstrong, P. 250, 329
Ashton, D. N. 337
Asian employees 28
ASLEF (Association of Locomotive Engineers and Firemen) and Miners' Strike of 1984-5 247
assertive apathy towards unionism 95-8, 125-7

352 *Index*

pacification of trade unions 3
Parsley, C. J. 335
Parsley, C. J:
  survey of union wage mark-up data
    221
part-time employees 20, 23
  in public service 115–16
  union influence and 47, 54
participation, HRM and employees'
  sense of 13–14
participative management style 131
participative populism 85–98
paternalism:
  in case-study firm 83
  ingrained 129–30
  in Swindon case-study firms 76
  unionization and 104
  weakening 103
paternalism 98
pay, favourability to unions and 45
pay bargaining 268
pay structures, union bargaining power
  and 47
Payne, J. 335
Penn, R. D. 246, 335
  analysis of locality unemployment
    255
  on engineering industry 254
  examines exclusion from skill
    277–81
  explains unionism in continental
    Europe 249
  exposes economism in Rochdale
    unionism 284–5
  on institutionalization of industrial
    relations in Rochdale 266
  occupational identity 273
  pension scheme membership 81
  on Rochdale specificity in 1980s
    245
  on sectoral spread of employment
    259
  shop stewards in textile industry
    264
  on union history in Rochdale 285 n.
peripheral employees 28
  growth 250
  stress on communication with 60–1
  union bargaining power and 47
  unionization of 276–7
personnel management, 'Neanderthal'
  approach favoured 102
Personnel Management (journal) 67,
  336

personnel policy:
  union bargaining power and 47
Phillips 214
Phillips, A. W. 214, 336
Phoenix Catering case 304
Piper Alpha oil-rig disaster 29, 312,
  306, 314, 316
Platt, J. 332
polarization 141
policing role for union 99
policy of employer:
  locality and 44–5
  new technology and 42–3
  pay-levels and 45
  product market and 44–6
Policy Studies Institute, *see* PSI
Polish *Solidarity* movement and British
  unions 246
political science, limitations of view of
  industrial relations in 1980s 134
political socialization, unions and
  162–3
political values, resistance to change
  and 111
politics, dogmatism in 113–14
Pollert, A. 336
populism among management 85–98
positive feedback, employee performance and 81
post-industrial theory 20
post-industrial work context 99
Prandy, K. 336
precarious employment 66
premium on wages, *see* 'trade union
  mark-up'
price of labour:
  problems in measuring 218
principled anti-unionism 171
private health insurance 81
private pension plans 80
private sector as client of public service
  112–13
privatization 72
  attitudes to unionism and 72–3
  logic of the programme 64
  rejection by government advisers
    114–15
  threat to employment system 110
  threat to unionism of 131
probabilities of joining a trade union
  211, 213
product market:
  accelerating changes in 1980s 13
  employer policy and 44–6

trade union (*cont.*):
  optimism over future of 250–2, 284–5
  organizing a new industry 286–7
  perception of failure in North Sea oil 299
  peripheral work and 251–2
  pessimism over future of 250–2, 284–5
  policing role 99
  possible revival of support 128–9
  postwar membership peak 175
  pressure group role 120
  public sector and 17
  recognition in Rochdale 258–69
  recruitment in North Sea Oil industry 287
  relations with state 120
  representation, *see* representation
  resilience of local institutions 284–5
  retreat after failed 1979 oil strike 293
  rights promoted by Tony Benn 295
  role in improving communications 36–7
  SCELI evidence of individual support 163
  significance for policy 217
  solidarity weakening 1980s 246
  strategy in North Sea oilfield 303–4
  survival in Swindon 10
  TECs and 281
  wage mark-up 13, 18
Trade Union and Labour Relations Act (1974) 295
Trades Union Congress, *see* TUC
traditional industries, institutionalized industrial relations in 45
traditionalism among branch officers 27–8
training:
  change in provision 281
  company specific 100
  consequences for control system 117
  constraint on management strategy 86
  deficits 86–7, 96–7
  neglect in case-study firm 78–9
Training Agency 285
Training and Education Councils, *see* TEC
transfers, union bargaining power and 47
Transport and General Workers Unions, *see* TGWU

Transport Salaried Staffs Association, *see* TSSA
Travel to Work Area, *see* TTWA
tripartite bargaining, *see* corporatism
tripartite institutions unions and 2
trust 83, 90
  effort to build 101–2
  example of 81
  growth of 17
  staff status and 80
team-specific study:
  in Rochdale 252–4
TSSA (Transport Salaried Staffs Association) 247
TTWA (Travel to Work Area) 138 n., 321,
TUC (Trades Union Congress) 26, 295
  disciplinary action (1982) 247
  dispute with EETPU 253
  Employment Policy Committee 246
  General council 246
  Leonard Murray as General Secretary 246
  offends Polish *Solidarity* movement 246
  Trades Union Congress
  Wembley Special Conference (1982) 247
Turner, H. A. 252, 254, 264, 269, 273, 338
turnover 267
  in North Sea oil industry 291
  unionism and lower 217

UCATT (Union of Construction Allied Trades and Technicians) 260, 290, 292
UDM (Union of Democratic Mineworkers) 246–9
UKOOA (United Kingdom Offshore Operators Association) 295, 306
'Uncle Alex Act' 79, 80
under-resourcing of union services 27–8
unemployed booster sample for SCELI 320–1
unemployment 33
  early 1980s 245
  little effect on union influence 54–6
  membership and 169–70
  NAIRU measure 233 n.
  policy and 44–5
  rates in SCELI localities 9
  unions and 216
  union influence and 63–4